THE SENSE AND NON-SENSE OF REVOLT

EUROPEAN PERSPECTIVES

THE SENSE AND NON-SENSE OF REVOLT

THE POWERS AND LIMITS OF PSYCHOANALYSIS

Volume 1

Julia Kristeva

Translated by Jeanine Herman

COLUMBIA UNIVERSITY PRESS

NEW YORK

Columbia University Press wishes to express its appreciation of assistance given by the government of France through Le Ministère de la Culture in the preparation of the translation.

Columbia University Press

Publishers Since 1893

New York   Chichester, West Sussex

Library of Congress Cataloging-in-Publication Data

Kristeva, Julia.

[Sens et non-sens de la révolte. English]

The sense and non-sense of revolt / Julia Kristeva ; translated by Jeanine Herman.

p. cm. — (European perspectives) (The powers and limits of psychoanalysis ; v. 1)

Includes bibliographical references and index.

ISBN 0–231–10996–2

1. Psychoanalysis and literature—France. 2. Psychoanalysis in literature—France. 3. French literature—20th century—History and criticism. I. Series.

PN56.P92 K75413 2000

840.9'353—dc21   99–049317

∞

Casebound editions of Columbia University Press books are printed on permanent and durable acid-free paper.

Printed in the United States of America

c 10 9 8 7 6 5 4 3 2 1

CONTENTS

EUROPEAN PERSPECTIVES
A Series in Social Thought and Cultural Criticism

Lawrence D. Kritzman, Editor

EUROPEAN PERSPECTIVES presents English translations of books by leading European thinkers. With both classic and outstanding contemporary works, the series aims to shape the major intellectual controversies of our day and to facilitate the tasks of historical understanding.

For a complete list of books in the series, see page 245.

ACKNOWLEDGMENTS

I would like to thank the students and auditors of my seminar at UFR, "Sciences des Textes et Documents," Université Paris 7-Denis Diderot, who made this work and its reconstruction possible. My thanks especially to Frédéric Bensaïd, who recorded the lectures and faithfully reproduced the text, and to Raymonde Coudert, who edited the final manuscript.

—J.K.

I wish to express my sincere thanks to Julia Kristeva for suggesting this project to me and to The MacDowell Colony, where many chapters of this book were translated. Thanks also to Jim Fletcher for the Aragon poems, Kristin Prevallet for the Freud archives, and David Strauss for *The Language of Psycho-Analysis*.

—J.H.

THE SENSE AND NON-SENSE OF REVOLT

1

What Revolt Today?

The title of this book is meant to evoke the current political state and the lack of revolt that characterizes it. I promise not to elude this aspect of the problem, but I will approach things from a bit of a distance: from the roots of memory, which is nothing other than language and the unconscious. There are two facets to the reflections presented here: the first concerns psychoanalysis, its history, and its present state; the second takes into consideration different literary texts.

I will explain first what I mean by "revolt" and why the problematic of the sense and non-sense of revolt is inscribed in a psychoanalytical perspective. A number of major texts of our time can be approached from this angle, and I have selected the works of three well-known authors, each linked, though differently, to rebellion in the twentieth century: namely, Aragon, Sartre, and Barthes.

Some psychoanalytical questions will allow us a more profound approach to these three authors. To begin quite naturally—some might say provocatively—I think it would be useful to look into the etymology of the word "revolt," a word that is widely used, if not banal, but that holds a few surprises. As a linguist by training, I sought out what linguists had to say about it.[1] Two semantic shifts mark the evolution of the word: the first implies the notion of movement, the second, that of space and time.

Movement

The Latin verb *volvere*, which is at the origin of "revolt," was initially far removed from politics. It produced derivatives with meanings—semes—such as "curve," "entourage," "turn," "return." In Old French, it can mean "to envelop," "curvature," "vault," and even "omelet," "to roll," and "to roll oneself in"; the extensions go as far as "to loaf about" (*galvauder*), "to repair," and "vaudeville" (*vaudevire*, "refrain"). If this surprises you, so much the better: surprise is never extraneous to revolt. Under Italian influence in the fifteenth and sixteenth centuries, *volutus, voluta*—in French *volute*, an architectural term—as well as *volta* and *voltare* suggest the idea of circular movement and, by extension, temporal return. *Volta* also means "time"—as in "one time" or "once"—hence, "turning back." Another direct derivative from Latin belongs in this lineage, the adjective *volubilis*, "that which turns with ease," as in *volubilitas linguae*; the French equivalent is *volubile* (voluble). And *volumen*, sheets of paper scrolled around a stick, with the spatial meaning of "wrapping" or "covering," results in "volume," which comes to mean "book" in the thirteenth century. (In a second usage the word acquired the more abstract meaning of "mass" and "thickness.") That the book has kinship with revolt might not be self-evident at first, but I will try to remedy this obfuscation.

The linguist Alain Rey stresses the cohesion of these diverse etymological evolutions, which start with a matrix and driving idea: "to twist, roll, wrap" (going back to the Sanskrit *varutram*, the Greek *elutron*, *eiluma*) and "covering," an object that serves as a wrapping. The idea of twisting or enveloping, a topological and technical concept, is dominant; it can even be found in the name of the Swedish car company, Volvo, "I roll." The old Indo-European forms **wel* and **welu* evoke a voluntary, artisanal act, resulting in the denomination of technical objects that protect and envelop. Today we are barely aware of the intrinsic links between "revolution" and "helix," "to rebel" (*se révolter*), and "to wallow" (*se vautrer*). But while I encourage readers to use etymology as a deciphering tool, do not rely solely on the appearance (or image) of a word and its meaning. Go further, go elsewhere, interpret. Interpretation, as I understand it, is itself a revolt.

"Evolution," in its first attested appearance in 1536, inherits the semes I have just mentioned but concerns only the movement of troops being deployed and redeployed. More interesting as far as the modern meaning of the word is that "to revolt" and "revolt," which come from Italian words that maintained the Latin meanings of "to return" and "to exchange," imply a diversion at the outset that will soon be assimilated to a rejection of authority. In sixteenth-century French, "to revolt" is a pure Italianism and signifies "to turn," "to avert" (to revolt the face elsewhere), or "to roll up" (thus hair was revolted). In 1501 the sense of a reversal of allegiance—siding with the enemy or religious abjuration—is attested, close to the Italianism "volte-face" (aboutface). Thus in Calvin ("If a city or a country revolted from its prince . . .") or in Théodore de Bèze ("Those who revolt from Jesus Christ . . .") the idea of abjuration is linked to that of cycle and return, sometimes indicating only a change of party. In the psychological sense, the word contains an idea of violence and excess in relation to a norm and corresponds to *émouvoir* (to move), hence *émeute* (riot) for "revolt."

In the sixteenth century, the word does not involve the notion of force but strictly indicates opposition: to leave (a party), to abjure (a belief), to turn away (from a dependency). Until the eighteenth century, the word "revolt" is not used for war, as is the series "rebel," "rebellion," but is used in the political and psychological domain: "It's always been allowed by right of war to fire revolt between one's enemies," Laodice says to Arsinoë, in Corneille's *Nicomedes*.[2] There is also reference to "feelings in revolt."[3]

The historical and political sense of the word prevails until the end of the seventeenth century and beginning of the eighteenth: in *The Age of Louis XIV*, Voltaire uses "revolt" to mean civil war, unrest, cabal, insurrection, war, and revolution when speaking of Mazarin's time.[4] The relationship between "revolt" and "revolution" is not yet clearly established, revolution maintaining its celestial origins until 1700.

Time and Space

Turning to the semantic line of time and space, the Latin verb *revolvere* engenders intellectual meanings: "to consult" or "reread" (Horace) and "to tell" (Virgil). "Revolution" appears later, entering the French language in scholarly astronomical and chronological vocabularies. In the Middle Ages, the word "revolution" is used to mark the end of a period of time that has "evolved"; it signifies completion, an occurrence, or a completed duration (the seven days of the week). In the fourteenth century, the notion of space is added: mirrors, interlocking objects, the projection of images.[5] The revolution of human affairs is a stopping point in a preexisting curve. Gradually, the term comes to signify change, mutation. In 1550, and for a century afterward, it is applied to another semantic field, that of politics: thus the revolution of time leads to the revolution of State.[6] In the second half of the seventeenth century, in the context of the Fronde and the period that followed, from Gondi to Retz and Bossuet, the word's political sense of conflict or social upheaval is confirmed.[7] In the eighteenth century, "revolution" becomes more specific and widespread, with parallels frequently drawn between planetary and political mutations.[8]

That's all I have to say about the evolution of the term "revolt," but I hope I have given you an idea of the richness of its polyvalence; I wanted to wrest it, etymologically, from the overly narrow political sense it has taken in our time. From these various etymological uses, I would like you to remember what I will call the "plasticity" of the term throughout its history, as well as its dependence on historical context. I have made passing reference to its links with astronomy but also with Protestantism, the Fronde, and the Revolution to show how rooted this plasticity is in scientific and political history. This preoccupation will guide the following reflections.

In the series of rather disparate semes I proposed, a number of them ought to be thought of in relation to this book's title, which emphasizes the impact, as much as the impasses, of revolt ("the sense and non-sense"): the non-sense suggested by words such as *galvaudage* (sullying, idling about) and *vaudeville* but also the uncertainties and randomness implicit in "reversal," "abjuration," "change," "detour," which repeat and transform, as well as the semes "curve," "quarrel," and "book"; "cycle," "stalling," and "upheaval"; and finally, "recovery," "unfolding," and the somewhat bland "reassessment." Also worth noting are the classic, though very different, uses of this notion by clans, tradesmen, and diverse social groups (artisans, astronomers, meteorologists), as well as its uses in psychology and politics.

In short, revolt twists and turns—indeed, veers off—depending on history. It is up to us to complete it. But why now? Why, given the plasticity I have briefly described, grapple with revolt now? What do I mean to convey in the present context, if it is true that historical context must be taken into account in order to renew the sense of the word? In response, allow me to make a point to which I will not return but which I would like to place on the implicit horizon of this book. This political observation supports a reflection I have expressed and pursued on various occasions that concerns the moment we are traversing and, to my mind, particularly justifies the necessity of reexamining the notion of revolt.

A Normalizing and Pervertible Order

The postindustrial and post-Communist democracies we live in, with their affairs and scandals, share characteristics that humanity has never confronted. Two of these accompany the society of the image, or of the spectacle, and justify the attempt to rethink the notion of revolt even while they seem to exclude the possibility of it: the status of *power* and that of the *individual*.

The Power Vacuum

As watchers and readers of the media, we all know what the power vacuum means: the absence of plans, disorder, all the things we speak of and that political parties show the effects of, that we as citizens show the effects of. Yet in spite of this anarchy (who governs? who is going where?), signs of a new world order do exist, and if examined closely this order appears to be both normalizing and falsifiable, normalizing *but* falsifiable. This is what grounds my inquiry into the possibility of revolt.

Consider the status of the legal system, of law: we no longer speak of culpability but of public menace; we no longer speak of fault (in an automobile accident, for example) but of damages. Instead of responsibility, there is liability; the idea of responsibility-without-fault is becoming acceptable; the right to punish is fading before administrative repression; the theatricality of the trial is disappearing in favor of the proliferation of delaying techniques. Crime cannot be found at the same time as prohibition; as a result, people are increasingly excited when they think they have unearthed a guilty party, a scapegoat. Look at the scandals judges, politicians, journalists, businesspeople are involved in. Crime has become theatrically media-friendly. I do not contest the benefits of this situation for democracy: perhaps we have in fact arrived at a so-called liberal society in which there is no surveillance and no punishment except in these theatrically mediatized cases that become a sort of catharsis of the citizen's nonexistent guilt. Though we are not punished, we are, in effect, normalized: in place of the prohibition or power that cannot be found, disciplinary and administrative punishments multiply, repressing or, rather, normalizing everyone.[9]

This regulation—invisible power, nonpunitive legislation, delaying tactics, on the one hand, and media theatricalization, the fear of getting caught up, of being theatricalized in turn, on the other—supposes and engenders the breaches and transgressions that accompany business, speculation, and Mafia activity. The causes for this are multiple, but on the legal level, it is possible to describe what allows for them in terms of normalization, on the one hand, and perversification, on the other. There are no longer laws but measures. (What progress! How reassuring for democracy!) Measures are susceptible to appeals and delays, to interpretations and falsifications. This means that, in the end, the new world order normalizes and corrupts; it is at once normalizing and pervertible. Examples of this abound in all countries. Note, for example, the importance of stock market speculation on industrial production; bookkeeping leads to the accumulation of capital, on the right as on the left, and to the falsification of true wealth, which even recently was still measured in terms of production and industrial capacities. This example may clarify my idea of the new world order as a normalizing and falsifiable order. It is neither totalitarianism nor fascism (as is said in Italy particularly), though we have a tendency to resuscitate these terms in order to continue thinking according to old schemas. Still, the current normalizing and falsifiable order is formidable in another way: indirect and redirectable repression. Faced with these impasses, shouldn't we try to determine how a new regulation of power and transgression has come to replace the totalitarianisms of yesteryear and stop letting old terms like "fascism" and "totalitarianism" distract us?

The Patrimonial Individual

Because literature reveals the singularity of experience, it is worth looking at what is becoming of the individual, the singular subject, in this new normalizing and pervertible economic order. Consider the status of the individual in the face of biological technologies. The human being tends to disappear as a person with rights, since he/she is negotiated as possessing organs that are convertible into cash. We are exiting the era of the subject and entering that of the patrimonial individual: "I" am not a subject, as psychoanalysis continues to assert, attempting the rescue—indeed, the salvation—of subjectivity; "I" am not a transcendental subject either, as classical philosophy would have it. Instead, "I" am, quite simply, the owner of my genetic or organo-physiological patrimony; "I" possess my organs, and that only in the best-case scenario, for there are countries where organs are stolen in order to be sold. The whole question is whether my patrimony should be remunerated or free: whether "I" can enrich myself or, as an altruist, forgo payment in the name of humanity or whether "I," as a victim, am dispossessed of it. Some provisions set forth by the European Economic Community concerning the dynamics of the sale of bodies have even found that, thanks to biotechnological advances, the patrimonial individual may favor European economic development. Happily, speculations such as these incite resistance and are challenged by many jurists. Nevertheless, the primacy of the market economy over the body is certainly something to worry about, perhaps even to get dramatic about, to protest before things are firmly established, before it is definitely too late. Again, I am not discussing the democratic advantages that this new world order may entail; they are no doubt considerable. Still, I would underscore that an essential aspect of the European culture of revolt and art is in peril, that the very notion of culture as revolt and of art as revolt is in peril, submerged as we are in the culture of entertainment, the culture of performance, the culture of the show.

The Culture of Revolt

The European tradition, where this phenomenon is most manifest, has an experience of culture that is at once inherent in the social fact and active as its critical conscience. Europeans are cultured in the sense that culture is their critical conscience; it suffices to think of Cartesian doubt, the freethinking of the Enlightenment, Hegelian negativity, Marx's thought, Freud's unconscious, not to mention Zola's *J'accuse* and formal revolts such as Bauhaus and surrealism, Artaud and Stockhausen, Picasso, Pollock, and Francis Bacon.

The great moments of twentieth-century art and culture are moments of formal and metaphysical revolt. Stalinism no doubt marked the strangling of the culture of revolt, its deviation into terror and bureaucracy. Can one recapture the spirit itself and extricate new forms from it beyond the two impasses where we are caught today: the failure of rebellious ideologies, on the one hand, and the surge of consumer culture, on the other? The very possibility of culture depends on our response.

Just under the surface of this question is another we could legitimately ask: what is the necessity of this culture of revolt? Why relentlessly attempt to resuscitate forms of cultures whose antecedents lie in Cartesian doubt and Hegelian negativity, the Freudian unconscious and the avant-garde? Aren't they simply lost forever? Why should we want to find modern responses to these past experiences? After the death of ideologies, shouldn't we just be content with entertainment culture, show culture, and complacent commentary?

We shouldn't! I will try to demonstrate why through a discussion of Freud, for in listening to human experience, psychoanalysis ultimately communicates this: happiness exists only at the price of a revolt. None of us has pleasure without confronting an obstacle, prohibition, authority, or law that allows us to realize ourselves as autonomous and free. The revolt revealed to accompany the private experience of happiness is an integral part of the pleasure principle. Furthermore, on the social level, the normalizing order is far from perfect and fails to support the excluded: jobless youth, the poor in the projects, the homeless, the unemployed, and foreigners, among many others. When the excluded have no culture of revolt and must content themselves with regressive ideologies, with shows and entertainments that far from satisfy the demand of pleasure, they become rioters.

The question I would like to examine—from the somewhat narrow though not socially irrelevant perspectives of private life, psychological life, art, and literature—is the necessity of a culture of revolt in a society that is alive and developing, not stagnating. In fact, if such a culture did not exist, life would become a life of death, that is, a life of physical and moral violence, barbarity. This is a matter of the survival of our civilizations and their freest and most enlightened components. There is an urgent need to develop the culture of revolt starting with our aesthetic heritage and to find new variants of it. Heidegger thought only religion could save us; faced with the religious and political impasses of our time, an experience of revolt may be the only thing that can save us from the automation of humanity that is threatening us. This revolt is under way, but it has not yet found its voice, any more than it has found the harmony likely to give it the dignity of Beauty. And it might not.

That's where we are, and I see no other role for literary criticism and theory than to illuminate the experiences of formal and philosophical revolt that might keep our inner lives alive, this psychological space we call a soul and that is no doubt the hidden side, the invisible and indispensable source of what is Beautiful. Starting here, I will try to integrate the notion of the culture of revolt in the realms of art and literature, understood as experiences, and to raise the stakes. This means going beyond the notion of text—the elaboration of which I have contributed to, along with so many others—which has become a form of dogma in the best universities in France, as well as in the United States and other, more exotic places. In its stead, I will try to introduce the notion of experience, which includes the pleasure principle as well as the rebirth of meaning for the other, which can only be understood in view of the experience of revolt.

My writing a book and your reading it might seem evidence that culture is still possible, that it goes without saying, and that there can be only one version of it. Allow me to express my concern about this notion. Our modern world has reached a point in its development where a certain type of culture and art, if not all culture and all art, is threatened, indeed, impossible. Not, as I have said, the art or culture of the show, or the art or culture of consensual information favored by the media, but specifically the art and culture of revolt. Even when examples of this culture are produced, they take on such strange and stark forms that their meanings are lost on the audience. At that point, it is our responsibility to be interpreters, givers of meaning. For this reason, I am including critical work in the contemporary aesthetic experience: more than ever, we are faced with the necessary and inevitable osmosis between production and interpretation, a process that also implies a redefinition of the distinction between the critic, on the one hand, and the writer or artist, on the other.

It is not at all certain that a culture and art of revolt can see the light of day when prohibition and power have taken the forms of falsifiable normalization that I have described or when the individual has become a patrimonial ensemble of accessories with market value. If this is the case, who can revolt, and against what? Can a patrimony of organs revolt against a normalizing order? How? Through remote-controlled images? If we want to talk about art and culture in this context, clarification is necessary: what culture are we talking about?

I do not have the answer, but I propose a reflection. I submit that past experience, the memory of it, and particularly the memory of the Second World War, the Holocaust, and the fall of Communism, should make us attentive to our cultural tradition, which has advanced a thought and an artistic experience of the human subject. This subjectivity is coextensive to time—an individual's time, history's time, being's time—more clearly and more explicitly than anywhere else. *We are subjects, and there is time.* From Bergson to Heidegger, from Proust to Artaud, Aragon, Sartre, Barthes, different figures of subjectivity have been thought out and put into words or given form in our contemporary culture. Likewise, various modalities of time lead us not to imagine an end of history (as some have been able to do in the United States or Japan) but to try to bring new figures of temporality to the fore.

Let us, then, contemplate and highlight the experiences of writers attentive to the dramas of subjectivity and to different approaches to time. They will allow us to consider the historical moment as well as the multiple, ruptured temporality that men and women experience today, that shuttles them from fundamentalism or nationalism to biotechnology. Let us not be afraid to examine meticulously these explorations of subjective space, these complexities, these impasses; let us not be afraid to raise the debate concerning the experience of time. People today are eager for introspection and prayer: art and culture respond to this need, particularly the unusual, even ugly forms that artists are now proposing. Often, they are aware of their place as rebels in the new normalizing and pervertible order. But they also sometimes revel in a rudimentary—or, on the contrary, refined—minimalism. The role of the art critic then becomes essential to clarifying the subjective and historical experience of the writer or painter. Rather than falling asleep in the new normalizing order, let us try to rekindle the flame (easily extinguishable) of the culture of revolt.

The Lost Foundation

The question I would like to ask at the outset can be formulated this way: Is the Beautiful still possible? Does Beauty still exist? If the answer is yes, as I think it is (for what other antidote to the collapse of fantastic ideologies, what other antidote to death, than Beauty?), then what Beauty does one observe in contemporary works of art? I will draw on a few examples from the 1993 Venice Biennale to guide this brief inquiry.

When I attended this event, I had—and still have—the impression that the examples of modern art being presented were not situated within the same history of the Beautiful offered by museums, including museums of modern art of the last twenty or thirty years. Certainly present were the perfection and technical mastery of the American artist Louise Bourgeois, who transforms trauma into fetish, and the skulls of the French sculptor Reynaud, who in a graceful and Cartesian way alleviates an obsession with death. But there was also something different that appeared to be the emblem of this biennale and perhaps even of contemporary art. Two works particularly struck me, for they seemed to bear a symbolic meaning of which the artists who made them may not have been aware. These two installations, or, if you prefer, sculptures, one by the German artist Hans Haacke, the other by the American artist Robert Wilson, in different ways represented the collapse of a foundation. Haacke's unusual installation had visitors walk on ground that shifted, crumbled; Wilson's ground did not erode but caved in, sank. A field of ruins, on the one hand; sinking ground, on the other. Viewers were fascinated, overwhelmed by volume, as if a troubling question had physically seized them in these two spaces. Loss of certainty, loss of memory. Political, moral, aesthetic loss?

To me, these artistic expressions resonate—in the furthest reaches of our culture's memory—with the Bible, particularly, Psalm 118, which talks of builders rejecting a stone that then becomes a cornerstone. This is done through God, and it is marvelous in our eyes. A song of glory and joy follows: *Exultate, Jubilate*, a hymn found in Catholic ritual, other rituals celebrating foundations, and Mozart.

We are a long way from that. We can no longer exult or be jubilant about our foundations. Artists no longer have pedestals. Art is no longer certain it can be this cornerstone. The ground is sinking; the foundation no longer exists. A great artist, the writer Marcel Proust, was able to celebrate the cornerstone in the image of the cobblestones of Saint Mark's in Venice, to extract from it a metaphor for art made from the vestiges of these traditions. This cornerstone may return at some point, but today it is crumbling. And we are anxious and unsettled. We don't know where to go. Are we still capable of going anywhere? We are confronted with the destruction of our foundation. Part of our pedestal is falling into ruin.

Yet there is an exquisite ambiguity to this moment, harrowing though it is, for it is not solely negative. The simple fact that an installation has been created in a place where the foundations are disintegrating gives rise to a question as well as to anxiety. This is the sense of Haacke's and Wilson's constructions: a question, a sub-version, a re-volt in the etymological sense of the word (a return toward the invisible, a refusal and displacement). And this question is a sign of life—certainly a modest, humble, minimal one but already a detour, a revelation, a shifting of the collapse—and it is deeply affecting. Of course, it isn't quite jubilation or exultation, as the response being formulated is minute, but it is a sign of life nevertheless, a timid promise, anguished and yet existent.

Many young artists make installations rather than simple art objects. Are these merely signs of an incapacity to produce a distinct and intense object? An inability to concentrate metaphysical and aesthetic energy within a frame, on a piece of wood, in bronze or marble? Perhaps. But I think something else is at stake. In an installation, the entire body is called on to participate through its senses—sight, of course, but also hearing, touch, sometimes smell. As if instead of creating an object, these artists seek to situate us in a space at the borders of the sacred and ask us not to contemplate images but to commune with beings, an unquestionably tentative and sometimes unvarnished communion but a call nonetheless. And seeing these young artists' installations, tangles, bundles, pipes, fragments, and various mechanical objects, I got the impression that beyond the malaise of a lost foundation, they were communicating this: the ultimate goal of art is perhaps what was once celebrated as incarnation. I mean by that the desire to make one feel—through abstraction, form, color, volume, sensation—a real experience.

Contemporary art installations aspire to incarnation but also to narration. These installations have a history: the history of Germany, the history of prehistoric man, the history of Russia, as well as more modest personal histories. An installation invites us to tell our story, to participate, through it and our sensation, in a communion with being. It also produces an unsettling complicity with our regressions, for when faced with these fragments, these flashes of sensations, these disseminated objects, you no longer know who you are. You are on the verge of vertigo, a black hole, a fragmentation of psychical life that some call psychosis or autism. Is it not the fearsome privilege of contemporary art to accompany us in these new maladies of the soul?

And yet I think we are experiencing a low period. I tried to compare the current situation with the end of the Roman Empire in my novel *The Old Man and the Wolves*.[10] Back then, however, a new religion was emerging, one that was already astonishing, though its arts and splendors had yet to come. Today, I am not certain that a new religion is arriving or that this would even be desirable. But I think we all need an experience, by which I mean something unknown, surprise, pain, or delight, and then comprehension of this impact. Is it still possible? Perhaps not. Perhaps charlatanism is today's currency, and everything is both spectacle and merchandise, while those we call marginal have definitively become excluded. In this context, obviously, one has to be very demanding, that is, disappointed. Personally, once over the disappointment, I prefer to welcome these experiences: I keep my curiosity on call, expectant.

Freud Again: Rebellion and Sacrifice

Parallel to the etymological and semiological references I have given for the term "revolt" (recalling its plasticity, its social, political, ethical motivations), two occurrences of "revolt" in Freud show the rigor and deep-rootedness of the word in both the history of psychoanalysis and its current state. At issue here are oedipal revolt, on the one hand, and, on the other, the return of the archaic, in the sense of the repressed but also the timelessness (*zeitlos*) of the drive.[11]

I will return to the Oedipus complex at length in a later chapter, but in order to anchor the notion of revolt firmly in Freudian thought, I would like to remind you here that, according to Freud, the oedipal is a component of the human psyche composed of two evolutions: on the one hand, from a structural point of view, the Oedipus complex and the incest taboo organize the psyche of the speaking being; on the other, according to a speculation that is less historical than historic, Freud attributes the origin of civilization to nothing less than the murder of the father, which means that the transmission and permanence of the oedipal over generations can be understood in light of a phylogenetic hypothesis.

Why is the oedipal permanent in all humans? Why must the subject live through the oedipal as a child and then see it repeated in various metamorphoses throughout his/her life? Freud responds to these questions in *Totem and Taboo*,[12] telling a story that is not as subjective as one might like to think and that should not necessarily be filed away as part of Freud's private "novel" or Freud's "folly."

To summarize, at the origin, primitive men lived in hordes dominated by a fearsome male who demanded total submission from his sons and prohibited access to women, the sexual enjoyment of whom he reserved for himself. One day, the sons plotted a conspiracy and revolted (there we are!) against the father: they killed him and ate him. After this totemic meal, they identified with him, and after this primary ceremony of humanity, which saw the concomitance of revolt and feast (remember this concomitance!), they replaced the dead father with the image of the father, with the totem symbol of power, the figure of the ancestor. From then on, guilt and repentance cemented the bond, the social pact, among the sons, among the brothers; they felt guilty and banded together as a result of this guilt, and "the dead father became stronger than the living one had been" (p. 143). The dead man elicited such guilt in the brothers that he became all-powerful, forcing them to keep themselves in check, to curb their desires through a sense of wrongdoing. The impulse of affection—which existed simultaneously with the impulse of hatred—was transformed into repentance and sealed the social link that first appeared as a religious link.

It is important to know that, for Freud, the social order is fundamentally religious. Which leads us to a first question: if the rebellious man is a religious man, what happens when the man is no longer religious? Is he still rebellious? How so? It is no doubt unnecessary to remind you that religion can make man docile and has no qualms about doing so. Read Nietzsche's indignations against

Christianity; these are more pertinent than facile secularisms. Furthermore, the social and/or religious link is also (though not only, keeping Nietzsche in mind) where revolt finds its conditions of possibility, hence its openings and traps, which are where I am headed. If art and literature are in fact a continuation of the sacred by other means (and not unaware of desacralization but, on the contrary, quite aware of it), this could not be more topical.

But let us return to our Freudian fable: the social link is founded as a religious link, the brothers deny themselves the women, rules of exogamic exchange are elaborated. The brothers, who have become social beings, resorb the feminine, renounce it. This feminine is the feminine of women, as objects of desire, but also the brothers' feminine, in the sense of their passive desire for the father, their love for and fascination with the father. Freud asserts that it is this repressed homosexuality that provides the basis for the social contract: guilt and repressed homosexuality; one synthesizes that which keeps one in check in the name of the father. *Homo religiosis* is born, shaped by feelings of guilt and obedience. It is in this context that Freud speaks of an "uprising": "The *tumultuous mob* of brothers were filled with the same contradictory feelings which we can see at work in the ambivalent father-complexes of our children and of our neurotic patients" (p. 143; emphasis mine). And Freud emphasizes the necessity to mimic this revolt: not to reproduce it exactly but to represent it in the form of a festive or sacrificial commemoration, composed of the joy of the initial crime subjacent to the religious sentiment, to guilt, to repentance, or to propitiation. After emphasizing the need for "remembrance of the triumph over the father," Freud goes on:

> Satisfaction over that triumph led to the institution of the memorial festival of the totem meal, in which the *restrictions* of deferred obedience no longer held. Thus it became a duty to *repeat* the crime of parricide again and again in the *sacrifice* of the totem animal, whenever, as a result of the changing conditions of life, the cherished fruit of the crime—appropriation of the paternal attributes—threatened to disappear. We shall not be surprised to find that *the element of filial rebelliousness* also emerges, in the later products of religions, often in the strangest disguises and transformations.
>
> (p. 145; emphasis mine)

I will let you appreciate the richness of Freud's text, and I point out that the "fruit" of this rebellion is the appropriation of the father's qualities; the "fruit" is subjacent to the "guilt." Like the religious experience, Freud's text emphasizes the guilt following the rebellion, but he is also the first to underscore the "fruit" of this rebellion and to invite us to think of situations where it "threatens to disappear," because it is then, and only then, that guilty obedience yields to the necessity to repeat the rebellion, particularly in the form of ritual sacrifice. When pleasure is no longer found in bonds, we start the revolt all over again. Religion allows us to do this by means of ritual sacrifice, a coded revolt.

One might ask how the rebellion can be repeated in other forms. Let us say, to anticipate, that when the sacred-social bond founded on guilt weakens, the logical—psychological—demand reappears to restart the rebellion (this is a function of the sacred as symbolic commemoration of the crime). But in certain situations wherein the bond and/or guilt is weakened, it is impossible or at least very difficult to recapture the festive "fruit" procured through the imaginary or symbolic reiteration of the rebellious act that is the sacred celebration.

Why does one sacrifice? Why does one enter into a religious pact and embrace fundamentalism, of whatever sort? Because, Freud tells us, the benefits we extract from the social contract threaten to disappear "as a result of the changing conditions of life": unemployment, exclusion, lack of money, failure in work, dissatisfactions of every kind. From then on, assimilation to the social link disintegrates; the profit "I" find in my integration in the *socius* collapses. What does this profit consist of? It is nothing other than the "appropriation of the paternal attributes." In other words, "I" felt flattered to be promoted to the level of someone who could, if not be the father, at least acquire his qualities, identify with his power; "I" was associated with this power; "I" was not excluded; "I" was one of those who obeyed him and were satisfied with that. But sometimes this identification with power no longer works; "I" feel excluded; "I" can no longer locate power, which has become normalizing and falsifiable. What happens then?

"We shall not be surprised to find that the element of filial rebelliousness also emerges," Freud remarks, and this is when revolt is set in motion, "in the *later* products of religions, often in the strangest disguises and transformations." What Freud calls a reappearance of defiance are cathartic experiences, rituals that have one or several (religious) meanings expended in an ordered profusion of signs (chants, dances, invocations, prayers, etc.). Thus we see the development of new attempts at rebellion, different from the primary revolt that was the murder of the father, in the form of religious worship and its pageantry, which today we consider aesthetic or artistic. A sacrificial situation is reproduced through which an imaginary power (which is not immediately political but has this latent vocation) is established and activated. Each participant hopes to satisfy the need to confront an authority in his/her imagination; it becomes possible not only to protest indefinitely (the rite is repeated) but also to renew the rite, in a way, with the dazzling expenditures that accompany religious celebrations: dances, trances, and other festivities inseparable from the scene of the sacrifice.

The problematic Freud broadly outlines here—condensed from a problematic of authority, of transgression as murder, of mimesis or representation, and of art as expenditure—is that there is a need for sacrifice in the sense of a remembrance and representation of the initial murder. As a speaking animal (capable of psychological representation, the results of which are thought and language), the human being needs to recall the qualities of the father (which Lacan will call the "paternal function") if and only if he mimics the transgression of his authority or the revolt against this identity. This reprise of the primary rebellion can take different forms: either a simple representation of the murder (these are the variants of sacrifices that all religions perform), or an acting out (where religious members of one community sacrifice religious members of another community), or in a *sublimated* form (as in the expenditure of festivities such as dances, incantations, rites, a crucible of what will become art).

The question I would like to ask (and whose gravity surely is obvious) is, hasn't this logic, which Freud brought to the fore and which characterizes the religious, social, and artistic man, reached a saturation point? Perhaps this is where we are: neither guilty nor responsible but consequently incapable of revolt.

The second occurrence of the theme of revolt in Freud is found in an October 8, 1936, letter to the philosopher and psychoanalyst Ludwig Binswanger. Objecting to Binswanger's philosophical flights and metaphysical speculations, which he finds far removed from both the clinic and the scientific thought he considers to be his own, Freud writes: "I have always dwelt only in the ground floor and basement of the building. . . . In that you are the conservative, I am the revolutionary. Had I only another life of work before me I should dare to offer even those highly born people a home in my lowly dwelling."[13] (Translation: you are highly placed; I would like to offer people like you who deign to accord me some attention a place in this basement where I am trying to develop a revolutionary spirit.) It is easy to establish the juncture between this image of the "lowly," "revolutionary" house and the series of archaeological metaphors in Freud whereby the unconscious is presented as invisible, hidden away, low. The comparison I am suggesting shows that the word "revolutionary" used by Freud has nothing to do with moral, much less political, revolt; it simply signifies the possibility that psychoanalysis has to access the archaic, to overturn conscious meaning. However—and this is where Freud's apparent modesty is revealed to be extreme ambition— someone who accesses the archaic and the impossible temporality that is timelessness (the unconscious has been unaware of time since *The Interpretation of Dreams*) is not only benevolent and indulgent but "revolutionary," in all the malleable senses of the word I presented at the start of this chapter. In short, Freud is a revolutionary in search of lost time.

This is the second direction I will try to explore: rebellion as access to the archaic, to what I will call an impossible temporalizing, which, as I said, will be the topic of a later chapter devoted to a discussion of time according to Freud. I take the term "temporalizing" from Heidegger, which he uses to demonstrate that even in ecstasy, even in an ecstatic state where time seems suspended, time, supposed time, is always already there. On the other hand, Freud was perhaps the only one to posit what he called "non-time," the "timeless" (*zeitlos* in German), time undone.

The return, or access, to the archaic as access to a timeless temporality: this is the experience whose analysis I propose here and that the great literary texts, particularly *Remembrance of Things Past*, allow us to approach. The access to the archaic, to timelessness, to "pure embodied time," to use Proust's expression, also prepares us for benevolence. Isn't a good analyst one who welcomes us with benevolence, with indulgence, without scores to settle, calmly, in a lowly dwelling, as Freud says, and in this sense, a revolutionary one, giving us access to our own "lowly dwelling"?

This image brings me back to the lost foundation and the installations of destroyed habitats I spoke of while describing the Venice Biennale. Robert Wilson's installation was called *Memory/Loss*. I found in it the access to the archaic that Proust symbolizes magnificently in *Remembrance*. You entered a great hall, took off your shoes, and walked on cracked clay that gave beneath you and made you feel as though you were losing your footing. A projector illuminated a bust of a man with a shaved head. A text was handed out, and a story was told of a strange people: it was their custom to shave the heads of future slaves and then expose them to the sun. This caused their hair to grow inside as opposed to outside their skulls, which in turn led them to lose their memories. By telling us this fable with the aid of light, texture, and sound, Wilson invited us to experience the threat of the loss of memory that the normalizing order imposes on us.

For me, the analytical revolt, in the sense of the oedipal revolt and the return to the archaic, is an antidote to the threat of lost memory that certain contemporary artists seem to perceive. I propose three figures of revolt based on the Freudian experience:

- revolt as the transgression of a prohibition;
- revolt as repetition, working-through, working-out; and
- revolt as displacement, combinatives, games.

Logically independent—in social behaviors, for example—these figures are nevertheless interdependent in the psychological experience, where they are imbricated in the psychical apparatus as well as in artistic or literary works.

Why Aragon, Sartre, and Barthes? Or, More Analytically, Who's Afraid of Aragon, Sartre, and Barthes?

Besides the chance encounters and historical influences that have shaped my own course, I consider Aragon, Sartre, and Barthes representative of three essential challenges that have marked the century. Even today we have trouble assessing the upheaval their experiences have brought to mindsets, ideas, literature, and language.[14]

In the wake of surrealism and having succumbed to Stalin's attraction, Aragon's poetic writing links sexual jouissance to the jouissance of language. This approach has inspired French poets from the troubadours to Rimbaud. Georges Bataille proposed a meditation on it, inspired by mystics, Hegel, and Freud. Antonin Artaud burned with the sonorous intensities of a body whose fibers, set ablaze, challenged the facilities of sex and psychological identity: a refusal that toppled into psychosis. Aragon conducts this deidentification of sex and language to two unsustainable points: the pleasure of power and the intoxication of lying. Neither true nor false, literary revolt is plausible, as Aristotle's *Poetics* already asserted. With Aragon, the plausible is pushed to the extremes of identity games—the extremes of sexual roles, the extremes of ideological opinions, the extreme virtuosity of words—and confronts revolt with the risks of compromise and cynicism.

Sartre meanwhile anchors this debate on the other and being in the literary experience (read *Nausea* and *Being and Nothingness* at the same time), a debate that Hegel and Heidegger's philosophy deployed on academic terrain and that French thought has in large part tried to dispel. But having transfused being into the other and vice versa, Sartre applies this vision of being-as-other to politics and to all human words as long as they are in a political context. One might regret the resulting politicization of the being-as-other that leads to certain engagements that curiously forget to question their own bad consciences. But one cannot forget the simultaneous elevation of the political to the level of being-as-other and the virtually mystical implications that Sartre achieves in the literary context (reread his plays, *Nausea*, and *The Words*) and subsequently in politics. In his incisive book, Francis Jeanson rightly questions the beliefs of Sartre the atheist: Sartre's atheism is not a rationalism but a complete engagement in the being-as-other of human existence.[15] We must continue this questioning if we want to find the possible or impossible meaning of modern atheism.

Finally, Barthes caused a scandal in the sixties, when ideologies were far from dead, by declaring in substance that everything ideological was semiological and by pulverizing the polished surface of ideas, beliefs, myths, fashions, texts in a polyphony of logics, semantic networks, and intertexts. The new priests that govern the media of France today are still upset with this musician of meaning for revealing—and for teaching us to reveal—all that is left unsaid under the appearance of messages, phenomena, and images.

For different reasons, each justifiable, these three experiences provoke fascination and, especially today, rejection. I will come back to the psychological and political reasons for such an attitude. Yet it seems important to underscore right away the common impetus that incites and characterizes the specific resistance toward these authors' works. The innovation of their texts, which has yet to be fully appreciated, resides in the revolt against identity: the identity of sex and meaning, of ideas and politics, of being and the other.

The demands of identity do not stem solely from a rationalist or Cartesian ideology that these three writers, in their specific manners, disturb. These demands are rooted in the speaking being's need to defend identity, which is a biological and psychological necessity and which monotheistic religion perfects and sanctifies. Loosening the strictures concerning "one's own" and the "identical," "true" and "false," "good" and "bad" becomes necessary for survival, because symbolic organizations, like organisms, endure on the condition of renewal and joy. Destroying them in a movement of revolt, however, leads to the risk of new defenses, false and deadly in other ways. In any case, the revolt against the One, which stands out in the experiences of Aragon, Sartre, and Barthes, raises the question of another structuring of subjectivity. Another humanity, we might say peremptorily, can be heard not only in their thought but also—and this is essential, for it signals the depth of the phenomenon—in their language: a humanity that takes the risk of confronting religion and the metaphysics that nourishes it, confronting the meaning of language.

This challenge is sizable and laden with compromises, mistakes, failures. Something new took place in Europe, the irruption of which Freud theorized with the discovery of the unconscious and which is manifested in the radical movements marking the shared thought-language destiny at the heart of what is still called literature and, indeed, philosophy. The unity of the speaking being, sealed by consciousness, is influenced by a network of biology and meaning, so that series of heterogeneous representations constitute our psychical apparatus. "We," "me," "I" are formed of multiple facets, and this polyphony— which depresses us or allows us pleasure, which nullifies or glorifies us—

resonates in the polysemy of our verbal exchanges, extracts thought from the yoke of the rational, and reconciles an eccentric subject to the pulse of being. To write and/or to think can become, in this perspective, a constant calling into question of the psyche as well as the world.

It is no longer a matter of conforming to the universal (in the best of cases, everyone aspiring to the same values, human rights, for example) or asserting one's difference (ethnic, religious, sexual) as untouchable and sacred; still less of fighting one of these tendencies with the other or simply and skillfully combining them. It is a matter of pushing the need for the universal *and* the need for singularity to the limit in each individual, making this simultaneous movement the source of both thought and language. "There is meaning": this will be my universal. And "I" use the words of the tribe to inscribe my singularity. *Je est un autre* ("I is another"): this will be my difference, and "I" will express my specificity by distorting the nevertheless necessary clichés of the codes of communication and by constantly deconstructing ideas/concepts/ideologies/philosophies that "I" have inherited. The borders of philosophy and literature break down in favor of a *process* of meaning and the speaking being, meanings emitted and values received.

Other eras have had this experience. Its radicalness, however, is unique in our century, one of education and information. The intensity of the avant-garde movements, their impact on political debates as well as on the desires of youth, has lent it the value of a mass movement. Those devoted to old ways of thinking are keeping watch: they do not understand, or understand too well, and oppose when they do not censure. Repressive returns to systems foregrounding the needs of identity are resurfacing: nationalism, traditionalism, conservatism, fundamentalism, and so on. Thought is content to build archives: we take stock and kneel down before the relics of the past in a museumlike culture or, in the case of popular variants, in a culture of distraction. We could spend years doing this. But revolt has taken place, it has not been erased, it can be read, and it offers itself to a rootless humanity now governed by the relativism of images as well as monetary and humanitarian indifference. Nonetheless the capacity for enthusiasm, doubt, and the pleasure of inquiry has perhaps not been entirely lost. This is at the heart of the ultimate defense of human life: the meaning of language and the architecture of the idea in the human mind. This at least is the presupposition of this book, or, if you like, this is my belief.

2

The Sacred and Revolt: Various Logics

In the previous chapter, I discussed an aspect of the organization of sacred space as Freud defined it in *Totem and Taboo* (1912–1913), recalling how the sons' murder of the father was repeated during the religious ritual in the form of sacrifice. If you read or reread Freud's text, you will see that he links the question of the sacred to the double taboo affecting the prehistoric community: on the one hand, the murder of the father; on the other, relations with the mother. Freud thus considers the two points of the oedipal triangle, the two constitutive elements of the oedipal, when he describes the advent and organization of sacred space.

Taint

Let us take a moment to examine the separation from the maternal space, which leads back to the incest prohibition. Seen from this angle, the sacred appears to be a desire for purification.[1] But purity can be dangerous, as Bernard-Henri Lévy and others have rightly said.[2] This is not a question the media has bothered to develop—it is not a hot topic—and yet it is truly of capital importance. What does one purify through a ritual? And what does one purify oneself of, having understood that all religions are rites of purification? It suffices to think of various systems of ablution: the washing of the feet, confession, and so on. Art and literature are rites as well: recall that Aristotle considered them catharses (in French, *purifications*).

As I wrote in *Powers of Horror*, according to a host of anthropologists who studied the question in detail and examined different purification rituals in societies throughout history, purification—eliminating taint—presents an enigma. What is defilement? What is dirty? In certain societies, defilement is identified with substances that must not be eaten. Rules are decreed in the form of food taboos such as those in Judaism, Hinduism, and so on. And if one examines the food taboos or the desires for purification in various religions, it seems at first that purification is recommended or imposed when the border between two elements or two identities has not held and thus these elements or identities blur. For example, the high and the low or the land and the sea must not be mixed; consequently, certain animals that live on land and in the sea or that possess attributes normally associated with land *and* sea are considered impure. Faced with such food taboos, the modern individual concludes that *the impure is that which does not respect boundaries*, that which mixes structures and identities. Now, identity must be kept autonomous and structurally pure in order to assure the survival not only of the living but also of the *socius*. And this corresponds to an archaic demand: "archaic" from the point of view of the history of societies that survive only by differentiating themselves from others, establishing rigorous but guarded links with them. Yet this so-called archaism trips us up more often than we might think, despite advances toward intermingling. I will come back to this.

The second rule, which does not exclude the first but is often concealed by it, ultimately sees the impure as the maternal. Why the maternal? Again, two explanations come to the fore. First, the speaking being's relationship with maternal space is precisely an "archaic" relationship in which borders are nonexistent or unstable, a relationship of osmosis in which separation, if it is under way, is never absolutely clear. This is the realm of narcissism and the instability of borders between mother and child, in the preoedipal mode of the psyche. Second, if we look at the question in religious terms, we see that the social and symbolic pact that I discussed earlier — brothers rebelling against the father's authority in order to establish a *socius* — is a transversal link that is constituted by the evacuation of the maternal: in order to establish the symbolic pact, one has to get rid of the domestic, corporal, maternal container. And even though maternal religions exist, they are always already on a path toward splitting the symbolic being from its psychological and maternal basis. The constitution of the sacred therefore requires separation from the physiological and its framework, the maternal and the carnal, which in fundamentalist monotheism are connoted negatively and sometimes even considered pagan or diabolical. Mystics and artists alike make use of subtle transgressions and skillful mixtures in a magnificent, parallel history.

I will not go further into this debate, although I did want to mention that purification, the elimination of taint, and protection against the maternal are at the heart of the constitution of the sacred and can be read beneath the surface of *Totem and Taboo*. But the question of the feminine and the maternal is of only secondary interest to Freud, who instead emphasizes the exclusion of the sons and the murder of the father, the abolishing of his tyranny and the constitution of the symbolic pact between the brothers.

An Archaeology of Purity

The most virulent aspects of certain religions today that take the form of fundamentalism and other obscurantisms are presented as so many desires for purification. But analysis should not stop there. The tendency toward purification leads insidiously to the demarcation of a place of purity designated by an officiant, a religious member, a place that might be represented by the following schema.

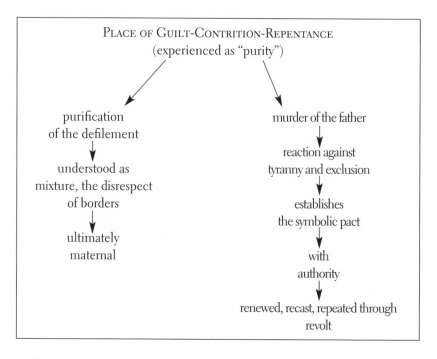

FIGURE 2.1

The pure and absolute subject—call him the purifier—defends himself against the maternal from which he is separating through antitaint rituals, while at the same time defending himself against the murder of the father through feelings of guilt, contrition, repentance. Therefore what appears to be purity in the eyes of the religion and the purifiers is only an obsessional surface that conceals a veritable architecture of purity, which I present schematically in figure 2.1.[3] It is probably impossible to question the validity of this so-called purity—or to fight the various forms of fundamentalism and violence that appear to be the sorry privilege of this end of the century—by looking exclusively at its surface and not taking into consideration what produces it, namely, the disgust with taint and the consequent contrition, repentance, and guilt that present themselves as qualities of religion but also profoundly constitute the psychical life of the being capable of symbolicity: the speaking being. It is thus important to examine the unconscious thoughts and desires that accompany the murder of the father, the abolished exclusion, and the constitution of the symbolic pact, an examination that will return us to the core of this book's subject, that is, revolt.

To abolish the feeling of exclusion, to be included at all costs, are the slogans and claims not only of religions but also of totalitarianisms and fundamentalisms. For this, the purifier wants to confront an authority (value or law), to revolt against it while also being included in it. The purifier is a complex subject: he recognizes authority, value, law, but he claims their power must be broadened, rebelling against a restricted power in order to include a greater number of the purified, the "brothers." This evolution of access to power may be accompanied by contrition ("Alas, I have killed the father, rebelling against him"), and in the ideal hypothesis, certain abuses of power may be renounced as a result ("I" share power with others; "I" therefore renounce certain privileges for the brothers' benefit), but most often the attraction that authority and law represent imposes on the purifier a paranoid spiral of persecution and revenge. Revolt against exclusion is resolved in the renewal of exclusion at the lower echelons of the social edifice ("I" include myself at the top; "I" exclude those at the bottom).

In the Freudian fable, the father embodies the position of authority, value, and law against which the sons rebel. Their revolt consists in this: they identify with the father and take his place, an integration that constitutes the collective pact, the inclusion forging the link that will be the *socius*. Thanks to this, the brothers no longer feel excluded but rather have the imaginary certainty of being identified with the power that, prior to the revolt, oppressed them. The benefit Freud observes in this process is one of identification with and inclusion in the law, authority, power. The sense of exclusion that, in our day, is provoked by economic crisis or the condition of foreignness, ethnic or otherwise, may be in some sense cured, or in any case relieved, in a religious space where the individual thinks he can benefit from identification through inclusion within a symbolic community. He moves from a place of national, social, political exclusion to a place of symbolic inclusion; he gains access to a position of power he considered inaccessible until then. The feeling of exclusion is reduced, erased by the symbolic and fantasmatic mise-en-scène of inclusion and identification with a so-called higher power.

Thus, by overemphasizing the purification and "dangerous purity" that religious ties offer, we run the risk of forgetting two things: that the feeling of purification is a benefit after the fact, following repentance, and that the initial libidinal impulse is a violence that involves desiring the father (authority) and taking him (it), in eros and unto death. Violence, repressed in the mind of the believer, remains implied, unconscious, an encoded libido. In fact, if this jouissance were absent, if this pleasure of violence blocked, Freud asserts, the benefit of inclusion would be lessened. And, as I observed in chapter 1, historically if a religion gave its followers the impression that it could not satisfy their need for identity, inclusion, purity—in other words, that it lacked enthusiasm and passion, that it was weakening, declining—then the followers would repeat the act of violence, the sacrifice, either in a strictly ritual form or by acting out. First, rites would be reactivated, the symbolic significance of dogmas reinvigorated, their expansion reinforced, and their influence made to dominate, and then more actual, active measures taken, from persecution to the physical elimination of those outside the religion, indeed, any religion.

I hope I have shown that ideologies that claim to fight religions by assigning them a place of absolute and dangerous purity do not acknowledge the jouissance that the revolt underlying this purity conceals. If you are convinced that revolt is revealed beneath purity, if you agree that "I" can neither include myself nor identify myself without abolishing the authority that oppressed me before and that in this act of abolition-identification lies all the violence of consuming rage and murder, then a crucial question is raised: what modern modes might re-create what was in the not-so-distant past the jouissance of the religious man? Are we capable of this revolt? Not in the actual, concrete form of acting-out, not in the form of violence, inflicted or sustained, but in a new symbolic form? And if we are no longer capable of it, why not? This is an important question, and allow me to emphasize it, for it concerns nothing less than the surpassing of *Homo religiosis*. Is it possible? Even the question of art and literature is not extraneous to it.

One of the reasons for our incapacity to implement revolt symbolically perhaps resides in the fact that authority, value, and law have become empty, flimsy forms. Here I remind you of advanced democracies governed by a normalizing and pervertible order as an ensemble of structures where power is at once spectacular and vacant, where the legal oscillates between permissiveness and fragility, where scandals and accusations are mises-en-scène organized for the media, and where it is possible, if not easy, to circumvent the law.

As for the wish to be included in the values linked to human dignity, difficulties arise regarding the notion of "rights" and even of "human." It has been said often enough that human rights represent the last bastion against the loss of values for the subject as defined by the founding principles of the Republic, that is, for the subject who is not the transcendental subject and who does not confuse himself with the code—the defenses—of any of the religions constituting the memory of the increasingly heterogeneous populations that are mixing today in Europe and elsewhere. Now, before our eyes, these values, guaranteed until now by human rights, are dissolving under the pressure of technology and the market, threatened by what jurists call "the patrimonial person," that is, the human being as an assemblage of organs that are more or less negotiable, that can be transplanted, converted into cash, bequeathed, and the like. Moreover, democracies' frank abandonment of great political, ethnic, and religious conflicts in favor of military and barbarous powers—as seen in the former Yugoslavia—throws grave discredit on these values that we now call, more and more naturally, so-called values.

Finally, revolt as a producer of purity in our modern world is endangered by an easy—not to say perverse—fit between law and transgression; it is spoiled by constant authorization, if not incentives, made by the law itself, to transgress the law and to be included.

Thus at least two things make revolt in this context problematic. The first has to do with the flimsiness of the prohibition; the second has to do with the fact that the possibility of revolt involves a jouissance that we do not acknowledge, because the very human being that is the locus of it is dispersed into organs and images, and the new maladies of this deliquescent and centerless soul are confined to passivity and complaint.

Priests and the Turbulent Boys

While examining the texts of Mallarmé and Lautréamont, I came across several figures of revolt and its variants or failures in the religious history of Indo-European societies. As suggested by the title of the work in which I developed these questions, *Revolution in Poetic Language*, revolt was already the central subject.[4] The power vacuum and lack of values were not yet issues when I wrote that book in the 1970s; the change no doubt appeared in a more obvious, more drastic, more threatening way after the recent collapse of communism. On a political level, however, the evolution in question has probably been under way since the end of the French Revolution and the development of democracy that followed. But I leave this question open for now to return to the profound logic of the passageways and impasses of the revolt internal to our cultural memory.

In *Revolution in Poetic Language*, I looked at two figures first examined by Georges Dumézil: on the one hand, the priest, who assumes what Bernard-Henri Lévy calls purity and, I would add, guilt and repentance, as aspects of the religious and cultural pact (I am speaking here of religious culture but perhaps of culture in general as well); on the other hand, what Dumézil calls the "turbulent boy," that is, the one who represents the jouissance, rupture, displacement, and revolt underlying purity, repentance, and the renewal of the pact.[5] The dual logic that structures the living, renewable identity and that the oedipal allows us to glimpse—that is, law, on the one hand; revolt and violence, on the other—seemed divided in the Indo-European pantheon between two distinct figures. The dialectic inherent in the process of revolt, inherent in the constitution of all sacred or social space, was distributed as if the function of purity had been delegated to certain individuals and the function of revolt to others, although one must keep in mind that these two categories converge and one is never possible without the other.

In the Mithraic system of sovereignty of the Indo-European pantheon described by Dumézil, the priest, called flamen or brahman, serves the idealizing part of the religious pact that has reached a form of stability, allowing ties to be formed: inclusion has been achieved, and a temporary equilibrium, assumed by the priest, has been established; the priest enjoys this stability or peace, Mithraism seems to say.

The rebellious sensualist is entirely different. Gandharva, half-horse/half-man, is the Indian centaur enamored of music, dance, and poetry, arts forbidden to the legislator and priest.[6] He heralds an underground economy: the facilitation of revolt and its underlying jouissance. The dual human and animal nature thus revealed seems to indicate, as though by metaphor, ardor and violence, a force difficult for anthropology to contemplate, a "going to the limit," the metaphor of the horse suggesting the vigor of the drive and a psychical and extrapsychical setting-into-motion that we have difficulty symbolizing.

In Revolution in Poetic Language, I proposed that the function of the horsemen was accounted for in our modern cultures by art and aesthetics—if we accept that sacred space and symbolic space coincide. On the one hand, there is the discourse of the norm and purity, subsuming a social harmony whose symbolic peace the priest celebrates; on the other, there is singing, dancing, painting, the use of words, the exultation of syllables, and the introduction of fantasies in narrative, which first give way to sacred incantation and then are gradually detached from the religious scene in secular literature. This experience, considered "aesthetic" starting with Kant, in fact recaptures the violence and nonsubmission that are an integral part of the social space. Dumézil demonstrates this forcefully: the "turbulent boys" are destructive, but they also promote fertility and joy during feasts. It is during feasts that sacred possibility is unleashed. I say possibility and not purity—that which precedes purity and exceeds it, the jouissance of protest, indeed, of destruction—since the feast is the chance to break down what exists in order to construct a new balance or, more commonly, to return to old habits.

No doubt revolt culture should consider the possibility or impossibility of establishing and elaborating values, pacts, and spaces of purity. But do we have consistent values or purities to propose today? Haven't the systems that were supposed to protect the last paradisiacal values of a future society where all men would be brothers shown how difficult it is to maintain ideals without exerting the most arbitrary violence? Moreover, shouldn't we consider this: spaces of purity are secretly sustained by a possibility of expenditure where man brushes up against his animality and where the drive jostles codes in order to try to modify them? When successful, this leads to celebration through dance, which is different from walking, just as poetry is different from language. And religion satisfies the desire for transgression.

The old dialectical model of the law and its transgression in fact remains valid for organizing religious space and the art that is its by-product. If, for example, we ask why certain people return to religion or find refuge in it, we can suppose that it is not only to connect with or attain a pure value: it is also because religion gives each and every person what we might call "warmed-over" fantasies, softened and nonviolent but charged with a certain aggression, which fulfill the obscure desire for pleasurable revolt and, with it, a certain horse-man quality. As for the *secular* loci where this law/transgression articulation is possible, these are obviously places invested by the arts.

Transgression, Anamnesis, Games

To sum up, Freud's text poses the following question: if one agrees to accept the constitution of the sacred space that I have outlined, where some take the side of the law (our modern priests) and some rebel against it (our horse-boys), what are the links between the law and the prohibition? Of course, if one considers law obsolete, prohibition weak, and values empty or flimsy, a certain dialectical link between law and transgression is impossible. Many devote themselves to reinvesting purity in values: we do not lack for priests, especially in the media, but where are the horse-boys? The figures of this transgression have been brought to the fore from Hegel to Bataille; the history of the twentieth century is rife with the image of the intrinsically antiestablishment intellectual (you know about erotic literature as subversion; you know that Georges Bataille's *Blue of Noon* and some of his other novels illustrate this problematic, which I will not address here).[7] Though it remains fascinating and rich in meaning, it is not, in my view, something we can replay in the context of the end of this century. More enraged, and heavily indebted to psychosis, is the rejection of the law and being itself hammered out in the writing of Antonin Artaud. You may also be familiar with the rather smug deployment of perversion as revolt against the new puritan order. Such forms seem relegated to an old space where people still believed in the solidity of the prohibition. On the other hand, if prohibition is obsolete, if values are losing steam, if power is elusive, if the spectacle unfolds relentlessly, if pornography is accepted and diffused everywhere, who can rebel? Against whom, against what? In other words, in this case, it is the law/transgression dialectic that is made problematic and that runs the risk of crystallizing in spaces of repression such as the Islamic world and its *fatwas*. The decree against the writer Salman Rushdie and the call for his murder for his bold "blasphemy," illustrating a revolt culture in action that we Westerners willingly support, is not something we have within secular democracy. François Mitterrand is not an ayatollah, and no one in France wants to rebel against the republic. The prohibition/transgression dialectic cannot take the same forms in Islamic societies as in democracies where life is still fairly pleasant, where sexual permissiveness—less prevalent before 1968, one must admit—is considerable, despite the return to conformist tendencies, and where, consequently, eroticism itself is no longer a pretext for revolt. What can one do, then, to rebel in such a situation, when the margin for maneuvering is so reduced?

At this point, I propose a brief return to Freud, where we can detect at least three figures of revolt. First, there is the one just discussed, which might be called ancestral, which constitutes the social as well as sacred link; this no doubt seems very circumscribed and somewhat archaic for democracies today. Another of Freud's inventions is the notion of analytical space as a time of revolt. I use the term "revolt" here not in the sense of transgression but to describe the process of the analysand's retrieving his memory and beginning his work of anamnesis with the analyst, whom he refers to as a norm, if only because the analyst is the subject who is supposed to know, embodying the prohibition and its limits. It is in no way normative, conformist, or antipsychiatric to assert that the salutary analysand/analyst configuration inscribes the law at the heart of the analytical adventure. In the Freudian perspective, which already goes beyond the Hegelian dialectic, it seems that what is essential in anamnesis is not the confrontation between prohibition and transgression but rather the movements of repetition, working-through, working-out internal to the free association in transference. It is the course of memory that takes on the Nietzschean vision of an "eternal return" and permits a renewal of the whole subject. Repetition, working-through, working-out are logics that, in appearance only, are less conflictual than transgression, softer forms of the displacement of prohibition as the return of the past and possible renewal of the psychical space.

Consider the analytical situation. A patient goes to an analyst in order to remember his past, his traumas, his feeling of exclusion. A traumatic event has led him to cut himself off from his family, his circle of friends, the symbolic pact: "I" am unable to express myself, "I" am inhibited, "I" am depressed, "I" am marginalized because "I" have this or that sexuality. If the trauma can be understood as a psychical form of exclusion, it will be undone by analysis. This is the sacred space I described earlier, except that the logic of the analytical pact (the transference) is not that of a transgression, or inclusion in a group that is already there, or a taking of power, but a displacement of the traumatism, a progressive, incessant, and perhaps even interminable displacement, as in Freud's "interminable analysis." And to what will this displacement lead the analysand? To the possibility of working-out, working-through, and therefore to the construction of a veritable culture where displacement constitutes its source and essence. "I" undertake the narrative; "I" tell of familial or social situations in a way that is stranger and truer each time. "I" am a budding narrator. You may recognize here the Proustian "embodied time," "the search for lost time." In the best cases, analysis is an invitation to become the narrator, the novelist, of one's own story.

Memory put into words and the implication of the drive in these words—which create a style—would be one of the possible variants of revolt culture: again, not in the sense of prohibition/transgression but in the sense of anamnesis as repetition, working-through, working-out or, to replace the Freudian problematic with a Proustian one more accessible to students of literature, "the search for lost time" through narrative enunciation. Which leads me to think that in our civilization—given the impasses of religious forms of revolt as well as conflictual or dialectical political forms of revolt (prohibition/transgression)—psychoanalysis, on the one hand, and a certain literature, on the other, perhaps constitute possible instances of revolt culture. Provided we understand the word "revolt" as it is etymologically accepted: as return, displacement, plasticity of the proper, movement toward the infinite and the indefinite, as I discussed in the first chapter.

A third and final configuration will appear when I speak of the style and thought of Aragon, Sartre, and Barthes, that of the *combinatory* or the *game* as possible instances of revolt. Here, again, it is not a question of the confrontation between prohibition and transgression, of these dated dialectical forms, though they are still possible in certain contexts, but of *topologies*, spatial configurations that are more supple and probably more appropriate to this situation whose difficulty I continue to underscore: how does the patrimonial person that each of us risks becoming confront a power vacuum, armed for discourse with only a remote control? In other words, how, in our societies of the spectacle, does one revolt in the absence of real political power?

Throughout this book, I will try to clarify the two logics of revolt I have just described. But first I would like to explain why I did not refer to Mauss and pot-latch when I evoked the necessity for jouissance and violence in revolt.

There are a number of things I have not made reference to, but I could have talked about Mauss, who I deal with rather extensively in *Revolution in Poetic Language*. It would be equally possible, in discussing the pure and the impure, to cite Mary Douglas's work on the maternal element in the ambiguous figures of defilement. Still other anthropological models could be summoned to echo what I am saying about revolt as sacred space and its realization today. Keep in mind that they take at least two forms: some plunge into fundamentalism, others into nihilism and despair ("Nothing can be done"). How can one revolt when one is an ensemble of organs? And against whom?

The Permanence of the Divine and/or the Immanence of Language

Before going on to Aragon, Sartre, and Barthes, in the next few chapters I will introduce a few aspects of Freudian thought that strike me as important for a better understanding of the place of prohibition and jouissance, as well as the relations between them: in other words, various positions relating to the links that are not necessarily figures of transgression. I will try to analyze the profound logic of what constitutes this "higher side of man," as Freud wrote, which is nothing other than the intimate associate of the symbolic link with which, against which, and in which men and women revolt: language.

In this examination of Freudian models of language, notions of power and prohibition refer to the paternal figure, the murder of the father, and the institution of the symbolic prohibition. For all human beings, the instance of the paternal function, the function of authority, is given in an immanent manner in our aptitude for language. In other words, language is an immanent god, unless you would prefer to think of God as a metaphorical extrapolation of immanence. The secular belief—whose foundations we are still seeking, which must neither be too reductive nor too lethal—might be described as this: with language, we will be better able to think about the meaning of a statement such as "God is within us." If God is within us, it is because we are speaking beings. And it is worth looking at grammar and all the decorative appearances of language, as well as the place of language in the human being's constitution, autonomy, and relationship with others and with his own body, while taking into account all the parameters that Freudian thought sets in motion and that prevent this thought from being linguistic thought, even though it deals with language.

So if I speak of Freudian models of language, it is to situate what seems to me to be the central position of language in Freud, a place that Lacan had the good sense to underscore. This approach to Freud however may have been too crudely or even mistakenly interpreted; Lacan's reading started to head toward what he himself called "linguisterie," a structural approach to language that reduced the signifying functioning of human beings to a rudimentary linguistic schema. This is not at all the case with Freud. As a chronological reading of his texts shows, there are at least three models of language in Freud. These three models, which may at first appear far removed from the problematic of revolt, will allow us to define the imbrication of language in a more complex dynamic that includes both the drive and sacrifice and to address the social link, and the place of literature within it, in another way.

3

The Metamorphoses of "Language" in the Freudian Discovery (Freudian Models of Language)

The Site of Language: Heterogeneous Series with No Subject

The first of the three Freudian models of language can be found in *On Aphasia* (1891) and in "Project for a Scientific Psychology" (1895).[1] The second, a more directly psychoanalytical model, is essentially outlined in *The Interpretation of Dreams* (1900).[2]

Asymptote

The first model originates in an observation that brings us back to the notions of prohibition and transgression and the dualism Freud repeatedly addresses under different names. Freud noted an inadequacy, an imbalance, between the sexual and the verbal. What the speaking being *says* does not subsume sexuality. Sexuality cannot be spoken or, in any case, cannot be entirely spoken. Lacan took up this idea when he asserted that "jouissance is not everything" (*la jouissance n'est pas toute*) and that "the truth cannot tell itself entirely" (*la vérité ne peut pas se dire toute*). Sexual desire is only apprehended by language and intellect to a very small degree, if at all: "I" develop my intellect, "I" develop my language, but a part of my subjectivity functions under a sexual regime represented neither by language nor intellect. Sexual desire is, in sum, asymptotic to language and intellect. This asymptote may be due to neurosis: the gap between the language of neurotics and their sexuality is blatant, one could say. But another more essential hypothesis could also be advanced: that this is a component traceable to the immaturity of *infans*.[3]

Human beings, who are speaking beings, are born without the power to speak and, in this way, are more immature than animals who quickly manage to assume the life of their species, including its code of communication. Humans require a long learning period to acquire language, and this immaturity of *infans* is reflected later in the gap between man's biological aspect, whose maturation follows its own paths, and the symbolic aspect constituted by the acquisition and development of language. The particularity of our species, immature at birth, with an initial linguistic incapacity, carves out the asymptote between the sexual and the verbal and prevents the gap between them from one day being filled.

In the two hypotheses (neurosis or constituent immaturity), according to Freud, this asymptote induces if not an absence of translation then at least a flawed translation between unconscious representation and words. We may have unconscious representations, inscriptions in the deep layers of our psyches, of our activities—particularly sexual traumas we have undergone, other sexual experiences, or even our biology—but words bear witness to these experiences much later, if at all. Therefore, if the translation is flawed, or if it falters to the point of producing symptoms, an intermediary is required, in this case, psychoanalysis, in order to try to transmit unconscious representations across the gap of this asymptote, into words.

Freud was preoccupied by the observation of this hiatus in his earliest work and, of course, sought a means to fill it. This, we should recall, occurred between 1881 and 1895, when Freud was a neurologist, before psychoanalysis conceptualized this gap as a "repression," "cut," "splitting," "split," and so forth, based on a variety of structures. Freud's work on aphasia essentially used the theories of Meynert and Wernicke but displaced them. What do these theories say and what does Freud's displacement consist of? His predecessors supposed that peripheral sensorial data—what "I" hear, what "I" see—trigger a stimulation of the peripheral centers that is then conveyed to the brain, producing in it a *univocal* projection: hence the idea that nerve centers give commands to which "I" respond. The well-known form of the reflex arc typifies the articulation of this trajectory.

Freud replaced the idea of univocal projection with a *series* of levels of representations, in order to obtain what he called the psychological schema of word-presentation.[4] This combines a "closed complex" called *word-presentation* (centered on *sound-image* and including a *reading-image*, a *writing-image*, and a *motor-image*) and an "open complex" called *object-* or *thing-presentation* (centered on the *visual image* and including *tactile images*, *acoustic images*, etc.). A single representation is not enough for "I" to speak; two are needed—word-presentation and thing-presentation—that will work together. In addition, each of these representations is a series composed of several levels in itself. For example, if I imagine the thing "train," the sound level, visual level, tactile level, and so on of this representation constitute a complex, stratified set, which I will call a *layered* representation of the object or thing. Moreover, word-presentation, too, is composed of several elements of representation. The word "train" comprises not only its acoustic representation but also its reading-image, for "I" know how this word is spelled; the spelling of "train" is added to the sound "train." "I" must also consider graphic representation, because "I" can write, and therefore the representation of my motivity comes into play. Thus, as far as words are concerned, Freud positioned complex representations in series or levels: this polyphony and heterogeneity constituted the essence of his conception of language, at least at this point in his work.

It is useless to point out that the preceding description is very different from that of the sign proposed by Saussure: the signifier and the signified. Though one could say that word-presentation recalls the signifier and that object- or thing-presentation evokes the signified, both elements in Freud are composed of multiple strata, and this is far from the Saussurian images of a sheet of paper with its recto and verso. Instead, what we see unfold is a truly layered model of the system of psychical representation or, as Freud says in his text on aphasia, a "speech apparatus" made up of series of representations.

Heterogeneity

I would like to emphasize the *heterogeneity* inherent in what I call the first Freudian model of language (thing-presentation/word-presentation). Not only is the energetic facilitation—what Freud would later call *drive*—considerable in this model, but the types of representability or representation in question here are unwedged from language. Freud uses at least two registers of representation: one involves words and in part resembles the signifier of Saussurian semiology (as would be the case of the sound-image, although this is also dependent on other sensorial images of the word and cannot be assimilated to a linguistic signifier pure and simple); the other involves objects and evokes something pictorial and invested with energy, for which we do not, strictly speaking, have a semiological term. Keep in mind, in any case, that starting with his work on aphasia, Freud formulated different levels of representation and, more profoundly still, a heterogeneity of these levels marked in this way: language is certainly the organizer, but one must also consider the representations of things, which, while linked to words, are not part of the same domain of representation. In this sense, the psychical apparatus is made up of a series of representations—in the plural—whose differences have yet to be fully explored.

Freud sorts out this complex arrangement in "Project" (which, I remind you, dates from 1895), emphasizing the energetic aspect of psychical representatives. (This aspect was dismissed during the linguistic period of French psychoanalysis, in particular by Lacan himself. It is making a comeback today, with cognitivism and the attention given to the biological, but it is unfortunately being taken up in a monistic conception of the operations of the mind.) Freud maintains the principle of heterogeneity and remains essentially dualist. There are two systems, he explains in substance: the external *phi* system and the internal *psy* system, which can be joined or separated according to the passage of the quantitative charge Q, which transforms into a qualitative or psychological charge. Light hits my eye, so "I" see; my skin is burnt, so "I" feel (touch); my eardrum vibrates, so "I" hear; and so on. The energetic quantity surging in the perceptual system is propagated along the nerves in order to arrive at the brain and, thanks to a system of filters, resistances, and protections, manages to inscribe a *trace*, the foundation of memory.

Intermediary

It is at this point that Freud assigns an *intermediary role* to language, which has not been sufficiently underscored or even noted. We think we have said it all when we repeat after Lacan that "the subconscious is structured like a language," and we neglect the contribution of Freud, who, as a prudent man of science, sought to reconcile the "body" (energy) and the "mind" (representation) without eliminating any of these levels. He thus introduces a subsystem that serves as a junction between the quantitative (energetic) and the psychological (representation): verbal associations ([R.thing/R.word] + [R.thing/R.word] + etc.) allow thought to invest certain mnemic traces, assuring attention and making knowledge possible. Situated between thought and energy, language allows thought to reach and stabilize energy; it allows attention to be fixed and thought to be deployed; in sum, it balances the sensorial and/or the quantitative (the energetic, the libidinal) and abstraction. When I outline the second Freudian model of language, you will understand the essential role of language as a carrier wave of anamnesis and how it allows the passage of the abstract signified to unconscious and even corporal trauma, which permits psychoanalysis to use it as a laboratory for its investigations into the desired rebirth of the subject. But starting with "Project," language constitutes the subsystem situated between *phi* and *psy*: language is *at once phi* and *psy*, physical and psychological. It is physical because I articulate, because my words are sensorial, visual, sonorous, and so on. It is rooted in the physical world and in the quantitative charge of excitation. And it is also rooted in the psychological imprint. This dual nature allows it to be at the crossroads of the body and mind. Here is how Freud describes the process in his own terminology: verbal associations "put thought-processes on a level with perceptual processes, lend them reality and *make memory of them possible*."[5]

Those who have read Proust and my reflections on his work know that thought and perception become amalgamated in the writer's sentences.[6] It is true that everyday language and especially metalanguage (what I am using here, for example) do not make obvious Freud's assertion that language puts thought and perception on the same level. Abstract thought exists, and it in fact dissociates and unwedges itself from the perceptive. But Freud did not study abstract or mathematical languages. He targeted language in the current sense of the term, not an automated code, as might too easily be imagined, but the language the child learns, that of passionate and amorous communication. What interested him as an analyst, and what he would base psychoanalysis on as a result of the particularity of the amorous language he observed in the clinic, were the thought processes and perceptual processes situated on the same level. What kind of speech affects both thought and perception? Not intellectual arguments and vague abstractions but stories. Thus Freud would ask his patients to say whatever came to mind, to free-associate, to tell him stories, silly trifles. It was there that he would find what he needed, and what the patient needed, investigating the equivalence between thought and perception and particularly their original tie, hallucination.

Let us return to the text: "[Speech associations] put thought-processes on a level with perceptual processes, lend them reality and *make memory of them possible*." Not just any memory, of course, but precisely the perceptual memory that has escaped my thought, that "I" have repressed. Language, by making thought slip toward the perceptual, allows me to recapture a perceptual memory lost for reasons "I" am unaware of. Situated between energetic charge and perception (pain, for example), on the one hand, and logical activity ("ideas," "thoughts": these are Freud's terms), on the other, language acts as an interface and favors *knowledge* and *consciousness* (the preconscious-conscious system) while being supported by a substratum of heterogeneous representations (neuronic excitations, perceptions, sensations).

You are discovering, I think, what you may have been unaware of, namely, the complexity of the Freudian conception of language, which the structuralist period certainly highlighted but also oversimplified. We are invited to go beyond simple linguistic structure—"subject/verb/object" or "signifier/signified"—because language is a much more complex practice than we can imagine within the confines of semiology, whether that of Saussure or of Peirce. The neuronic data are neither erased nor absorbed; they are subjacent, structured, coded in order to obtain value solely by virtue of their relations with other elements. This is where Freud does in fact shift neurology toward a sort of structuralism *avant la lettre*: language is composed of a neuronic or quantitative substratum, but it does not become language until these stimulations are linked with other elements in order to form a structure that makes sense for the other: the other-recipient, as well as the other that "I" become to myself in listening to myself. The neuronic is overdetermined by the organization that is provided by the already-there (the *déjà-là*) of language, by the *socius*, by those who speak before me and to me (think, for example, of the child raised by wolves who never spoke).

Freud thus sketches out a site of language in the brain itself, contingent on stimulation (system Q), distinct from it, doubly articulated (R.thing/R.word), and with no need for a transcendental subject. It has two levels: a horizontal one, with articulation in linguistic categories, representations of things and words, that takes on meaning in the hearing of language; and a vertical one, with the neuronic stimulation where the drive will subsequently secure itself. The function of the psychical apparatus is thus to assure the translation among the three registers that are neuronic excitation, thing-presentation, and word-presentation, with failures in this translatability provoking various symptoms and pathologies. As you may have noticed, Freud never mentions a subject; he does not need a subject to articulate this dynamic. This notion will appear much later, in *Metapsychology*, as "subject of the drive," in the sense of agency and not the sense we use today. The study on aphasia develops a sort of non-centered combinatory that articulates the neuronic register, the R.thing/R.word organization, the listening of the other, but not the transcendental subject. Nor is there, I must stress, an unconscious organizer.

Freud will set aside the heterogeneity of what I call his "layered" conception of language in his subsequent work, when he develops the model of the dream as the royal path of the unconscious.[7] When Freud compares the unconscious to the dream, he asserts that the dream and/or the unconscious are not language but have to do instead with a drive reservoir that is articulated but based on *another* logic made up of displacements and condensations, like hieroglyphics and puzzles. It is as if Freud simplified his first model (neuronal, R.thing/R.word), which issued from the study of aphasias, in order to discover a logic proper to the functioning of the unconscious, perhaps to allow the deciphering of dreams without becoming mired in endless complications and to dissociate an autonomous psychoanalysis from neurobiology. But this "simplification" will not be without its consequences and will in turn require the development of a third model, introduced in 1910, which Freud will maintain until the end of his life, which will be the basis for a clinic and a theory of individuation, as well as the relationship to the other, and which will inscribe the murder of the father and the separation from the mother in transference. Far from being evacuated, language will then be integrated into Freudian thought with individuation as a condition of civilization. It will be understood as a stratum within a process that I propose calling *signifiance*, a term expressing the process, dynamic, and movement of meaning, not reduced to language but encompassing it.

To conclude, I underline once again the heterogeneity of Freud's first model of language. Certain psychoanalytical theories of the seventies will take it up, as will analysts faced with the clinical necessity of thinking about infralinguistic psychological functioning, either in psychosis or in poetry[8]: in 1970 W. R. Bion outlined his theory of symbolizing alpha function and nonsymbolized beta elements; in 1973 I made a distinction between the semiotic and the symbolic to point out the heterogeneity of verbal and infraverbal representations; and in 1975 Piera Aulagnier proposed pictograms as places of meaning articulation in psychosis.[9] Analysis was thus led to reengage and interpret this first Freudian model of language and to develop strategies to consider this truth: the psyche is not reduced to language, even if language is its organizer.

The Optimistic Model of Language Justifies "Free Association"

An Unconscious Under the Dominion of the Conscious

I have proposed a voyage through the Freudian models of language beginning with two of Freud's preanalytical studies: On Aphasia of 1891 and "Project for a Scientific Psychology" of 1895. The truly psychoanalytical model of language appears later in Freud, when he tackles the analytical practice and establishes the device of treatment, founded on the fundamental rule of free association. This model is essentially worked out in The Interpretation of Dreams of 1900. One might define it as an optimistic model, close to the structural conception of language. It is on this second model that Lacan will later rely to construct his own theory. I have already mentioned the idea that Freud's invitation to the patient to tell a story profoundly modified the traditional conception of language. And I would stress that it is indeed the story, and not signs or syntax, that allowed this modification to occur. I will come back to this in detail, but for now I would like to underscore another aspect of the second Freudian model as it appears in The Interpretation of Dreams.

What happened between 1892 (after the work on aphasia and the great neurological period) and 1900 (after the treatment of hysterical patients and the work on dreams)? Freud became convinced of the capacity of the associative story to translate unconscious traumatic contents, to illuminate them, and indeed to displace them. Listening to his patients confirmed his hypothesis, and this was what he would attempt to thematize.

Language is made up of "preconscious intermediate links" as Freud would point out later in The Ego and the Id (1923).[10] But starting with The Interpretation of Dreams, he asserted that the unconscious is dominated by the preconscious in treatment, for this occurs through language, on which treatment is based. In other words, language constitutes an intermediate zone, an interface between the unconscious and the conscious, and allows the former to be dominated by the latter. Language is not in the unconscious; the unconscious is not language; however, they do not exist independently of each other. (Those tempted to believe in the so-called biological purity of the Freudian unconscious, please take note.)

An ambiguity remains, however, because Freud defined the unconscious as both a reservoir of drives and as an agency dominated by the conscious, which opens the door to a linguistic interpretation of the unconscious.[11] "The only course which psychotherapy can pursue," Freud continued in *The Interpretation of Dreams*, "is to bring the Ucs. under the dominion of the Pcs."[12] As a psychoanalyst or psychotherapist, I understand the unconscious—can theoretically imagine it—as the domain of drives, independent of language; but it is always already under the dominion of the preconscious and the conscious, and I can only understand it through the intermediary of language. Thus by respecting the "fundamental rule of free association," the patient "reveals" not his biological surface or his libidinal surface (or rather depths) but, says Freud, "his *mental surface*, from instant to instant,"[13] namely his traumas, his drives, everything that causes psychological symptoms, and this in the form of language. Domain of the preconscious, language has the power to go further than conscious language and as far as unconscious oblivion. This is its force and its power: to conjoin the "mental surface" and unconscious oblivion. And this is the effectiveness, in therapy, of the fundamental rule of free association where language serves as fertile soil and has the capacity to pick out the memory trace as well as the unconscious libidinal charge, precisely because of the thing-presentation/word-presentation heterogeneity in the first model, which here is no longer hypostatized. Indeed, if the end of *The Interpretation of Dreams* takes up the model of "Project" (unconscious/preconscious/conscious), it is not to accentuate the quantitative charge that circulates among neurons or other aspects of the first stratified model but to depart from these quantitative and biological aspects and instead chart the *progressive* passage (the progress) of the dream's instinctual force, furnished by the unconscious in preconscious thought and thus linguistically formed and destined finally, and solely, to the conscious.

For the successful dominion of the conscious over the subconscious, the model of the unconscious must in turn be influenced by the linguistic conscious. Not only is language the intermediary between the unconscious and the conscious, but, so that the analyst can better understand it, so that "I" can see myself as a speaking and conscious subject, a structure must be conferred on it that *resembles* the linguistic conscious, that represents a certain audible, comprehensible linguistic form. Thus the dream, thought to be an exemplary actualization of the unconscious, its "royal path," according to *The*

Interpretation of Dreams, is certainly modeled as an other scene but also equipped from the start with a grammar and a rhetoric (displacement-condensation-overdetermination joining metonymy and metaphor) in the manner of conscious language. In other words, language is preconscious, it has a biological foundation and a mental surface, but it is articulated based on rules drawn from the language sciences. As for the dream, Freud would rid it of its mystery and hieroglyphic esotericism (which was nevertheless postulated) in order to compare it to language.

You see now why I qualify this second model as optimistic. Because the unconscious is articulated like a language, "I" can decipher it, "I" can discover its rules; in addition, because it is situated in an intermediary position between different agencies, it will give me access to the unknowable, that is, to trauma. The unconscious—a theoretical construction—will for these two reasons be the promised land of analysis.

Who Has Had No Experience of Contradiction?

"The Antithetical Meanings of Primal Words," an article by Freud dating from 1910, which I situate in the same second, optimistic period of this model of language, is not very well known but was studied closely by several linguists, Emile Benveniste, in particular.[14] Freud established, you will recall, the nonexistence of contradiction or the absence of negation in the language of the dream and the unconscious. The dream is not aware of contradiction, there is no "no" in dreams, "no" does not exist for the unconscious. If, however, a contradiction, a "no" appeared in a dream, it would not be read as such but as the affirmation of a desire. "I did not dream of my mother," our patient tells us. "You *did* dream of your mother," Freud corrects. And just as there is no negation in the unconscious, there is no duration, or time (I will return later, and at length, to this notion of the suspension of time in the unconscious). Freud was delighted to find the same logic of the absence of contradiction, a feature of the unconscious, in "primal words" as described in Karl Abel's etymological speculations. (Though it has since been shown that this etymologist was wrong, at the time his propositions were not only accepted but well regarded.) In certain so-called primitive languages—including Latin—Abel explained, the same word might express two opposite ideas; the same word might signify "deep" and "high," for example. This shows, Freud adds, that primitive languages function like the unconscious, without contradiction, that they demonstrate in a way the functioning of the unconscious. The dream state and primal languages thus share the absence of contradiction.

How can one interpret this comparison of unconscious logic to that of "primal language"? In two ways, I think. On the one hand, Freud tends to erase the irreducible alterity of the unconscious in relation to the conscious, which he has nevertheless postulated, by discovering in this other scene a functioning identical to that of eminently conscious language. The unconscious has nothing to do with the conscious, he asserted in *The Interpretation of Dreams* but not long afterward claimed in "Primal Words" that language exists—that of primitive languages—that shares the properties of the unconscious. This may appear to be a direct result of Freud's intention, already mentioned, to place the unconscious under the dominion of the conscious. The unconscious is not an obscure, illogical, aberrant state of mind; the conscious is present in these secret and mysterious regions and dominates them.

On the other hand, and conversely, as a result of Freud's comparison of primitive languages and the unconscious, language traditionally considered conscious finds itself invested with paradoxical logics, unconscious logics: words, even primitive ones, act as a dream does. This would allow one to infer that a social practice might exist where words act as in dreams, and there may be other situations—poetry, myths—where conscious discourse also acts as dreams. This considerably expands, I'm sure you would agree, the field of the unconscious. An interpretation of the two scenes (conscious and unconscious) results, which no doubt satisfies the Freudian intuition of the human mind's permanent dualism (the unconscious is not the conscious) and for the moment (1910) does not call into question Freud's confidence in language as a link between the conscious and the unconscious; it consequently raises amnesia to the status of instinctual trauma. In other words, starting with the conscious, "I" can have access to the other scene; moreover, in certain situations in his conscious life, man behaves as though he were unveiling his unconscious. Access to the unconscious is thus possible.

This, in my opinion, is the fascination that Abel's proposition exerted over Freud. Thanks to this etymological "discovery," Freud could express what I call his "linguistic optimism," which consisted of positing that language is the control mechanism of unconscious traumas. I remind you nevertheless, that scholars such as Benveniste refuted Abel's thesis, which did not consider the position of the subject of the enunciation in the act of discourse. Indeed, if the same word signifies "deep" and "high," it is because the subject of the enunciation has moved; the subject is high atop a ladder when saying that a well is deep and at the bottom of the ladder when commenting on its height. In other words, it is the position of the subject of the enunciation that changes the perspective and adjusts the semantic differences, which are not therefore necessarily manifested in the words themselves. The interlocutor, on the other hand, is never led astray and does not confuse the meaning of identical words,

for the context of the discursive act—with the help of adverbs, personal pronouns, innuendoes, and even gestures—removes any ambiguity. There is no
oneiric functioning in the conscious, discursive act. Contrary to the dream,
language is a system of differences and discriminations and not the confusion
of opposites. As for Freud, he makes ideological use of Karl Abel's mistakes to
assert: I find the unconscious in words; thanks to words, I can reach the unconscious and thereby justify my optimistic model of language.

Mathesis *and Drive*

You will see that the third model is much less optimistic, but for now let us stay
with the second, and *The Interpretation of Dreams*, and consider Lacan's contribution. In my opinion, the Lacanian assertion that "the subconscious is structured like a language" constitutes a careful reading of this second Freud, whose
essential aim Lacan elucidates. I am not one of those who feel Lacan indulges
in an overly personal interpretation of Freud because he speaks of the signifier
and not the drive and who are content to point out the outrageousness of the
Lacanian reading. On the contrary, I think this reading applies all the rigor of
the philosophy and linguistics of the sixties to the second Freud, and this Lacanian rigor was certainly new. Nevertheless, the idea that language and the
unconscious are dominated by the conscious, that the unconscious is organized
like a grammar or rhetoric, is a Freudian position that does, in effect, support
the statement that "the subconscious is structured like a language."

The mathematicization of the unconscious pursued by the Lacanian
school and, in another way, the cognitivistic ascendancy over unconscious figures—the computational strategies applied today to conscious and unconscious processes—seem to me affiliated with this second Freudian program,
formulated in *The Interpretation of Dreams*: Psychotherapy's "task being to en-
sure that the unconscious processes are settled and forgotten. . . . *The only
course which psychotherapy can pursue is to bring the Ucs. under the dominion
of the Pcs.*"[15] This attempt to capture the unconscious in the conscious is, I
think, very clearly inscribed in the Freudian project at this moment. It is not
possible because language, as Freud understands it, is itself the place of this
domination of the unconscious by the conscious. (I would also like to point out
here that the unconscious of cognitivists has nothing to do with the Freudian
other scene and that it ignores the primary processes and the other logic that
governs sexual traumas; the cognitivistic pseudounconscious refers essentially
to automatic functionings and mechanical acts and concerns lack of attention
rather than the unconscious.)

If we harden the Lacanian line as I have traced it, we end up getting rid of what still constituted Freudian dualism at the heart of this second model, a dualism that situates language between the conscious and unconscious while at the same time maintaining the dualist drive/conscious vision. We thus liquidate the instinctual domain as well as the primary processes. This is the tendency of a certain current in French Lacanian and post-Lacanian psychoanalysis that considers the notion of the drive useless. The drive is a myth, adherents of this point of view are basically telling us, because we do not have access to it except through language. It is therefore useless to talk about drives; we should be content to talk about language.

The Freudian point of view is entirely different: the drive and the primary processes are irreducible to the secondary processes, though subject to their domination. Certain modern analytical currents, and cognitivists too, are free not to see either the pertinence or the usefulness of the drive and primary processes, but from then on they are situated outside the camp of psychoanalysis and the radicalness that testifies to the division of the speaking subject. I will have occasion to return to the ambiguity of the Lacanian clinic in this regard, but before passing on to the third Freudian model of language, I will sum up the features of the second:

- language's intermediary situation between the conscious and unconscious;
- the domination of the unconscious by language and by the conscious, which opens the way for a mathematicization of the unconscious and may lead to cognitivistic positions; and
- the maintenance of a dualism that preserves the existence of a drive reservoir, which certain epigoni would like to eliminate.

The Symbolic Pact and Phylogenesis: From *Signifiance* to Being

Most of those who greeted the advent of structuralism stick to the second model of language in Freud, which culminates in the texts from 1910 to 1912. Freudian thought is more complex, however, for he elaborates on his initial theories rather extensively, developing a conception of meaning that is no longer solely dependent on language, that becomes more complex, and that, because it poses problems, unveils the fertility of the analytical process, its irreducibility to what Lacan would criticize as "linguisterie." I hope I have shown how "linguisterie" might, in effect, have been deduced from the second model of *The Interpretation of Dreams*, but Freud moved away from this model to construct the one I will call the model of *signifiance*.

Assimilation-Hominization

A turning point in Freudian thought occurred around 1912–1914 and intensi-
fied with World War I and its effects on Freud's personality and analytical theory. Freud would in fact be seriously shaken by the tragedy of the war and its
effects on his family, his sons, and his method itself. *Totem and Taboo* (1912) already harbors the elements of the third model of language and emphasizes the
difference between acts that are repeated without having psychological representatives (in particular, the murder of the father), on the one hand, and, on
the other, an assimilation-identification with the agency of power represented
by the father that is effected through the totemic meal, which generated the
symbolic pact between the brothers.[16]

It may be useful to detail this process and to remember that in *Totem and
Taboo*, Freud gives a (fictional?) account of the essential stage of hominization
through which *Homo sapiens* becomes a social animal by identifying not with
the *tyranny* of the father (which once crushed him) but with the function of *authority* (which henceforth elevates him to the rank of subject of a culture). Simultaneously, Freud highlights two psychological strategies: *unrepresentable
acts* (coitus and murder will be two prototypes of this) versus *structuring representations* through identification with the father. In other words, the brothers
revolt against the father who took women away from them and accumulated all
power and kill him in the course of a violent act. This act is repeated at first without giving rise to a psychological representative and evokes what in our individual lives constitutes trauma: we have been affected by one or several acts,
sexual seduction or violence, which come back to us (as do our passive or violent reactions) without our being able to represent them to ourselves in order
to think about them, name them, master them, traverse them, forget them.
These traumas incite somaticizations, nonpsychical abreactions, symptoms,
maladies, behavioral disturbances, and acting out. Similarly, the killing of the
father of the primitive horde by the sons may be repeated in an obsessive manner, Freud thinks, without being represented in the human psyche, until the
devouring-assimilation, through the totemic meal, becomes a symbolic act of
psychological identification with the function of the father.

There has been no lack of criticism of Freud on this subject: this is his own
personal fantasy, his own delirium, a perfect example of the Freudian novel,
of Freudian subjectivity, and so on. We need not dismiss these suspicions, but
we must try to appreciate his theoretical contribution, to take his totemic fable
seriously. Through this scenario, beyond the problematics of prehistory, Freud
is trying to contemplate the traumatic acts his patients, and perhaps he himself, suffered during childhood. Why are these acts traumatic? Why do they incite other violent acts or somaticizations? Because they do not find represen-

tation. "I" have undergone such violent experiences, "I" have been so violently excluded, that "I" can only become a criminal or commit an act analogous to the one "I" underwent, even if "I" am unaware of it: taking drugs, for example, in order to obliterate my consciousness. In other words, the trauma causes a chain of acts that leave the suspense of the representation intact.

Now, Freud explains that the brothers who murdered the father of the primitive horde did not simply repeat the traumatic act endlessly but proceeded through the totemic meal to assimilate-identify with the power that traumatized them; that is, they ate the father and thereby assimilated him in both the concrete and metaphorical sense of the term: they became him, and he became them, and, in becoming power, they ceased to be excluded from it. Through this totemic meal, a trace of which is found in all religions, they contracted a symbolic pact and thus formed an ensemble, a culture. The subtlety is apparent, I hope: the brothers' revolt does not remain a simple unrepresentable act; a qualitative leap occurs whereby the sacred act henceforth constitutes a symbolic link. The sons, the brothers, become fathers in turn. *Totem and Taboo* places in narrative form a very important stage in hominization whereby *Homo sapiens* becomes a social animal, identifying not with the tyranny of the father but with his function of authority: this is the act of hominization, the act of culture.

The absence of women is glaring here, as you have no doubt noticed. I will later address the question of the feminine and the symbolic pact specifically, but for now it must be noted that in this text Freud remains discreet as to the fate of the brothers' femininity. How did they resolve their potentiality of being the wives of the father, that is, the submissive or passive victims of the paternal sexual drive, a potentiality suggested by the emphasis on the homosexual bond established among the brothers as they gathered around the dead father? Freud tells us even less about the fate of the women who, after the murder of the father and the creation of the pact, become objects of desire and exchange among the brothers. By saying nothing about the feminine, Freud remains faithful to the social pact—to the rule of the society that excludes women from the brothers' religion—and perhaps faithful to his own tendencies as well. Nevertheless, we ought to recognize that the founder of psychoanalysis had the honesty to express the homosexual substratum of the sacred understanding, the split of this social destiny into homosexual destiny, which he does not, however, investigate further. The brothers band together by repressing their femininity and distancing the sexual exchange of women from the sacred and social space. This will constitute the sphere of the private, the erotic, and the repressed.

Now I return to two psychological strategies Freud outlines in *Totem and Taboo*: on the one hand, unrepresentable acts, the prototypes of which are the murder of the father and coitus (for this is why the brothers reproach the father:

they desire the right to pleasure with women, and he has seized all the women); and, on the other hand, structuring representations through identification with the father. It is here that the notion of *signifiance* emerges, which has nothing linguistic about it, because Freud is investigating not the structure of language but the psychological dynamic and the dichotomy between *act* and *representation*, between the *unrepresentable* and the symbolic *contract surrounding authority*. These parameters, strictly speaking, have nothing to do with linguistics.

Narcissism, Melancholia, and the Death Drive

In the period following *Totem and Taboo*, Freud continues to refine his theory on variants of psychical representations, or formations, being careful not to put language at the forefront. In 1914 he defines narcissism as "a new psychical action," new because distinct from autoeroticism but anterior to the object triangulations in Oedipus.[17] Autoeroticism, narcissism, and the oedipal stage are thus gradually introduced in the life of the subject, and narcissism appears as a primary identity organization, a primary autonomization that is neither very strict nor very clear at this point, because we will have to wait for the oedipal triangulation for psychical autonomy to occur.[18]

As Freud underscores in his 1914 text, narcissism is characterized by instability. (Note in passing that the current use of the term "narcissism" is naive and erroneous, because it refers to a person who is full of himself, sure of himself, and triumphant, whereas the Freudian Narcissus does not know who he is at all and only invests in his image because he is not sure of his identity. In reality, then, narcissism is a borderline state between identity security and insecurity.) Why is this organization unstable, on the border? Because it is still too dependent on the other—in this case, the mother—from whom the subject is in the process of separating. It is a pseudoidentity on the way to constitution, not yet stabilized by the oedipal triangulation. Freud thus situates himself in a new perspective, quite different from the earlier linguistic optimism, in which he details the stages of what I call *signifiance*, which, instead of separating drives and words, is organized in intermediary structures.

In 1915 the term "subject," as opposed to "object," appeared in Freud's writings on the drive.[19] The subject, he says, is the subject of the drive, and not the subject of language. I must emphasize this point. Three polarities of psychical life are distinguished, which will articulate the Freudian metapsychology:

- subject (ego)–object (external world);
- pleasure-displeasure; and
- active-passive.

Let us explore the evolution of these elements of Freudian theory, which allow a definition of this third model of language that I call *signifiance*. In 1917 "Mourning and Melancholia" deepened the ambivalence between subject and object.[20] In melancholia, for example, the object is at once external and internal, at once loved and hated, and for this reason, it engenders depression: "I" was abandoned by my lover, a colleague at work hurt me, he/she is my enemy, and the like. But it does not stop there. It is impossible to change partners or plans, for the object that has caused me pain is not only hated but also loved and thus identified with me: "I" am this detestable other, "I" hate myself in his/her place, that is why he/she incites my depression, which sometimes goes as far as suicide, an impossible, disguised murder.

The fourth and last movement occurs in 1920, with the appearance of the extraordinary postulate of the death drive, which is the carrier wave of the life drive. Freud postulated the life drive as *libido* during the construction of the optimistic model in *The Interpretation of Dreams*, where he told us the dream is the realization of a desire acted on by a linking drive, a binding drive that founds desire, the sexual act, and love. But as the analysis of his patients gradually unfolded, Freud recognized that the binding drive is not the only thing that programs our physical life: there are also resistances to the optimal evolution of the subject and to analysis. He then posited the existence of another drive that goes against the life drive, which he called the death drive, the unbinding drive.[21]

We often fail to differentiate between the erotic drive and the death drive, between Eros and Thanatos. We should recall that Eros is linking, while Thanatos is unlinking: it cuts. Melancholia offers a striking representation of this: links with the other are cut, "I" isolate myself from the world, "I" withdraw into my sadness, "I" do not speak, "I" cry, "I" kill myself. And this unbinding that has cut me off from the world will end up cutting me off from myself, destroying my thought as it cuts off the continuity of representation. The most radical Freudian postulate, which has often been perceived as Freud's pessimism but perhaps at bottom is merely evidence of his lucidity, consists in positing the death drive as the most instinctual. An enigmatic postulate, to be sure, but it affirms that the carrier wave is the unbinding drive and the life drive is only a sort of calming, or ordering, of it. In other words, beneath the life drive, beneath eroticism, we must expect to find the diabolical work of the death drive.

Language, Source of Errors

What becomes of language as a result of this construction? How does it allow us to understand language? A detour is necessary before answering these questions. In the meantime, the resistances to analysis manifest themselves, preventing recovery, interrupting treatment, and blocking its process. These resistances did not make Freud reject the fundamental rule of free association (this so-called pessimism never made him say there are too many problems, the tool is useless; he never abandoned the initial basis of his theory) but instead led him constantly to modify his optimism about the effectiveness of the rule and to reevaluate language and establish the second topic. *The Ego and the Id* (1923) and the article "Negation" (*Die Verneinung*, 1925) will help us to understand this evolution in its initial stages and most confident phase.

First of all, with regard to the place of language, Freud maintained his theory that unconscious representations are distinct from verbal representations but capable of being associated with them and, as a result, capable, through language, of reaching consciousness. There is no language in the unconscious, which is a reservoir of drives; verbal representations exist in the realm of the preconscious; what is instinctual is therefore unconscious but can reach the conscious: "The real difference between a *Ucs.* and a *Pcs.* idea (thought)," Freud writes, is

> that the former is carried out on some material which remains unknown, whereas the latter (the *Pcs.*) is in addition brought into connection with word-presentations. This is the first attempt to indicate distinguishing marks for the two systems, the *Pcs.* and the *Ucs.*, other than their relation to consciousness. . . . Only something which has once been a *Cs. perception* can become conscious, and . . . anything *arising from within* (apart from feelings) that seeks to become conscious must try to transform itself into *external perceptions*: this becomes possible by means of memory-traces. . . . A word is after all the mnemic residue of a word that has been heard.[22]

The preconscious—which is verbal—has thus first been perceived; verbal stimulation has come from others through discourse that has been perceived and then forgotten; this forgotten perception has fallen into the unconscious where it has become a memory trace; and these words that are heard, welded to perceptions, their mnemic traces forgotten, are what preconscious words heard today will seek out. The psychical apparatus therefore engages in a double game with words: first, words have been sown in me like seeds, words "I" have perceived that have fallen into oblivion; they have formed mnemic traces onto which perceptions have been grafted, as well as drives emanating from within the body; finally, it is this unconscious conglomerate, ruled by the mnemic trace, that I recover through the intermediary of words as they presently function in my adult preconscious psyche.

In the second, optimistic model, what gave preconscious verbal representations their major role as the control lever of repression itself (and thus the power to transfer us from consciousness to the drive) were these verbal representations. Having once been perceptions[23]—in contrast to abstract ideas, which are consequently useless in treatment aiming to lift repression—they could, like all memory traces, become conscious again. It is because there were perceptions in words that these word-perceptions—the Freudian sign is a heterogeneous doublet—can be linked to the drive and therefore to the corporal, physical, traumatic investment and to linguistic representation, to consciousness. The words-doublets remain a crossroads among perception, the ancient memory trace, and consciousness, and it is starting at this crossroads that words—as Freud understands them—are able to become the essential tool of psychoanalysis. This applies to the optimistic model that Freud maintained until the end of his life.

But skepticism moved in, and an important change appeared in Freudian thought, probably as a result of his more extensive confrontation with psychosis: words, he stated, are not simply the guarantors of our ability to recapture perceptions or real memory traces; this advantage has a flip side. Words not only allow internal things to become conscious but, conversely, may also be the source of errors and hallucinations; it is not as easy as it seems to travel from perception to consciousness and vice versa. Language can cease to be the solid terrain that leads to truth. Freud considered this problem again in later texts, "Constructions in Analysis" (1937) and *An Outline of Psycho-Analysis* (1938).[24] Language "brings material in the ego into a firm connection with the mnemic residues of visual, but more particularly of auditory, perceptions. Thenceforward the perceptual periphery of the cortical layer can be excited to a much greater extent *from inside as well*, internal events such as passages of ideas and thought-processes can become conscious. . . . The equation 'perception = reality (external world)' *no longer holds. Errors*, which can now easily arise and do so regularly in dreams, are called *hallucinations*."[25]

Given these two limits of the power of language (resistance-hallucination), the rest of *The Ego and the Id*, which situates language in the preconscious, does not explore the linguistic problematic. It takes another path, the first step toward the second topic. It is heir to the subject of drives as well as the "father complex"[26] as established by the oedipal and by *Totem and Taboo*, which seeks out "the higher side of man" revealed in religion, morality, and social feeling.[27] Freud did not hypostatize this "higher side," thereby rendering it unknowable; on the contrary, he scrutinized it closely in the evolution of his patients, distinguishing in it identification, idealization, and sublimation. I call this the process of *signifiance*.

The goal Freud set for himself was not to define language but to open psychoanalysis to a vaster process of symbolization in which language had its place but was not the common denominator. In sum, verbal representations were maintained but temporarily put aside in favor of the more global process that Freud established in the second chapter of *The Ego and the Id*.

"Tired" or "Adolescent"

Before returning to the process of *signifiance* and approaching Freud's second topic via *The Ego and the Id*, I want to make a small digression and respond to a question I was asked: does speaking of psychoanalysis as a discourse of revolt mean that the couch is expected to rise up and take power? The question has a certain freshness, and it offers me the chance to make two clarifications.

First of all, I have pointed out that the term "revolt" must be understood in an etymological and Proustian sense. Add to this two well-known statements by Freud: "Where it was, there I must come about" [*Wo Es war, soll Ich werden* = Where it (id) was, there I (ego) must come about.—Trans.] and "I succeed where the paranoiac fails." The patient, the analysand, is thought to occupy the place of this "there." And this "there" is an anamnesis, a memory buried in the unconscious (which the return of the repressed makes available) or deposited in the person's history, including generational history and possibly phylogenesis (though this last perspective is debatable). In an even more untenable way, this place—where I must come about in my recollection—is a place where the namable and the unnamable, the instinctual and the symbolic, language and what is not language, are dissociated. It is a perilous place, a place of subjective incoherence, a difficult position for subjectivity.[28] Revolt here is not an advance toward "singing tomorrows" but, on the contrary, a return and a process.[29]

Why, given this, can't I stick to the term "recollection"? Why have I felt obliged to use the term "revolt," even if it means emphasizing its etymological sense? Precisely so as not to give the impression that the analytical experience and the literary experience, in different ways, consist of simple recollection, simple repetition of that which has taken place, but instead represent, as Mallarmé says, "a prior future." A modification, a displacement of the past, occurs and, by returning to painful places, especially if they are nerve centers, there is a reformulation of the psychological map (in the optimal hypothesis, of course). Lacan had a great line on the subject—"Psychoanalysis can make the imbecile cunning"—and this can also be seen: by repeating and appropriating his symptoms, the subject is fixed there; he repeats them and may even normalize himself with the entire universe manipulated by his symptoms, which are finally integrated, gratified, recognized. Certain analysts—such as Winnicott, in the pediatric perspective (with all the delicacy this presupposes)—see the end of an analysis as a rebirth. As for me, I prefer the term "revolt," because I want to address not only the analytical experience but also the literary one. And I want to point up the angry, even enraged, sense of this rebirth in literary texts, as well as in patients' free association. Those of you who have worked on such texts, particularly twentieth-century texts, know how much they are animated by a desire to overturn the world, oneself, the Other, love, and death. It is from this perspective that I associate the terms "repetition," "recollection," and "anamnesis" with that of "renewal" and propose to reflect on their condensation in the connotations of the word "revolt."

My second clarification has to do with the history of psychoanalysis and allows me to defend my own position. Years ago, Catherine Clément published a book called *Les Fils de Freud sont fatigués* to warn against a certain reassessment of analytical theories.[30] Her diagnosis seemed a bit pessimistic to me, but it was not devoid of truth. Indeed, perhaps "Freud's daughters," for oedipal reasons that I will outline soon, are even more fatigued than his sons. I think, for example, of Helene Deutsch, a disciple of Freud who introduced notions that are still used concerning "as-if" personalities called "false selves." She was interested in political movements, art, literature, and, above all, the states of the personality where we construct masks for ourselves, which she explored with her patients. These defensive procedures come in handy at times, although eventually we can no longer bear the weight of them, and their hazards then motivate the request for analysis.

Deutsch believed that one could not conduct analysis (and I think the same goes for interpreting literary texts) without maintaining a certain openness in one's own psychical apparatus, a flexibility that ultimately represents an aptitude for revolt. There was no use maintaining a position of normative truth—although the position of the "subject thought to know," as Lacan called it, is a necessary aspect of analysis—if the analyst was not also what Deutsch called "an eternal adolescent." This may sound odd, because we know that the eternal adolescent is immature and capriciously fragile, moving from depression to hysteria, from amorous infatuation to disappointment. But eternal adolescence also indicates a certain suppleness of agencies, an adaptability, a capacity to modify oneself according to the environment and the other, as well as against them. It is this aspect that it is important to cultivate, not only when one listens to patients but also when one reads literary texts. Then, and only then, will texts appear not as fetishes or dead objects corresponding to definite states of history or rhetoric but as so many experiences of psychical survival on the part of those who have engaged in the struggle and on our part as well.

And now for one last digression, a few words about Guy Debord's suicide, which was a cultural and literary event.[31] He was a rebellious man, and it was as a rebellious man that he diagnosed this society as a "society of the spectacle," whose cogs he revealed in the East as well as the West, whose evolution he analyzed in an ultraclassical manner, borrowing the tones of Cardinal de Retz, Bossuet, Saint-Simon, and finally Lautréamont when he was formulary and classically dense. It was certainly an act of revolt to adopt this style, and one may consider Debord's suicide the ultimate gesture of revolt as well. Unless—as certain of his friends and associates fear and regret—it was an involuntary affirmation of the all-powerfulness of the spectacle that had managed to force its most violent detractor into a voluntary and dramatic annihilation that was immediately celebrated and nullified. Is all pathetic resistance to the spectacle destined to be reduced and remote-controlled? Does the spectacle feed on spectacular death? The question is worth asking, if only to try to step "outside the ranks" where the murderous align, to use Kafka's phrase, to step to the side, into the invisible labyrinth of inquiry, into a clamorous struggle against morality, or simply to search for a style. Indeed, to denounce something in a classically bombastic way clearly required admirable courage. To seek, in the negative, to arrive "where it was" is another path I will try to illuminate in this book; it does not contrast with Debord's but is connected to it, discreetly.

As you can see, even the most untenable revolt leads me to acts of language—and to their traps. Here I return to the third model of language that seems to me to be sketched out in Freudian theory and that I have begun to explain as a process of *signifiance* founded on the negative.

Without analyzing language, strictly speaking, Freud includes it in the signifying capacity of speaking beings, the *signifiance* that interests the semiotician and that Freud calls, in *The Ego and the Id*, the "higher side of man." According to Freud, it is made accessible to the psychoanalytical experience through three modalities that I will detail here and then illustrate with a clinical example. These modalities are *identification*, *idealization*, and *sublimation*, found in the analytical as well as aesthetic experience.

Einfühlung

The first variant of identification—which Freud called "primary"—occurs with an imaginary schema, with "the father of the individual's own personal prehistory," which is totally different from libidinal object–cathexis.[32] This phenomenon recurs with amorous idealization in the lover's discourse. This is a very archaic stage in the development of the future speaking being, brought into play with a schema that Freud refers to as an archaic occurrence of paternity. This has nothing to do with the subsequent father who forbids, the oedipal father, the father of the law. Direct and immediate, this primary identification—Freud speaks of an *Einfühlung*—is a sort of flash, not unlike the hypothesis of the irruption of language in human history (a hypothesis taken up by Lévi-Strauss according to which the evolution of language occurred all at once rather than slowly through the acquisition of rudiments leading progressively to total proficiency).[33]

Although the primary identity occurs with the father in the individual's "own personal prehistory" and seems at the outset connoted in the masculine, Freud points out that it also creates an ambivalence, for this archaic father comprises the characteristics of both parents. Is this an identification with the phallic mother? Not really. At this archaic stage of the psychical evolution, the subject already moves away from the mother/child dyad and toward a third pole, not yet a symbolic agency but already the beginning of the thirdness prefigured by the mother's desire for someone other than the child (her father? the child's father? an extrafamilial or symbolic agency?). In the uncertainty of this disengagement, however, an imaginary space is sketched out where this loving third party is found, the "father of the individual's prehistory," the keystone of our loves and imagination.

With this primary identification—degree zero of identity, according to Freud—I will try to put into perspective two more recent propositions concerning the archaisms of the subject: Lacan's "mirror stage" and Didier Anzieu's "ego-skin."[34]

The mirror stage is thought to constitute the primordial stage of an imaginary identification. Influenced by the maternal relationship, the image of the ego is already recognized as separate from the mother's, though dependent on her presence.

The tactile contact with the maternal container is primordial in another way: the sensitivity of the skin furnishes a primary delimitation of the future ego vis-à-vis the rest of the world that the mother announces. It is on this skin surface that the numerous difficulties of individuation will be played out, from eczema to the most diverse eruptions, concerning the boundaries not only of the skin but also of psychical endurance. Skin as a surface of perception and projection of the ego is the substrata of the mirror, the first container able to reassure, to calm, to give the child a certain autonomy, on which the narcissistic image may be supported and without which the mirror will smash into pieces. The psychotic fragmentation of the subject suggests a damaged skin as well as a mirror without silvering. And although these "skin" and "mirror" stages are maternal in the identification of the subject, they are dependent on the "father of the individual's prehistory."

If it is true that the skin is the first container, the archaic limit of the ego, and that the mirror is the first vector of represented and representable identity on the other sensorial vector that is the gaze, what are the conditions for both of them occurring and becoming optimal containers? The answer is to be found in the "father of prehistory." This primary thirdness allows a space between the mother and the child; perhaps it prevents osmosis as well as the merciless war where self-destruction alternates with destruction of the other. For this reason, the "father of the individual's own personal prehistory"—well before the oedipal prohibition—is a barrier against infantile psychosis.

Later, in the aesthetic experience, it is this figure of the loving father—which so many religions celebrate, particularly the Christian religion, forgetting the war of Oedipus against Laius and denying the revolt of the son against the law—on which the artist relies when, in paintings or texts, he depicts the diabolical or abject figure of a woman-mother from whom it is vital that he separate. The idealization of the father, the beatific reparation of his image that supports these experiences, in effect constitutes a denial of the oedipal reality. It is indispensable to note, however, that this denial is in some way counterbalanced by the rehabilitation of the "father of the individual's own personal prehistory," thanks to which the subject is not mired in perversion but finds the resources (imaginary, strictly speaking) to continue the revolt integral to his autonomy and to his creative freedom. The artist's debt to the maternal grandfather or uncle, and, of course, the religious allegiances that lead him to celebrate the sacred figures of paternity in the religion of his choice, function in this same vein.

Sublimation

After this initial phase of subjectification, two additional stages detail the *signifiance* Freud points out in the second topic. First, the ego primitively identified with the "father of prehistory" takes *itself* for the object or rather may become the object of the id: look, you can love me, "I" so resemble the object! Note what the sublimatory process consists of. Initially identified with the father of the "individual's own personal prehistory," the ego invests itself: that is, it loves itself insofar as it is identified with the imaginary loving father, and this love is not a sexual libido but a narcissistic one. "The transformation of object-libido into narcissistic libido . . . obviously implies an abandonment of sexual aims, a desexualization—a kind of sublimation, therefore."[35] Such a transformation leads to the dissociation or defusion of different drives (particularly the two principal ones, of life and death) and liberates the death drive. Here we confront a strange capacity of the ego identified with the imaginary father of

"the individual's prehistory." By disengaging from the drives to become ho-
minized and gain access to the imaginary that will lead to linguistic representation, the ego deeroticizes itself and, in so doing, exposes itself to the death
drive: "By thus getting hold of the libido from the object-cathexes, setting itself up *as sole love-object*, and desexualizing or sublimating the libido of the id,
the ego is working in opposition to the purposes of Eros and placing itself at
the service of the opposing instinctual impulses" (p. 45).

Isn't this outrageous? Narcissus placing himself at the service of the death
drive! Freud is telling us that the death drive is inscribed *at the outset* in the
process of subjectification, or the constitution of the ego as the initial and indispensable stage in the transformation of the drive into *signifiance*. Put otherwise, even more paradoxically, it is the death drive that consolidates the narcissistic ego and allows the prospect of investing not an erotic object (a partner)
but a pseudo-object, a production of the ego itself, that is quite simply its own
aptitude to imagine, to signify, to speak, to think: the ego invests *signifiance*
when it deeroticizes and utilizes the death drive internal to its narcissism. You
must admit, at the very least, it's dramatic! Language abandoned in favor of a
vaster process that I have called *signifiance* and that Freud calls "the thought
process" or "intellectualization" leads the founder of psychoanalysis to relate
the idealization-sublimation-religion-culture series to . . . the death drive.

We know the superego's tendency toward this: if it cannot repudiate its
acoustic origins, if its verbal representations (notions and abstractions) make it
accessible to consciousness, and if the cathectic energy of these contents come
from the id, the superego embraces sadism and rages against the ego: "What is
now holding sway in the super-ego is, as it were, a pure culture of the death instinct" (p. 54). Kleinians have moreover remarked that when language manifests itself in the child, the future speaking subject goes through a depressive
phase: he experiences—and, through the affect of sadness, depicts—his separation from the mother. Only following this melancholic experience is he able
to recapture the lost object (the mother) in the imagination: first by seeing her
and then by naming her, transforming echolalia into veritable linguistic
signs.[36]

Once again I emphasize the ambiguity at the heart of sublimation, as well
as in any access to the symbolic that sublimation illuminates. At the core of
this narcissistic withdrawal, the death drive invests Narcissus and threatens his
integrity. The thought process is set in motion at the price of this threat. The
psychical apparatus uses the negative and assumes its risks in order to produce
what André Green calls "the work of the negative," which Freud developed in
his text "Negation."[37] The death drive, reflected on the ego, makes a qualitative leap to inscribe not *relations* with the other but representations with it in

the excrescence of the ego that the psyche becomes. Although not limited to sublimation alone, the psyche is founded by it through and through, for it is the capacity of *signifiance* (representation-language-thought) based on sublimation that structures all the other psychical manifestations.

This, in sum, represents a profound integration of the Hegelian dialectic into Freudian thought. The libido detached from the object turns toward Narcissus and threatens him. What will act as a counterbalance and prevent Narcissus from being destroyed? It is a new object, which is not mommy or daddy, the breast or any other external erotic object, or the body itself, but an artificial, internal object that Narcissus is capable of producing: his own representations, speech, sounds, colors, and so forth. This alchemy of sublimation, which Freud placed at the heart of the ability to think, is of the greatest interest to us in understanding the work of writers.

"Negation" comes back to language, after temporarily abandoning it, and reconsiders it not in light of word-presentation/thing-presentation, the unconscious, preconscious verbal/conscious, but of the overall process of *signifiance* established in *The Ego and the Id*, this intricate connection among sublimation, idealization, and the death drive, as opposed to the erotic drive. In "Negation," Freud postulates an instinctual rejection (*Ausstossung-Verwerfung*) that, by being repeated, transforms into a negation (*Verneinung*) and posits and thus affirms both the *denial* of the instinctual content and the symbolic *representation* of it: "I" do not love my mother = "I" admit (under the condition of negation) that "I" love her (the unconscious content itself). Language is intrinsically inscribed in a process of negativity that is strongly Hegelian and once again takes up the mechanism of identification-sublimation that Freud applied to the drive of the id to bring about the ego.[38] With the article on negation, the dynamic of the second topic was transported to the very heart of the linguistic sign and the capacity of symbolization.

I recommend reading *The Ego and the Id* alongside "Negation." You will see that Freud is proposing *something other than a model of language*, namely, a model of *signifiance* that presupposes language and its instinctual substrata but grasps language and the drive through the work of the negative. This work leads from the presignifier to the sign and to the superior stages of a stratified subjectivity (the id, the ego, and the superego) that affect each other in a circular or spiral process. "Thus in the id, which is capable of being inherited, are harbored residues of the existences of countless egos; and, when the ego forms its super-ego out of the id, it may perhaps only be reviving shapes of former egos and be bringing them to resurrection."[39]

Lacanians have often asked me where "the object a" would be in, say, Barthes's work. In other words, they have wanted to know how to locate the object of desire in a text or textual theory. Well, "the object a" in literature and literary theory is language; not this or that lover, fetish, or social code located on a thematic or psychological level but language. Extreme narcissism? Not solely, because language, and nothing else, leads to exteriority. If the moment of sublimation has failed, however, the signs of language will not be invested in any way, and thought processes will have no interest for the subject. Hallucination, or psychosis, is the result of this failure. And as for writers, they assume this alchemy of sublimation most intensely. I am not trying to suggest that sublimation is only an aesthetic activity. In aesthetic activity, however, this rather dangerous dynamic is hypostatized; its objects—sounds, colors, words, and so on—become a narcissistically invested production as well as a mode of life with others. Yet the mechanism of sublimation is indispensable and subjacent to the thought process in every speaking being.

Phylogenesis or Being?

The negativity of *signifiance* is not the only characteristic of this third model that we might deduce from Freudian thought. The most troubling aspect of the enigmatic fable of *Totem and Taboo* consists less in explaining ontogenesis with phylogenesis than in asserting the real (nonfantasmatic) character of *acts* attributed to *Homo sapiens* of the glacial period. The brothers did not have a *fantasy* of murdering or devouring the father, Freud maintains, though prudent friends and disciples encouraged him to abandon this hypothesis; they *really* killed and ate him.

We might be content to uphold that Freud needed this "reality" of phylogenesis in order to link individuals' psychical destinies to earlier human history. I would go further. Given the incommensurable periods Freud evokes and the fact that they suppose monumental human mutations (in the Nietzschean sense) rather than real events that can be located in a historical progression, Freud's main concern seems to be to open the subjective destiny to the historic and to the transsubjective appeal of a ray of light in what Heidegger calls Being. The problem is stated in paleontological or Darwinian terms, as befits a Viennese doctor suspicious of philosophy.

Thus Freud explains bisexuality either ontogenetically, through the impotence of neoteny and the evolution of the Oedipus complex, or phylogenetically: "According to one psycho-analytical hypothesis, . . . [it] is a heritage of the cultural development necessitated by the glacial epoch. We see, then, that the differentiation of the super-ego from the ego is no matter of chance; it represents the most important characteristics of the development both of the individual and of the species; indeed, by giving permanent expression to the influence of the parents it perpetuates the existence of factors to which it owes its origin" (p. 31). Moreover, the factors that organize the differentiation of the psychical apparatus into id and ego, or, more generally, the negativity that generates a stratified signifying functioning, are attributed not only to primitive man "but even to much simpler organisms, for it is the inevitable expression of the influence of the external world" (p. 35).

Freud's phylogenesis was a response to the necessity that had emerged to contemplate the extrapsychical. Against panpsychology and the negativity of the *signifiance* whose layers he was refining, he called on (Nietzschean) "monumental history" or "an external reality" (to use his terminology) distinct from psychical activity and yet inseparable from *signifiance*. This historic outside that *does not signify* in the linguistic sense of the term (because Freud takes examples from primitive man, inferior organisms, or inorganic matter) nevertheless persists in the id and in its conflicts with the ego and continues in the heir to the id, the superego. "The struggle which once raged in the deepest strata of the mind, and was not brought to an end by rapid sublimation and identification, is now continued in a higher region, like the Battle of the Huns in Kaulbach's painting" (p. 36). Freud multiplied the metaphors, constantly examining primitive history as an external reality resistant to psychical and more narrowly linguistic representation as well as a source of its signifying negativity. I remind you that Freud abandoned language, here, in the narrow sense of a grammatical or rhetorical system, in order to speak of it as an inter- and intrasubjective dynamic.

Freud's heirs—André Green, in particular—tend to interpret this new phylogenetic fable as a rehabilitation of the archaic, or as an invitation to include generations anterior to the subject in the psychical destiny of the subject itself, or even as a project using Hegelian history to provide an optimal interpretation of the unconscious. Only Lacan took a path unforeseeable to Freud, a path suggested to him by contemporary philosophy, which was concerned with bypassing metaphysics and investigating the pre-Socratic being. In the wake of this later Freud, I will situate the Lacanian formulation of the speaking subject as *parlêtre*: a play on words echoing Heidegger's *Dasein* that expresses the unavoidable insistence of *being* (outside-subject, outside-language) at the heart of human speech as it unfolds its negativity. *Da*, there, "I" speak, thrown out, cast out as "I" am, by being. My speech joins the historic meaning that exceeds the subjective signification of my discourse.

When Freud compares this to a delirium in "Constructions in Analysis" (1937), it is useful to recall what he wrote to Ferenczi on October 6, 1910: "I succeed where the paranoiac fails." Delirium takes words for things and fails at symbolization, while at the same time repudiating the other and projecting drives onto it, the death drive, in particular. In other words, words do not take the place of symbolic protection, the paternal function is obsolete, the pact with the other is abolished, in the place of the other "I" put my death drive, which "I" henceforth believe I receive from outside. In this logic, which is that of the paranoiac, the outside, the other, and language are not preserved. Yet in its mad truth, psychosis unveils the heterogeneity of the psychical apparatus sustained and activated by an outside transmuted into other as well as language and constantly threatened by this same outside. Freud's extreme daring, which is clear today, was not rejecting the delirious latency integral to the psychical apparatus given over to rebellious being. Freud was not content to protect himself from it through the reality testing that a certain psychoanalytical approach has retained from his work. If he succeeded where the paranoiac failed, it was because he constantly returned to the *historic*: being, the transpsychical; the transsubjective. To what end?

Is "Free Association" Only a Language?

The field of discourse—and interpretation—can be understood as a narration nourished by sensations/mnemic traces transposed (*métaphorein*) into narrative signs that are invested themselves; the human being is a speaking being inhabited by Eros-Thanatos and by a third component that is neither language nor drive but overdetermines both: *signifiance*. The two scenes of the conscious and the unconscious adjoin a third: the extrapsychical. There is a horizon of being outside the psychical where human subjectivity is inscribed without being reduced, where psychical life is exceeded by *signifiance*. Freud defined the capacity to idealize and to sublimate by forming an ego from the id; Bion speaks of function K (knowing), added to L (love) and H (hate); André Green proposes an objectifying function that transforms activity (sublimation) into object-possession through the ego ("I" love, "I" desire *my* work, *my* thought, *my* language). Freud the analyst devoted his last years to the works of sublimation by deciphering art and religion; at the same time, in treatment, he tried to draw patients to narrative activity focused on being as both source and otherness.

Note the difference with regard to the initial discovery of the unconscious: the issue is no longer the *structure* of language as such but the fantasmatic *narrative* (fable, tale, myth) constructed with the material of this language. What else is this if not the full value, recaptured, of the so-called fundamental rule of free association? Tell me your fantasies, put the sadomasochism of your drives, your parents, your grandparents, transgenerational and primitive histories in narrative form; make yourself an animal, plant, amoeba, rock; make the unrepresentable enter representation. The Word can reveal your truths to you by reconciling you with . . . whom? Not merely with yourself but with the other of the psychical, indeed, the other of language. There is no modern word for this. It was *logos* for the pre-Socratics. The Greeks said "being." Lacan did not hesitate to adopt this interpretation. Most analysts recoil from it, because they do not see how to integrate the notion of being into the clinic and they remain resistant, for good reason, to German phenomenologists—Binswanger, for example—who, by dint of investigating the extrapsychical and the extrasubjective, made inquiry into the human being so noble and abstract that sexuality was obliterated and human experience ended up dissolving. Freud, on the contrary, taught us to sexualize being, to alter it, to decipher the other in it, in the sense of an instinctual conflict, of "you" and the feminine-masculine.

The *signifiance* I am trying to elucidate in my reading of Freud is far vaster than the cognitivists' "mind," modeled on logic when not on computer science. A *signifiance* open to being and presented here and now in the structures of narration: something to revive your interest, as interpreters of sacred or literary texts, which I hope I have not numbed with this analytical detour.

Once Again Sublimation: Resexualized

At this point in the investigation of the "higher side" of man that Freud focused on, we must not forget the pitfall that the founder of psychoanalysis never underestimated: left to itself, sublimation disentangles the mixed drives, extricates the death drive, and exposes the ego to melancholia. Too often we emphasize the link between art and melancholia[40] instead of bluntly asking the question: how does one avoid succumbing to it? The answer is simple: by resexualizing the sublimatory activity, by sexualizing words, colors, and sounds. This is done either by introducing erotic fantasies into the narration or plastic representation (Sade, Diderot, Proust, Genet, Céline, Joyce, etc.) that real erotic activities may or may not accompany—artists thereby put the Freudian conception of a language underpinned by the dramaturgy of unconscious drives into action, whereas analysis, by contrast, tries to translate them or work them out. Or by concentrating rather exclusively on the sublimatory act itself and its product (a book, composing music, playing an instrument), which take the place of autoeroticism, especially when encouraged by social rewards or idealizing religious assurances (Bach).

Aside from great aesthetic performances, themselves often conflictual and threatened, sublimatory activity leaves the speaking subject exposed to this other aspect of *signifiance* that is the death drive. Freud brilliantly pointed out its power, not because he was the victim of a sorrow or a tendency to devalorize works of art—which, on the contrary, he esteemed highly—but because of an exemplary lucidity that linked the fate of meaning to the destiny of negativity.

The incomplete and open state of this third stage of Freudian thought on the subject of language seen in the light of vaster preoccupations is very beneficial: there is no Freudian dogma concerning language (as there is with "original fantasies," "drives," etc.). The complexity of the Freudian inquiry in this field offers contemporary psychoanalysis fertile areas of research. Here are a few:

1. The heterogeneity of the site of language (the first model) leads one to contemplate various types of representation (word-presentation/thing-presentation) and to refine them into sensations, which have given phenomenologists such a hard time and which cognitivists today believe they can subsume within logical categories.

2. The preponderance of verbalization (the "fundamental rule") should lead us to examine not only the facility of the narrative in approaching fantasmatic contents but also its limits in this regard.

3. Serious consideration of the nonverbalizable psychical act allows diagnosis of operational psychosomatic functionings or operational fantasmatic constructions made of images and split from words.[41]

4. The opening of the psyche to the dimension of being as psychical exteriority can be approached by a broadening of the rhetorical or sublimatory capacities of the analyst and the analysand, without which the real is absent from the psyche in psychosis. English analysts' interest in Beauty in the treatment of autism and other disturbances is a step in this direction.[42]

Does the Lacanian conception of language respond to these avenues left unexplored by Freud? I said earlier that Lacan's formulation "the subconscious is structured like a language" was an interpretation of the optimistic model of *The Interpretation of Dreams*. Later, Lacan's warnings against "linguisterie" and his portmanteau word *lalangue* opened analysis to the translinguistic and the infantile. The "paternal function" according to Lacan resonates pertinently with the preoccupations of *Totem and Taboo* and *The Ego and the Id*. The major difference between Lacan and Freud resides in the postulate according to which the heterogeneity of the drive would be impossible to enunciate in the field of free association. Nevertheless, the practice of scansion and even the short session, which lead to psychodrama rather than psychoanalysis, indicate a consideration of the unrepresentable, the unverbalizable, that operates within the psychical apparatus and is plainly revealed in countertransference. The one who seemed to hypostatize language as a control lever of therapy ultimately gave language the least possibility to express itself there, as if the extralinguistic rebounded and sent transference and countertransference, patients and analysts, back to prelinguistic psychical representations or acting without representation. Others in England and France (W. R. Bion, Piera Aulagnier, myself) have tried to furnish concepts of this, to allow it within treatment, to interpret it.

The three models in the complex course of Freudian thought on language (or the signifying process specific to human beings) that I have schematically outlined here should be understood in resonance with each other and together, based on our means of transference and countertransference, allowed to expand our various registers of *signifiance*, listening, and interpretation.

Dangers and Benefits of Free Association

I will end with a clinical vignette that will allow you to penetrate the complexity of the third model in the experience of a patient and that demonstrates two limits of the fundamental rule of free association: first, the difficulty of inscribing the symptom in language and, consequently, the recourse to the compromise of the sublimation (poetic writing); second, the psychical confusion (hallucination) that the verbal translation of the drive provokes and the subsequent necessity to go outside, to the cultural or historical, in order to modulate the translation of the drives into psychical representations.

A bulimic patient managed to rid herself of her symptoms after a year of face-to-face analytical psychotherapy. She began a sexual relationship with a man, which she said she found more satisfying than the rare relationships she had had before, until she realized during a visit that her partner resembled her mother. The vomiting started again, and on top of it, the patient could no longer curtail it in her usual manner: writing poetic texts, which previously had given expression to her violence while fragmenting the world, people, and language itself. The vomiting, which "emptied" her, was also evacuated, "emptied," from the sessions; only a few allusions and a show of secret sorrow suggested an alternative to this jouissance as painful as it was private. I advanced that the vomiting was a speechless writing, severing and excising internal matter and the patient's body itself. A rich associative discourse followed, as the patient tried to put into words specific olfactory, tactile, and auditory sensations internal to her attacks, with an obvious exhibitionistic pleasure in seduction but also with aggression toward me, to which the pleasure of mentalization, leading things to words and vice versa, was added. Note how the dramaturgy of this narrative of sensorial naming was at once pleasure and attack. Note also that language hovered between what Freud called thing-presentation and word-presentation; words were not dissociated but attached to things the patient experienced sensorially.

The putting into words of her perceptions was soon followed by the memory, in a dream, of her first episode of binging and purging, which occurred when she was a little girl, on vacation by the seaside with her parents and sharing a bedroom with them. The account of this episode revealed an erotic conflict (desire for the mother *and* the father) and led the patient to a grave difficulty, as if the words of the story had confronted her with an experience contemplated but still *active*, traumatic. After recounting the dream, the patient seemed almost paralyzed, plunged in verbal and mental confusion; she forgot words, even sentences, and then fell silent. For a few sessions, she was unable to pick up the thread of the story or even discuss her complaint, a performance that was usually economical but very logically constructed. *The verbalization of the trauma had threatened verbal construction itself*, as if the expulsion of matter (the symptom of vomiting) had affected her words, emptying not only her stomach but also her syntax and signs themselves of their meaning. When she managed to speak again, her speech resembled her poems: sparse, obscure. I made out the words "sea" (*mer*), "water," "viscosity," "death," "mother" (*mère*), "stream," "horror," and "dejection." The patient was a reader of Céline; she had even written a thesis on him. The first scene of vomiting in her childhood, which she had tried to recount to me, an attempt that had placed her in this state of mental and linguistic confusion, made me think of an analogous scene in *Death on the Installment Plan* in which the narrator and his mother are seized by violent and abject vomiting during a sea voyage to England. I told the patient about this association, which I thought might have been preconscious for her and which, for me, was a linguistic, rhetorical, and cultural reference point to set against her linguistic and mental confusion: "Your malaise calls to mind *Mort à crédit* [*Death on the Installment Plan*]." I noticed that the words "mort à crédit" could be applied to the analytical situation: giving the analyst credit for making the old subject die. My intervention could also have been taken as a narcissistic gratification, a sublimatory aid. The patient told me that she had always felt disgust and fascination for this text and its author. She associated on her master's thesis, remastering her thoughts and words. In the following sessions, she made associations between Céline's text, which she had just reread, and her own attempts to go further in putting her attacks into words. She abandoned poetry and began to write short stories. In them, she talked about her hatred for a man and a woman: for her boyfriend, for her mother, and, discreetly but rather clearly, for me and my "abstractions." The symptoms—bulimia, vomiting—once again disappeared. A new narrative, of violent cruelty, had swallowed it.

I didn't know if this was progress: the patient continued to have difficulties with her boyfriend, her mother, and her coworkers. But we were caught—the patient, myself, and words—in a construction where language again became narrative and, clearly supported by a sublimatory gratification (Céline's text), took over the conflict that had previously played itself out in the autoeroticism of the stomach, the esophagus, and the mouth.

Is speech in an analytical situation a narrative that stages one's own murder for the other (the analyst) and the other's murder for oneself in order to defer death from the living body? The wordless symptom was deadly. The poetic writing, tangled in itself, phobic, and apparently protective, was a powerless mausoleum in the face of the destructive attacks. On the other hand, free association for someone—the analyst—to swallow and vomit had at first endangered my patient. Situated in the context of treatment and in the transsubjective context of cultural history, it then allowed speech to preserve the life of this woman, who had been annihilating herself in the symptom and through poetry.

After an extremely violent session that dealt with her boyfriend and myself, the patient concluded that analysis was the only place where she could allow herself to be *tender*. Tender *with*? Or tender *toward*? The paradox of her statement made me understand that the violence vomited in words allowed her to be tender with . . . her instinctual being (mute force, waste product, amoeba, or hominid of the glacial period: the Freudian fable is calling us), inasmuch as she was able to give words to this being.

Is language the tenderness of the *parlêtre*? *Tender to the parlêtre* through free association? Beyond hallucination and cruelty,[43] isn't language (or better yet, narrative) within therapy a reconciliation between word-presentation and thing-presentation that makes us perceive—unconsciously—that meaning communicated to someone else shelters us (temporarily) from death?

Language, as Freud would have us understand it, is this sublimation that uses signs and syntax in a narration in order to allow passage from the being external to the subject to the other that makes me a subject. But is this solely a matter of language? Or is it what Freud the rationalist called in his third model, with a certain infelicity, the "higher side"? Analysts are left to listen indefinitely to the infinite folds that form language, the unknown. Moreover, where is this language? Does it exist outside the specific listening of the analyst who broadens it and narrows it, proposes models of it according to his own "higher side," his own *significance*? What remains of language after Freud? An artifact dependent on the "higher side" of the subject of the interpretation?

In any case, the language of the analyst is not the language of the linguist. But what control, what tension, what tenderness! These are the paths of revolt, in the sense I give it in this book.

4

Oedipus Again; or, Phallic Monism

The Conscious/Unconscious versus Knowledge

Before going on to Oedipus, I will conclude my remarks on the three models of language in Freud by responding to a question concerning the link that may be established in the solitude of analytical treatment.

A great analyst, Michel de M'Uzan, asked in his seminar one day: what is the analyst's *organ*? The brain? The unconscious? The erogenous zones? Analysts no doubt use all these as well as personality, history, rhetoric, culture, and politics. Consequently, we also use our capacity for revolt as I am trying to define it here. Solitude then becomes an open solitude, and a link is possible between the experiences of those who are attempting to speak.

Now I will return to free association, which provided Freud with the complex model of language on which he based his experiment. Why free association? Why the narrative? This, at bottom, is what interests us as literary scholars. What are the stories that Freud asked his patients to tell? Stories full of gaps, silences, awkwardness—in a way, novels deprived of an audience.

The free association Freud bequeaths us as an essential tool of analysis is not the language sign, the language sentence, but the *narrative*. To associate is to recount, to develop a narrative activated by drives and sensations, in which phylogenesis is implicated. Moreover, this narrative is bordered by *acts*—which are unrepresentable in the sense that their intensity destabilizes language—as well as by the *feminine*, which we have seen obscured, absorbed, and resorbed in the pact among the brothers. Finally, this narrative is tuned in to being, the being of monumental history that Freud intuited through phylogenesis. *Narrative, drives, sensations, acts, the feminine in being*: Freud invites us to see all these in the free associations of patients. The analyst is led to see sexual difference situated in being; this being evokes something along the lines of the sacred but is dissociated neither from the cosmos nor monumental history nor, for that matter, from the history of the species or the history of the world. The analyst tries to understand the act, in particular the sexual act, by receiving words, bearers of sensations and drives well beyond the signifier-signified system. In addition, he keeps himself alert to the aura beyond language and even to the extrapsychical, which modifies the codes of language by introducing disturbances, lapses, ellipses, silences, rhetorical figures, and, indeed, different myths for both sexes.

We are no longer in the realm of psychology and even less in that of psychiatry: the serene *significance* opens the analyst's listening to being, certainly, but to a curiously altered being. Our memory, awakened by the narrative sexed in transference, indeed constitutes an unconscious Other (Lacan capitalized it) that inhabits us. We are at the heart of an unsettling strangeness here, and at the same time this memory, however outrageous, is invested by the narrative that restores it to us, that submits it to the domination of the conscious, that deciphers in language and addresses an Other.

This is a major stumbling block for cognitivist theories, which cannot conceive the Other except as an addressee, a double of "myself" and, as such, knowable insofar as identical to "myself." Now, the history of philosophy—particularly, Descartes, Husserl, and Heidegger—teaches us that there is a logical obligation ("I think, therefore I am") whereby my relationship to others implies a relationship of being to being and not of knowledge to knowledge. This means that, insofar as the other is himself, "I" cannot *know* him as such but only *think* of him in his own being, in his being as an other. If "I" try to think of him, I make the wager that since he is not me, he is different from me, he exists differently than me. "I" therefore make a wager of otherness, a wager in the Pascalian sense, the validity of which nothing can prove to me and which is absolute transcendence. Sartre, as I will show, put this brilliantly in *Being and Nothingness*: in order to accede to the other, to absolute immanence, "we must ask absolute immanence to throw us into absolute transcendence."[1] The immanence where I am deep within myself ("I" love myself, "I" hate myself, "I" accept myself or kill myself: basically, "I" contemplate myself) is only possible in relation to an other; this has been said often enough. What is more difficult is to think that this other exists differently from me, that he is not simply a mirror image of myself; it is up to me to convince myself that there is an other whose being is radically "not me." People have managed to do it, in a way, insofar as they have imagined an other who goes beyond them and who is not them, whom they have placed above them and who reigns over the world.

The Freudian revolution proposes that this absolute transcendence is quite simply what makes us speak by making us other-beings, which implies that, far from resembling others, being is always continuously other. This is Freud's post- or anti-Cartesian wager: an ego addresses another ego, of course, but in fact it is a subject ("I," who *thinks* and *is*) addressing another subject in being. The other is of being, the other is not me, the other is also a being but in another way from me. And it is because the other is a being other than me that I am not simply me but also a subject and that the being that bears us is plural, altered. This is what analysis sounds out: not the complacent communication of ego to ego (though this may be necessary when certain egos are in shreds and need urgently to be reconstituted, through psychotherapy, for example) but an altered subject's relationship to another being. It is a somewhat ascetic practice, perhaps, but it does not exclude exchanges between egos, decentered by the other and brimming with their "own" unconscious otherness.

In the ideal hypothesis, the patient delivers a narrative as a subject address-ing another subject, a subject who constructs himself in this narrative rela-tionship to the other subject. This difficulty cannot be reduced to interpsychi-cal dialogue or "intercognition," for it is matter not of knowledge to knowledge but consciousness to consciousness. In other words: "I" is not a cognitive strat-egy; "I is another." "I" transcends its enclosure as a strategy of knowledge, which it also is. When I say that it transcends this cognitive enclosure, it is not merely that "I" is wrought by this other scene of the unconscious that has to do with another logic (drives, primary processes, etc.); it also means that "I" (which is of being) is constituted as such in relation to the other, which I de-tailed by going over various stages of individuation. The other is not a redou-bling of the ego but a complex dynamic that takes us from language to *signifi-ance* and being, which, if you follow my reading of Freud, is not appeased in the serenity that Heidegger finds in it but split to begin with, by letting the other-being of the unconscious appear. There is a piling-up of otherness: the addressee is an other-being; "I" is an other-being; these others are altered by contemplating each other. Far from being absolutized as the summit of a pyra-mid from which the other gazes at me with an implacable and severe eye, the problematic of psychoanalytical alterity opens a space of interlocking alteri-ties. Only this interlocking of alterities can give subjectivity an infinite dimen-sion, a dimension of creativity. For by gaining access to my other-being, I gain access to the other-being of the other, and in this plural decentering I have the chance to put into words-colors-sounds . . . what? Not a strategy of knowledge but a sort of advent of plural and heterogeneous psychical potentialities that make "my" psyche a life in being.

What I have just said rejoins several criticisms previously set forth by Mer-leau-Ponty concerning a type of psychoanalysis that he saw as mired in "ob-jectivism":[2] the subject's dependence on the object (mother or father) is rei-fied; even the drive is seen as a fact of the conscious (objectifiable force or objectified representation); the topography of the psychical apparatus leads to a realism of agencies; the analytical process is thought of in terms of identity and law (same/other, law/transgression, as if psychoanalysis were an extension of an existence according to the law where man has been situated from Saint Paul to Nietzsche); we reduce psychoanalysis to a technique; and so on. How-

ever, though psychoanalysis does in fact too often objectify and psychologize
the analysand and transference itself, it is essential to emphasize the fact that
the Freudian discovery opens the path, at the heart of scientific rationality, to
a knowledge and to a transformation of the psyche as a life in being, transversal to psychological objectification. Therein lies its most radical revolt.

Having scaled these heights, let us return to the classic Oedipus, which has
its own set of difficulties.

Oedipus Revisited: Sophocles and Freud

Has the Oedipus complex today become a commonplace of psychoanalysis?
And, as such, does it still merit our attention? Do we still need to talk about it?
These questions have often crossed my mind, and I hope to convince readers
that returning to Oedipus is not only important but indispensable.

Quite recently, its central place in the debate was confirmed to me during a
lecture I gave at the Ecole Nationale des Ponts-et-Chaussées. I thought it worth-
while to discuss Oedipus at some length. A young lady in the audience got up
to say: "Madame, why aren't you talking about the father? I lost my mother
when I was very young. My father raised me. The father must always be spoken
of. Everything I am, I owe to him." She was preaching to the converted, perhaps without knowing it: I, too, owe everything I am to the father, in a way,
though as an analyst and also as a writer, things are a bit more complicated for
me. But a young girl at the Ponts cannot know everything, even if she already
knows a lot, and a lot more than a lot of others, and has gotten to the point of
stating brusque truths on the father, unrefined truths but truths nonetheless.

The father is never spoken of enough. Of course, in my practice as an analyst, I continually deal with the debt to the father, often expressed as demand
or complaint (as during the lecture I just mentioned)—indeed, as protest—
and rarely as desire. Yet by relying precisely on this debt toward the father, I
will try to speak of other debts, particularly vis-à-vis the "dark continent," the
maternal continent. For now, however, I will attempt to introduce you to
Oedipus, because Freud poses the question of the father using the complex of
the same name.

Oedipus Rex

The earliest Freudian reference to Oedipus occurs in a letter to Fliess on October 15, 1897: "I have found, in my own case too, falling in love with the
mother and jealousy of the father, and I now regard it as a universal event of

early childhood. . . . If that is so, we can understand the riveting power of *Oedipus Rex*."[3] The Greek myth was able to capture a compulsion that everyone recognizes because everyone feels it. We have all contained within us the seeds of an Oedipus at one point.

There are two Oedipuses, as you know: *Oedipus the King* and *Oedipus at Colonus*, which is the story of the blind king who withdraws with his daughter to die at Colonus, in other words, the story of the death of the father. Wanting to leave a testament of his art, Sophocles made *Oedipus at Colonus* the longest play of the Greek repertory. But Freud was referring to his *Oedipus the King*, a play that dates from circa 320 B.C. If you reread this text, you will not fail to be struck by what is called the "Greek miracle," a major aspect of which is bringing forth what we continue to consider our inner life: love, hate, guilt, defilement—the defilement that designates desire as desire for incest and death—without which there is neither happiness nor unhappiness. Given how many years separate us from this text, we can only be impressed by the paradox of this temporality linking such an ancient truth to one so close to us. *Oedipus the King* was written twenty-three centuries ago, and for almost a century, we continuously return, with Freud, to the topicality of this play. Why this permanence? Is it because it is still alive, we are all constituted this way, and we have simply subjectified or psychologized the same logic that for the Greeks was a fate inflicted by the gods? And what if, at the same time and on the contrary, the constellation of desire, transgression, happiness, and unhappiness that Sophocles put before us were henceforth threatened?

Perhaps Freud revisited Sophocles in order to contemplate this threat. In any case, he recognized that the miracle—of a psyche taking into account desire, law, transgression, defilement, and guilt—had occurred there, there and not in China or India. In Greece we find the origins of, if not the desiring subject— which, as a subject, must await the Judaic interpellation and the Christian incarnation in order to be designated and contemplated—than at least its logic. The logic of the desiring subject is just another side of the logic of the philosophical subject, which we often forget; it is also another side of the subject of science, for the philosophical subject and the subject of science, as Plato (427–347 B.C.) and Aristotle (384–322 B.C.) bequeath them to us, appear around the same time as the tragedy. Obviously, what Sophocles says does not fall from the sky; it is borne by myths and preceded by the epic, incantatory narration of Greek history. But it is through Sophocles' tragedy that these words are crystallized in the oedipal subject (to get back to the interest of Freud) that is at once tragic, philosophical, and scientific. It is what we are, it is what the best among us are (by "best" I mean those who want to know; those who do not want to know are far more tragic), and it is what Sophocles formulated in *Oedipus the King*.

Here are two passages from the text that seem to me to define the problematic of the tragic man, this hidden side of the desiring man, also revealed to be clever and knowing. You remember that Oedipus killed his father at a crossroads in the shape of the Greek gamma (τ). Note that it is at this crossroads that Sophocles contemplated the division, the bifurcation between desire and murder. Note also that starting from there he describes to us in less geometric terms what will follow:

> Now I am found to be
> a sinner and a son of sinners. [The being of the subject is thus posited: "I
>   am Oedipus," desiring subject, subject of science and philosophical
>   subject; think of all these facets hidden in what follows.] Crossroads,
>   [the desire and the crime]
> and hidden glade, oak and the narrow way
> at the crossroads, that drank my father's blood
> offered you by my hands, do you remember
> still what I did as you looked on, and what
> I did when I came here? O marriage, marriage!
> you bred me and again when you had bred
> bred children of your child [Here the theme of incest is announced.] and
>   showed to men
> brides, wives and mothers and the foulest deeds
> that can be in this world of ours.
>
> Come—it's unfit to say what is unfit
> to do.—I beg of you in God's name hide me
> somewhere outside your country, yes, or kill me,
> or throw me into the sea, to be forever
> out of your sight. Approach and deign to touch me
> for all my wretchedness [Note the chain: happiness, unhappiness, guilt.],
>   and do not fear.
> No man but I can bear my evil doom. [He excludes himself from our community yet invites us to identify with his exclusion.][4]

The Chorus concludes, "Count no mortal happy till / he has passed the final limit of his life secure from pain" (2:76). Note the emphasis on the pain inherent in the human trajectory and thus the unhappiness beneath the appearance of happiness.

Here then is what so deeply affected Freud when he exhumed *Oedipus the*

King in 1895–1896 and spoke of it in a letter to his friend Fliess in 1897. He also summarized and explicated the story of Oedipus in *The Interpretation of Dreams* (1900). What interested him was precisely what Oedipus says in the passage I have just quoted. "Like Oedipus," Freud comments, "we live in ignorance of the desires that offend morality, the desires that nature has forced upon us and after their unveiling we may well prefer to avert our gaze from the scenes of *our* childhood. . . . There is an unmistakable reference to the fact that the Oedipus legend had its source in dream-material of immemorial antiquity, the content of which was the painful disturbance of the child's relations to its parents caused by the first impulses of sexuality."[5] "We live," "we may well prefer," "our childhood": based not only on the emotion that Sophocles' text incites in him and his own observations about himself—his own history, his personal relations with his father and his own children—but also on the stories of patients, Freud uses the Oedipus complex to interpret his reading and his thought.

The question is not whether the Greeks did or did not experience the Oedipus complex. A number of anthropologists and Hellenists have taken Freud to task, arguing that differences separate contemporary society and mentality from that of the ancient Greeks. This is a pointless quarrel. The analyst that Freud is in the midst of becoming finds in the logic of the tragic text the elements he rediscovers internalized/hidden/dreamed in the contemporary psychical experience. In the ins and outs of finding, thought work is produced: the psychoanalytical interpretation, the invention of the novelty that is psychoanalysis. Consequently, psychoanalysis is not tragedy, and Freud does not say the truth of Sophocles. The concept of Oedipus on which Freud worked after 1897 and that he developed in particular in *Three Essays on the Theory of Sexuality* (1905) did not appear until 1910 (thus relatively late) in the first of his "Contributions to the Psychology of Love."[6] Only twenty-six years after his letter to Fliess did Freud formulate the theory definitively, in "The Infantile Genital Organization" (1923) and "The Dissolution of the Oedipus Complex" (1924).

In "The Dissolution of the Oedipus Complex," Freud emphasizes what he calls "the central place" of this complex. "To an ever increasing extent the Oedipus complex [i.e., the incestuous desire for the mother and the desire to murder the father] reveals its importance as the central phenomenon of the sexual period of early childhood [i.e., the Oedipus complex organizes the sexual period of early childhood]. After that, its *dissolution* takes place [this is the latency period]; it succumbs to repression, as we say, and is followed by the latency period."[7] For now, note that Freud emphasizes the central place of the Oedipus complex as an organizer of the psychical life of early childhood.

In "The Infantile Genital Organization," Freud takes up the theses he already formulated in 1905 in *Three Essays*. But he modifies his concepts and gives them their final, definitive form, with the libidinal stages—oral, anal, and phallic—that he will not alter. Enumerating these stages he takes care to specify that what he calls "genital organization," after the oral, anal, and phallic stages, is contemporaneous with and a correlative of the blossoming of the Oedipus complex. (Please be sure to remember that this is a matter of *infantile* genital organization, to be distinguished from that of the adult.)

What is this infantile genital organization characterized by? By the primacy accorded to the penis, by both sexes. At the same time, Freud admits unreservedly that homosexual and heterosexual object choices, even if they are specified later, are manifested in childhood. Here one can observe three postulates of the Freudian conception of the organization of psychical life: Oedipus, phallic organization (the primacy of the penis), and the castration complex, because the penis in question will be thought of as threatened, especially since it is missing in women.

These ideas, which we see explicated in their definitive form in "The Infantile Genital Organization," had already been advanced by Freud earlier. Elements of them are present in texts such as "Little Hans" (1909) or "The Wolf Man" (1918), where Freud emphasizes the importance of the penis in his patients' psychical life and symptoms.[8] Later, he continues to maintain the primacy of the male sexual organ. In 1923 he asserts it for the boy as well as the girl, and this is where a number of major challenges arise, spurred by feminism, as you might suspect. I will examine this debate in my discussion of feminine sexuality, but let us start with the boy's point of view, as Freud explains it, and consider the primacy of the penis, or the phallus, in the boy's sexuality.

The Primacy of the Penis

Why is the penis the narcissistically invested organ? Because it is visible. (Lacan will valorize a variant of visibility with the "mirror stage," as I have mentioned.) Representation, as a subsequent psychical capacity, allows one to displace the narcissistic image of the face or any other object of need linked to the maternal presence, onto the eroticized visible thing that is the male sexual organ. Visible, then, and, in addition, eroticized. Why? Because of the erection observed, undergone, or experienced. Finally, the penis is an organ that is detached, in the dual sense of the word in French [*se détacher*, to stand out, to come loose.—Trans.]. Its tumescence/detumescence induces the threat of deprivation in the little boy, confirmed by the absence of the organ in the little girl, and provides the basis for the fantasy of castration. Starting with this latent absence, the penis can become the representative of other ordeals of separation and lack experienced earlier by the subject.

What other events are organized around the detachable character of the penis? Birth, oral deprivation, and anal separation. The penis ceases to be a physiological organ in order to become a phallus in the psychical experience, "the signifier of the lack," to use Lacanian terminology, because it may be lacking and because it subsumes other lacks already experienced. To this we must add that the signifier of the lack is the paradigm of the signifier itself, of all that signifies. The penis as phallus becomes, so to speak, the symbol of the signifier and the symbolic capacity.

I will discuss the copresence of eroticism in symbolization later; for now, it suffices to locate the link between Freud's and Lacan's reading of this moment in infantile genital organization. The investment of the penis is an investment of all that may be lacking and, starting from that, of all lack as paradigm of the signifiable and the signifier: corporal lack but also, in the field of representation, the thought that represents what is lacking.

Phallic Monism

A second question in the analytic theory surrounding Oedipus concerns "phallic monism," the notion that every human being unconsciously imagines every other human being to possess a penis. The theory of phallic monism supposes an ignorance of the vagina for both sexes. I will come back to this, but for now let me observe that this ignorance occurs differently in men and women. The theory of phallic monism implies not only that the subject of both sexes is unaware of the existence of a sexual organ other than the penis but also that, correlatively, the absence of the penis, or even castration, is considered a sort of "eye for an eye" punishment against the man or the woman: this punishment is inflicted on the man to punish him and on the woman at the outset, because she is not equipped with this "signifier" at birth.

The question then becomes who is responsible for the punishment, having deprived one sex (the female) of this organ and having the capacity to remove it from the other sex (the male). It is the father, as you may have guessed, who is fantasmatically responsible, who executes this punishment for both sexes. This is the theory of phallic monism; I am only summing up the doxa. I will add that it is a fantasy; at no moment does Freud say that this is what must be thought or what is definitively thought by the human being (although his prehistoric fable supposes that such a punishment might have taken place and, like the father's appropriation of the women, might have provoked the sons' revolt against this tyrant).

This fantasmatic organization depends on *infantile genital organization.* And I underscore this last idea, which has not, I think, been sufficiently acknowledged. Read "The Infantile Genital Organization," which posits the primacy of the phallus, and you will see that its author specifies that this concerns the development of the *child* and does not *in any way* coincide with adult genital organization: "The main characteristic of this 'infantile genital organization' is its difference from the definitive genital organization of the adult. This consists in the fact that, for both sexes, only one genital, namely the male one, comes into account. What is present, therefore, is not a primacy of genitals but a primacy of the *phallus.*"[9] Freud makes a clear distinction here that his later readers have had a tendency to neglect: he emphasizes the fact that it is a matter of a phallic organization localized at a certain moment in the subject's history, which endures as an unconscious fantasy but is not at all the optimal outcome of adult human sexuality. The optimal outcome would be the recognition of both sexes and relations between them. When one speaks of the primacy of the phallus, therefore, one must not lose sight of the fact that it is, I repeat, a matter of a *fantasy* linked to *infantile* genital sexuality. If some remain fixed there, it is their structure, but it is not the path Freud envisages in the development of the human psyche. This stage, these fantasmatic unconscious contents, are repressed in the adult, and Freud does not in any way identify phallic monism thus defined with completed adult sexuality, the advent of which he assumes and that is perhaps somewhat of a utopia. Perhaps none of us ever really accedes to this supposed genitality where we recognize our sexual difference and can have relations with beings of different sexes. Perhaps this is another utopic fantasy, indispensable to psychoanalytical theory this time, but rarely if ever attained by real subjects. Let us nevertheless continue to interpret the Freudian idea of a phallic phase as an organizing structure in no way exclusive of adult genitality. A fundamental organizing structure, certainly, but not definitive in psychosexual development.

To sum up these two texts, the Oedipus complex is a fantasmatic organization, essentially unconscious, because repressed, that organizes psychical life and supposes the primacy of the phallus insofar as the phallus is, on the one hand, a narcissistically and erotically invested organ and, on the other, the signifier of the lack, which makes it suited for identification with the symbolic order itself.

The inner workings of classical Freudian theory raise several questions: Is the Oedipus complex universal? Is it the same for the boy and the girl? Are there reversible oedipal stages that would imply homosexuality and heterosexuality?

The universality of the complex is in fact the universality of the triangular relationship that Freud maintains for all civilizations. "Triangular relationship" describes the child-father-mother link, with the father occupying the summit of the triangle, though the relationship may have variations. The role of the father, for example, may be occupied by a maternal uncle in matrilineal societies or, indeed, by a woman, hence the various configurations of Oedipus; but one never observes its nonexistence. The proof of this universality is the incest theory. Lévi-Strauss (whose reticence toward psychoanalysis you are no doubt aware of) nevertheless maintained the principal of the incest prohibition as the organizer of all societies. Now, what does this rule of the incest ban suppose? The recognition of *sexual difference*; the institution of marriage in various forms with—always—a contract between the two sexes; and, finally, the attribution of the child to the mother and the father, that is, the recognition of *generational difference*. Many commentators have been content to emphasize the fact that the Oedipus complex implies sexual difference, but we should remember that it also posits *generational difference*, marked in particular by initiation rites at puberty. The incest ban establishes not *one* but *two* differences: that of the sexes *and* that of generations. The structuring ban prohibits the maternal object and *at the same time* relations with another age group. Consequently, its perverse transgressions are manifested as much by the refusal of the other sex as by the abolition of generational difference.

It is often asked: Isn't incest for the man the mother-son relationship and for the woman the father-daughter relationship? Let us look at this.

If the Oedipus complex is a universal structure defining every subject (whether the subject is biologically a man or woman does not matter as long as he/she becomes a *subject*), incest characterizes the relationship with the mother. For all individuals, men or women, "incest" implies the return to the female parent, the mother, and this, I stress, goes for the girl as well as the boy. There is no lack of obscurity in Freud on this point, but keep in mind that primary incest—which one must call radical or structural, a corollary of the phallic desire and the murder of the father—is the sexual desire for the mother, *whether this desire emanates from the girl or boy*. This follows not only from the fact that the prototype of the subject in Freud is the boy but from an essential fact I am trying to underline here by emphasizing "phallic monism," namely, that the phallic reference is indispensable for *both* sexes as soon as they are constituted as *subjects* of the lack and/or the representation that culminates in the capacity to *think*. Starting there, the subject (man or woman) carries out a transgressive, tragic act in desiring the mother. (The configurations of this incestuous transgression are different depending on whether one is biologically male or female, but for now the universality is what is important.)

A last particularity of this universal Oedipus complex is that it declines, Freud tells us; it is destined to failure. Have we really contemplated the consequences of this decline for psychical life?

Oedipus and Failure

Though certainly a figure of revolt, the Freudian Oedipus is also one of *failure*, a failure that most of Freud's commentators say nothing about, so powerful is our unconscious desire for a transgressive figure that defies the law and breaches taboos. We might know that Sophocles' *Oedipus* is a *tragedy*, for his revolt is paid for with condemnation and severe punishment; we might read in Freud and observe in anyone that the genital oedipal impulse at the age of five ends in renunciation and that of adolescence is elaborated in a change of object. It doesn't matter. Oedipus remains a hero for the unconscious; we repress the universality and ineluctability of the oedipal failure. That the oedipal object is an object forever lost and sought is important to repeat forcefully, rereading the Freudian formulation:

> The early efflorescence of infantile sexual life is doomed to extinction because its wishes are incompatible with reality and with the inadequate stage of development which the child has reached. That efflorescence comes to an end in the most distressing circumstances and to the accompaniment of the most painful feelings. Loss of love and failure leave behind them a permanent injury to self-regard in the form of a narcissistic scar, which in my opinion . . . contributes more than anything to the "sense of inferiority."[10]

"In this way the Oedipus complex would go to its destruction from its lack of success, from the effects of its internal impossibility."[11]

Why this failure? There are many causes, which we would prefer not to acknowledge. First, the superego in the boy is afraid of castration, in the girl, afraid of losing the mother's love; then, the premature beings that we are have a regressive need to conserve the identification with the same sex that precedes the Oedipus and assures and protects us; finally and above all, the child, whatever the sex, feels the intergenerational inadequacy between itself and the desired or hated adult, an inadequacy that magnifies its parent at the same time that it sends back a devalorizing image and perception of its own weakness, of its infantile (physical, genital, mental) impotence.

The failure of the Oedipus is probably this intrapsychical condition that accompanies and consolidates the access to the symbolic function: the renunciation of infantile genitality inscribes impossibility at the heart of the psychical apparatus, and it is on this impossibility that an other unfolds, intrinsic to the matrix of meaning, which is precisely the inadequacy of the signified to the signifier and to the referent, what Saussure called "the arbitrariness of the sign." By relying on the impossibility of Oedipus, the arbitrariness of the sign already acquired during the "depressive position" is developed in thought,[12] and the speaking being invests thought as its privileged object, tentatively or brilliantly, as the history of culture and the academy attest. Moreover, the Greek man named Oedipus was himself subjected to the failure of the Oedipus complex, which explains how he learned to speak and to think and finally to become king: he had to renounce his complex with the substitute parents who raised him and to whom he owed everything—or, at least, his conscious being—namely, Polybus and Merope, who took him in as a child and with whom he apparently behaved normally, that is, like you and I, renouncing his genital impulse of the fifth year, at the risk of unleashing "the most distressing" and "painful feelings," as Freud says.

Here we are at a crossroads that is no less problematic than the one where Oedipus stood in Sophocles' text. Is the oedipal revolt absolutely necessary at the same time that its failure is necessary? How are we to understand the sense of this impasse? A particular destiny of the human being is in question here, the logic of which the Greek tragedy already illustrates forcefully. By harboring the desire for incest and murder as well as renouncing it, are we on a slope that inevitably leads to renouncing revolt or else to displacing it indefinitely, renewing it, refining it?

Perhaps the amorous link—and with some luck, a love relationship, and maybe even marriage (why not?)—consecrates both the failure of Oedipus ("I" abandon the drive of desire and death for mama/papa in favor of a new love object) and its renewal (this new object often translates my parents' traits, without being their substitute, and he/she also provides the genital, pregenital, and narcissistic satisfactions that the oedipal desires of long ago should have or could have offered me). The amorous couple thus succeeds at what has been called an "oedipal organization," a fragile success and one irremediably challenged by oedipal conflict, which is unleashed each time a disappointment or a new object disrupts the equilibrium.

The twofold danger threatening this oedipal revolt, at once indispensable and destined to failure, is all too clear. On the one hand, there is the definitive renunciation. From the ennui of monogamy, which normalizes and ends up extinguishing desire, to the social group, which impresses its constraints, numerous configurations of our socialization emphasize the impossible aspect of our oedipal structuring and doom the revolt to failure. On the other hand, there is the defiance of the man (more rarely the woman) who has never given up, at least in fantasy. Although he accedes to language and thought and thereby is constituted as a subject, the eccentric personality denies the renunciation and the castration that it implies, though these still organize him as the subject of a symbolic pact. Favored, perhaps, by an indulgent mother who, oh so frequently, has reasons to prefer her son to her husband or encouraged in his narcissism by a permissive or even perverse familial or social group, the eccentric subject does not want to know about failure and, not least, about the failure of the Oedipus. All-powerful, megalomaniac, feeling persecuted at the slightest sign of constraint from others who do not allow themselves to be manipulated as faithful intimates do, our "hero" is fixed at the oedipal level and uses it. He *appears* to be a rebel, for he violently rejects the symbolic pact whose norm wounds his narcissism as well as his impulse for genital—or, rather, anal—control over the incestuous mother. But his defiance keeps him outside the framework, and, starting from this eccentricity—not wanting to know that the impossible exists while at the same time using it—he cannot construct a veritable revolt but only the signs of a depressed or amused but definitively perverse marginality.

Between these two impasses, the path for revolt is narrow, as you might imagine: dealing with failure, keeping one's head up, taking new paths (eternal displacement, salubrious metonymy), leaving the nest, refashioning the wager of loving/killing over and over with new objects and strange signs: all this makes us autonomous, guilty, and thinking. Happy? In any case, amorous, for the amorous couple realizes the precariousness, as altruistic as it is inevitable, of the oedipal organization (understood at once as oedipal conflict *and* oedipal failure).

I will try to show that the experience of writing not only transposes or transcribes the amorous event in the body of language but quite often substitutes for it, when it does not surpass it. Writing as realization of the oedipal organization, as recognition of the failure and renewal of revolt: this is perhaps the secret of what we call sublimation.

Structural Oedipus for Both Sexes

In the current evolution, the boy feels a sexual desire for the mother and a desire for death for his rival, the father; inversely, the girl sexually desires the father and feels a jealous hatred toward the mother. Given this reversal, shouldn't we reserve the term "Oedipus complex" solely for the boy and use another term for the girl: the "Electra complex," for example, as Jung proposes?

Freud was ferociously opposed to this proposition. As for Lacan—who was brilliant, as you know—he did not bother himself with such minutiae. In a structural perspective, he preserved the universality of Oedipus and the incest prohibition *for both sexes*. Yet the rigor of this structuralism is still an oversimplification: when Lacan spoke of incest, he did not specify the sex of the subject in question. I will add that the subtle distinctions of "same," "other," and "Other" allow one to eliminate the question of the maternal. This is why I prefer Freud's theses, which, though imprecise and mutable, seem better able to help us understand how biological difference and the symbolic pact establish the Oedipus as a universal structure.

For the most part, controversies concerning Freudian theory and different currents of research in psychoanalysis bear on the question of the female Oedipus and its differences from the male Oedipus. As for Freud, he maintains it is the father who represents the fundamental reference for both sexes: it is the father the child wants to eliminate in order to inscribe himself in the law, and it is the attachment to the mother that the two sexes have to transgress.

Two Sides

I must emphasize, however, that although it is structural, even the Oedipus has two sides, which are described at the outset of Freudian theory. Freud calls them the "direct" or "positive" Oedipus and the "inverted" or "negative" Oedipus, respectively.

The direct or positive Oedipus is the incestuous desire for the parent of the opposite sex: the boy's desire for the mother, the girl's desire for the father. I underscore once again the position of the girl who must separate from her mother in order to desire the other sex, whereas the boy's desire exists within the continuity of his primary desire. But Freud recognizes the structural implications at stake here. For him, the Oedipus complex concerns girls and boys similarly, with specificities for each sex. The boy's incestuous desire for his mother, to whom he is initially linked by dependency, demand, and need for support, will subsequently be modulated as a desire for women. The girl, on the other hand, must free herself from this initial, exclusive attachment to the mother, which both sexes have: she must free herself from an "inverse" desire for the mother before she can bring her "direct" incestuous desires to bear on the father (and men). This is a notable difference.

For now, let us grant that inscription in the symbolic/phallic law through assimilation of the paternal place is structuring. In order to do this, the boy kills the father and desires the mother; for him, becoming a *symbolic subject* and becoming a *desiring subject* are one and the same. The destiny of the girl is completely different. She completes the same trajectory as the boy in order to become a subject—she takes the paternal phallic place, killing Laius and assimilating his attributes—but the heterosexual amorous choice requires that she take an additional course: she must desire the father and detach herself from the mother to whom she was initially linked by need and desire, tenderly and sexually. This second path, which is called a "direct" Oedipus, assures her erotic individuation as a woman who loves men. The first movement, called "inverted" Oedipus (to absorb/kill the father, to desire the mother), assures her structural place as subject. You may note however that in the direct/inverted doublet, only inverted Oedipus determines what is called a homosexual amorous choice, even though the *structure* itself of this inverted Oedipus (and not its physical realization) conditions the girl's access to thought and to the symbolic. This leads to questions concerning certain structural aspects of feminine homosexuality. Add to this structural homosexuality the archaic daughter-mother link that normal evolution abandons in favor of the daughter-father erotic choice, a link that will be called a link of primary homosexuality. Thus we have an endemic and ineluctable female homosexuality, subordinated to female heterosexuality, that does not cease to mobilize feminists in a rather dramatic way and, more lucidly, the great literature of remembrance/revolt, such as that of Proust and Albertine.

Precocious and Biphasic

A final remark will define the complexity of the oedipal organization more clearly. Is Oedipus ontogenetic or phylogenetic? In other words, is it inherited from the history of the species or is it constituted solely in the human being? The Oedipus complex appears late in the child's development: it refers to the genital phase between the ages of three and six. Nevertheless, Freud considers this stage, and consequently this complex, as being established progressively from the beginning of life. Moreover, in his texts on ontogenesis and phylogenesis, particularly *Totem and Taboo* (1912–1913), he situates the murder of the father in an archaic history of humanity and, even earlier, to the dawn of hominization. The crossing of an ontogenetic causality with a phylogenetic causality has led numerous analytical currents, from Melanie Klein to Lacan, to consider a precocious Oedipus, what Lacanians call "the always-already-there" (*le toujours-déjà-là*) of Oedipus, well before ages three to six. This "always-already-there" is explained in particular by the precondition of the paternal function and language. I will have occasion to speak of this again, but for now I will outline the classic postulates of Freudian theory.

The Oedipus complex intervenes between the age of three and six, after which the latency period sets in. Then, at puberty, the Oedipus is reactivated by the development of the subject's genital sexuality, that is, it culminates when biophysiological maturation makes the subject capable of genital sexuality.[13] These two occurrences of the Oedipus complex represent what is called the biphasism of human sexuality, which constitutes the definitive organization of the Oedipus, which in fact always accompanies human psychosexuality.

I will add a last word on early Oedipus. Melanie Klein, for example, situates the Oedipus phase much earlier than Freud does. She believes the incestuous desire for the mother and the desire to murder the father can be observed in the second semester of life, starting at six months. There is a schizoparanoid love/hate phase before the age of six months, during which the child both loves and rejects its mother. This phase is followed by the "depressive position," which I have often commented on. The breast, perceived by the child as the entire human person, is withdrawn; the child loses its mother; a depressive period sets in. Love and attachment, on the one hand, and an aggressive impulse, on the other, which initially converged on the mother's breast, will now be brought to bear on the two protagonists of the scene, the father and mother. There is a recognition of sexual difference; love is felt toward the mother, aggression toward the father.

Klein goes even further, and her position seems untenable to many: she considers the child's aggression toward the father as being directed toward the father's sexual organ in particular, while at the same time the child fantasizes the presence of this organ in the mother's body. A fantasy of coitus interruptus makes the child aggressive toward both parents, particularly toward the maternal body fantasized as containing a penis. The Kleinian fantasy, which supposes the three familial protagonists to be distinct at the outset, nevertheless refers to a universe of organs and drives that remains dual. Why is there not a third? Because, I think, of the absence of language in the Kleinian model of psychogenesis. The human being, the child Klein speaks of, is an *infans* in the etymological sense of the word: the child operates with imagos and does not seem to be motivated by the symbolic third that, at the outset and no doubt well before the child's birth, inscribes its "thirdness" in the mother-baby relationship and favors the development of thought. The paternal penis, which is so present and so incites the child's aggressivity, remains in Klein a maternal imago, a sort of other maternal breast, maleficent and competitive but not a third. It is here, I think, that Lacan's decisive contribution is situated, which should be explained because it shows how the place of the third—that is, the father who will be put to death by Oedipus—is the place of the symbolic (not *only* the symbolic but *also* the symbolic).

Sexuality-Thought Copresence

I propose a reinterpretation of the set of theories I have presented that remains close to the Freudian text and follows from it. This is my conception of psychoanalysis, and I will attempt to clarify it as a theory not of sexuality exclusively but of the development of thought copresent to sexuality. This is no doubt what characterizes the novelty of the psychoanalytical intervention and what has been disturbing about it since its foundation. Psychoanalysis neither biologizes nor sexualizes the essence of man but emphasizes the copresence of sexuality and thought. It is on this point that cognitivist theories could make an interesting contribution, for they constitute an attempt to construct a theory of thought in relation to biological and sensorial development. But this is also their limitation, for they pretend to do without sexual development.

I have already pointed out that Freudian psychoanalysis was founded on the asymptote between sexuality and language and that this gap between the two was readable in the first observations Freud made concerning hysterics: namely, the excitability of the hysteric, on the one hand, and the incongruence and inadequacy of this excitability with the thought of the other, as well as the absence of a juncture between the two. Having made this observation, Freud appeared to consider that language at once attests to the *abyss* between the two sides—excitability/thought—and possible *passageways*. Your excitation does not correspond to your thought; the proof is you cannot say it. Thrown over this abyss, however, is the bridge of language, for through language the two sides of excitability and thought will try to connect. You cannot say this traumatic excitability, but, more exactly, you say it without knowing it, unconsciously. This *other scene* of the unconscious will take shape in language, which will become the space of *another* translinguistic representation. It allows the transfer—Freud called it the "transference," a term he used first to characterize the functioning of the unconscious and then the link to the analyst—from instinctual conflicts to sensible or reasonable behaviors. From then on, the unconscious will provide the model for a transition between excitation stemming from the physiological, on the one hand, and conscious thought, on the other.

From the beginning of the Freudian inquiry into hysteria, psychoanalysis offers itself as a theory of what I call the copresence between sexuality and thought within language; it is neither a theory of sexuality in and of itself nor a biologization of the essence of man, as it is often reproached for being. Though Lacan highlighted this essential characteristic, it was already inscribed in the Freudian approach itself. As for Kleinian theory, even polished and refined, it sets up a silent universe, a wordless dramaturgy of energies and organs. Certain modern avatars of pre-Lacanianism are susceptible to the same criticisms. We forget that the psychogenesis of the child established by Freud is a psychogenesis of capacities of representation or thought, insofar as these capacities are linked to sexual conflicts. Freud, in sum, speaks of the way in which the child's thought is constituted in relation to his sexual conflicts. What happens? A range of heterogeneous elements is offered to the *infans*, a diversity of representations is put in place, particularly through the Oedipus; all of this ends in genitality as well as the active exercise of the symbolic function, that is, the mental capacity to speak, to reason, to be creative in language.

What are the stages of the genesis of the symbolic function, stages in which the Oedipus, while exerting an influence from the beginning of human life, occupies a pivotal place, always with the copresence of excitation and mental representation that will work its way to thought? The first is separation from the maternal object. Starting with this separation, Freud speaks of a primary identification with the "father of the individual's own personal prehistory." For the child to separate from the mother, a primary identification with this father is produced that is already the inscription of a third, with whom the child is not yet engaged in a struggle to the death. We might wonder to what extent religions celebrate this father with the miracle of the God of Love. Second is the mirror stage, that is, the identification of the self, visible through the gap that separates us from our body and the maternal body. Third comes narcissism, the investment of the ego: "I" love myself, me, "I" love my image, my body. Fourth is the depressive position, namely, the separation from the other and the investment of hallucinatory capacities: "I" hallucinate mama, and "I" invest these representations; "I" no longer invest the breast or the bottle; "I" invest what "I" imagine. This hallucinatory representation functions as a sort of footbridge favoring access to signs and to the linguistic capacity that replaces the earlier symbolic equivalents. We are in the presence of the first sublimation, which becomes intrinsic to the human condition; the investment of signs is translated by a surpassing of the depression, by a jubilation: "I" invest signs; I am happy with the pleasure that signs procure for me. The investment of language therefore necessitates a certain retreat of the libido in relation to the object: "I" do not invest the breast, "I" do not invest mama; "I" invest my own capacity to produce signs. This is the beginning of intellectual pleasure, a moment of extreme importance that continues in the sublimation subjacent to all creative activity, artistic creativity, for example.

After these stages, the oedipal conflict takes place. But the triangular relationship and the appearance of the oedipal agency—preceded by this procession: hallucination, representation, sublimation, and the investment of the sign—are established gradually. The oedipal conflict (incest, the murder of the father, and the trial of castration) includes the subject—already able to sketch out his autonomy, perceive himself as abandoned or separated, identify himself in the mirror, detach himself from his mother—in the signifying chain. The signifying chain is made up of three protagonists, and the subject situates himself in relation to three: "me, me, and me." He signifies as an "excluded third" demanding his rights and inserting himself into language, law, socialization and thus acceding to thought, in the sense of the capacity to formulate his place not only in society but also and consequently in the transsocial world. It is in the oedipal conflict that the symbolic capacity will, in sum, be measured, and it is here that the question of the father resurfaces, because this symbolic capacity will be referred to him specifically. Until the Oedipus complex, thought was not referred to the father as an obstacle but as a pole of identification: he loves "me" and protects "me" in order to separate "me" from the maternal container. Starting with Oedipus, thought will be referred to the father as the oedipal father, the third, an agency of the law. "I" must identify myself in relation to this law at the same time that "I" must separate myself from it in order to create my own place, the site of my expression: "I" have a place of my own.

This process of integration of the sexuality-thought-language copresence leads the child in the oedipal triangulation to locate — *repérer*, if you will — the separability of the father, a separability in the sense that the father is different, in the sense that he separates himself from the mother and child. He is a third, he is separated, and at the same time he is separable; he is not only a support, as the father of individual prehistory was, that of primary identification, father love; he may also be threatened: "I" can take his place, "I" can dislodge him, "I" can displace him, "I" can "differ" him, as Derrida says, with this term's unconscious psychoanalytical implication, the violence of the rejection attending *différance*. Because of the phallic investment, this separability of the law is referred to the father, who is not only the third but also the bearer of the penis endowed with all the imaginary implications I pointed out earlier.

While language is strongly implicated in the oedipal conflict, the little boy imagines an identification between the strange function he acquires progressively, which is speech, and the gratifying yet threatened oedipal experience, which is penile or phallic pleasure. This pleasure is at once referred to his own body (the real dimension), the father's body as the bearer of the penis (the imaginary dimension), and the social function the father represents (the symbolic dimension). In other words, during this oedipal experience that characterizes us as human beings, an equivalence is produced between phallic pleasure, on the one hand, and access to language — the function of speech the child acquires — on the other. This speech is a cold abstraction, extraneous to the body-to-body contact with the mother, to the warm dimension of echolalia, rhythms, perceptions, and sensations; extraneous to the sensory, it situates the subject in the frustration of the absence of objects that were once immediately satisfying. Speech is frustration but also compensation, for it is the source of new pleasures and new powers, which are the benefits contributed by the abstract: hallucinations, representations, and thought salvage and refashion what was lost. The complex experience of the access to language that I am describing here, which is consolidated through the Oedipus as a result of the child's neurophysiological evolution, demonstrates the copresence of thought and pleasure—all the more gratifying in that it is threatened (presence and lack)—that the little boy experiences with his genital organ, which is also his father's.

In this parallel between the sexual experience and the experience of thought, this transfer, this transference that articulates mental space, our interiority, occurs at a precise moment of the evolution that will be reactivated at puberty. Essential to this is the development of the repressed construction that is the symbolic phallus, a function of the father and language, which remains in our unconscious. Added to this is the imaginary phallus, which is phallic power accompanied by the threat of castration. Finally, there is the real power, that is, the erection, or powerlessness, impotence on the physiological level. Corresponding to these three levels are the surges as well as the disturbances of thought and language.

Presence and Death of the Father

This dynamic of simultaneity between eroticism and symbolism is present from the very start of the speaking being's life. The different stages of the dual neurological and psychical maturation impose it throughout the subject's existence. But during the oedipal ordeal, a first coincidence occurs between the investment of the phallus and its lack on the real and imaginary level in the little boy, on the one hand, and the order of language, on the other. The trial of the third (the Oedipus) accommodates not only the coincidence between the phallus and its lack and language but also, and consequently, a coincidence between the speaking-desiring subject and the place of the father as father of the law.

In this complex problematic, what does the term of lack signify? What is lacking? And how is it lacking? The lacking penis is castration. The lacking father is his absence or death. The paradigm that we have just elaborated thus comprises the penile organ (present/absent, powerful/powerless, impotent), the order of language (the real object/the signified through absence/the signifier of this signified), and the place of the father insofar as he is both *presence* and *death*. "The father is the dead father and nothing else," Lacanian theory tells us. This means he only exercises his signifying role of guarantor of authority if he is capable of lacking this authority. How? By being put to death, which is another, more dramatic form of absence. But the father is not "always already" dead "on his own." He dies by and through the subject, precisely, who must put him to death in order to become a subject. Here we find the logical necessity of the oedipal tragedy mentioned at the beginning. In effect, if the father is always there to block the horizon, if he does not become "dead," "I" have no chance of inscribing myself in the power that is corporal, penile power but also the symbolic power of language. Male or female, in order to find my place in the sun of the Intelligible and the Other, "I" must kill the father, holder of phallic or symbolic power, and at the same time wage a war against my drives in order to translate them into representations and thereby not only be an instinctual being but also a being who first hallucinates and imagines and finally thinks—with a little luck.

This split, or internal unfolding, that "I" force on myself in order to become a being of thought (although "it" is "always already there," "I" nevertheless necessary must become, "I" must acquire symbolic capacity, "I" must manifest it, "I" must represent, more and more, and better and better, throughout my evolution) finds its external correlate in the struggle—the revolt—against the paternal agency, in his being put to death, which is, once again, manifested in the tragedy. In order to become "myself," for the subject to become himself, the death of the father and/or the lacking signifier is necessary. The desire for the mother, an unconscious, incestuous desire, supports and propels this struggle to the death that consolidates access to thought.

There is no signifier that is not lacking, no father who does not become dead: these are the two aspects of the castration fantasy, fantasy because, of course, this is an imaginary construction, which does not at all mean that it is unessential: starting from this fantasy every subject is constructed as such, that is, as desiring and thinking. Perhaps you believe, as some do, that no one is obliged to be a subject, no one is obliged to posit himself as envious of the place of the father, desirous of occupying the place of the father, assuming a law and being put to death oneself, for, of course, if "I" put myself in the place of the father, "I" risk being subjected to the same hazards "I" inflict. The tragedy calls us to occupy this place of death and desire; it is even the condition for becoming a knowing, philosophizing, thinking subject. But are we necessarily forced to submit to this uncomfortable logic? Are we necessarily subjected to this crossroads, this gamma-shaped bifurcation where Oedipus stood? Can't we slip away and occupy other places in human history: The anti-Oedipus? Or the normalizing and corruptible new world order I described earlier, where we would be neither guilty nor responsible? Wouldn't this allow us to avoid having to confront the paternal function, to avoid being subjects in the sense I have just described, that is, in the classical sense, meaning the Greek, tragic, knowing, and thinking sense? But then, what would we be? Neither guilty nor responsible: Is that to say free? Or rather mechanized, roboticized, lobotomized, a sorry and embarrassing version of the human?

That said, the phallic issue as the Oedipus presents it to us—and which, once again, is linked to the destiny of the subject in our civilization, even if it is threatened by the hybrid forms I evoked—cannot be the sole issue. Civilizations exist in which the place of speaking beings, while structured in relation to power and law and thus referred to the father, is not thematized as such. These are civilizations in which the subject does not confront the phallus but the void—Taoism, for example—or the maternal. These are religions, "philosophies" in the non-Greek sense of the term, hence the quotation marks, human organizations that emphasize not the ordeal of power but other modulations of the symbolic-sexual copresence.

In this different preoedipal or transoedipal order, articulations of representation are produced that I define as "semiotic" [14] (Piera Aulagnier refers to them as pictograms) and that return above and beyond the oedipal barrier that constitutes the sign, the signifier, and the entire mental organization targeting univocal communication. These earlier elements return in symbolic organization, disturb it, modify it, and constitute highly curious signifying manifestations—for example, the symbolic practices that one finds in societies where writing is not based on the phoneme and the sign in the Western sense of the term but on gesture, calligraphy, and rhythm. In our societies, heirs to Greece, the Bible, and the gospels, the equivalent might be signifying practices that constitute revolt in relation to the law and the univocal signifier—for example, aesthetic practices, artistic practices that redistribute the phallic signifying order by causing the preoedipal register to intervene, with its procession of sensoriality, echolalia, and ambiguous meaning. Whatever these practices and manifestations (it is here that we seek experiences of revolt), it is indispensable to point out the structuring yet traversable role of phallic organization, which can be challenged.

The Freudian tradition has the advantage of having underscored the structuring role of Oedipus and the phallus. But it perhaps has the disadvantage of having done so without indicating forms of modification, transgression, and revolt vis-à-vis this order. In any case, we cannot speak of revolt without redefining the axis against which it is organized and elaborated in the psychical space of the speaking being.

The Phallic Mysteries

Before concluding this chapter, I would like mention several mythological references that are part of the history of religions and concern the importance of

the oedipal organization, as well as what we might call its phallic manifestation, a manifestation that in reality is its very essence, because the attack of the
paternal figure amounts to an ordeal vis-à-vis the phallus insofar as it is the representative of both the organ and the symbolic function.

   The observation was made long ago: all forms of the sacred, all ritual celebrations can be traced back to a phallic cult. It is a controversial observation, although it has been supported by numerous scholars who point to the mysteries
of our Greco-Roman world and find equivalent expressions of them in other
civilizations, for example, the mysteries of Eleusis, the Orphic mysteries, and
the Dionysiac mysteries in Rome. Some of these celebrate social cohesion
through a rite involving the veiling and unveiling of the phallus. In his library,
Freud had a work by the eighteenth-century anthropologist Richard Knight, *A
Discourse on the Worship of Priapus and Its Connection with the Mystic Theology of the Ancients,* in which the author maintained that the primitive cult of
the phallus is at the origin of all myth and thus the basis of every theology and
the core of Christianity. I have presented the Freudian version of the Oedipus-
phallus in an effort to establish the unconscious logic behind this imaginary.
Another author, Jacques-Antoine Dulaure, published a work in 1805 entitled
*Les Divinités génératrices; ou, Le Culte du phallus chez les Anciens et les Mod-
ernes.* "It would be difficult," he wrote in regard to the phallic cult, "to imagine
a sign that better expressed the signified thing." A sentence of interest for linguists, isn't it? I do not know if Lacan was aware of this book, and, needless to
say, for this author in 1805, the words "sign" and "signified" have no relationship to the signifier and the signified as we understand them after Saussure.
Still, they highlight the fact that in the phallic celebrations the phallus is a signifier, a sign in relation to a signified, this latter being nothing other than the
possibility of generation, the genital capacity, the power to procreate, the aptitude for being sexually creative. This creativity is no doubt cosmic, not necessarily the sexual desire of interest to psychoanalysts but an extension of it, which
Dulaure explains as the thing signified by a signifier or sign: the phallus.

   The binary logic that the phallus symbolizes is contained in the pres-
ence/absence dichotomy inherent in the threat of castration, or the referent/
sign dichotomy, or even that of every marked/unmarked signifying articulation. Here the phallus object plays a role of sealing the signifying dichotomy:
it organizes the sacred space in which the cult of our capacity to signify is developed. At the unconscious origin of the phallic cult we find the sacralization
of this capacity, which perhaps has nothing sacred about it except the signifying aptitude of the human being, his difference in relation to other species, the
ability to create meaning.

Given the prevalence of the phallus, it would be interesting to know what other sorts of logic, besides binary logic, the phallus organizes. Perhaps here one could contemplate the semiotic, the preverbal, and various forms of fluid, sensorial organizations: from pictograms to other pre- or translinguistic representations. Researching types of representations or psychical acts, which would not be those of the signifier and language, could have extremely important anthropological implications, as this would concern not only the maternal and the preoedipal but also other forms of the sacred, not the phallic sacred exclusively.

As a sort of conclusion, I would like to comment on a few Italian baroque sculptures: *Modesty* and *Veiled Christ*, found in the Sansevero chapel in Naples, and *Purity* in Venice (see figures 4.1, 4.2, and 4.3). *Modesty* (1751) and the magnificent *Purity* are by Antonio Corradini (1668–1752), a sculptor who worked in Venice, Este, and Naples. *Veiled Christ* is by Giuseppe Sammartino (1720–1793). As you know, not far from Naples, north of Pompeii at the Villa of the Mysteries,[15] the initiation rites of the Dionysian mysteries and phallic cults were celebrated with the veiling and unveiling of the phallus. The word "mystery" itself has the Greek root *muo (hidden, closed), from the Sanskrit *mukham* (mouth, hold, closure), rendered in Slavic languages as *muka* (pain, mystery). The mysteries were processions, rites that involved both showing and hiding what our anthropological author called the supreme sign, the phallus. This practice is found in humanity's sacred arena in various configurations that hide and show not only the phallus but all sorts of other desirable objects or objects that become desirable by being veiled/unveiled. Just think of the importance of the veil in temples not exclusively devoted to the phallus but housing other hidden forms, Jewish and Christian places of worship, for example.

It is hard not to be struck by the profusion of veils that dissimulate, as though to accentuate, the sacred figures from the Gospels, which are quite anthropomorphic and no longer phallic: Jesus and Mary, of course, but also allegories such as Modesty, Purity, Prudence, and so on. The baroque sculptor does not present us with phalluses, as did his predecessor, the painter of the Villa of Mysteries, but characters, incarnated forms, bodies. Yet he veils these bodies as the phallus was veiled in Pompeii. All art, all innovation—I will say in passing that the innovation of forms is both an ultimate and user-friendly revolt—is translated by work on the veiling and unveiling of tradition (that celebrating the human figure and, earlier, the phallic cults). The figures are sculpted in marble, covered by veils both marmoreal and gossamer through which we make out the figures perhaps more effectively than if they were bared. The veil expresses the divine presence/nonpresence, an invitation to see the object as it is, though it is hidden. And thus the question of presence and absence is taken up again in a new form.

The theme here is not castration or death but their *différance* in an economy that is, strictly speaking, infinite, like the multitude of folds of the veiling and unveiling. This secret, or discreet, reference to the phallic mysteries became a source of aesthetic innovation in the eighteenth century; baroque art was constituted, beyond mannerism, in an internal conflict with anthropomorphism. In effect, in the baroque art of two centuries ago, these veiled virtues and this dead, veiled Christ do not merely present us with theological signifieds; in this baroque veiling/unveiling we find beyond the forms themselves a kind of abstract art. For the essence of the virtuosity here involves the possibility of constructing folds that do not represent anything besides representation itself and its possible failure, namely, the cult of the unrepresentable, which is inverted in an apotheosis of the very art of representing, with all its limits.

When the phallus becomes the equivalent of representation and vice versa the questioning of one implies the questioning of the other. To hide/show, to examine what is showable, to veil it, to make the visible appear through that which obscures it, to center attention on the possibility of monstrance itself: this is an inquiry into the roots of phallic meaning and simultaneously into power and the sacred, which are its apotheosis. The baroque sculptor who managed to give a marble veil the aquatic fluidity of transparency in fact situated himself at the heart of the mystery, if it is true that the mystery resides in the emergence and extinction of representation and/or the phallus. There is no phallus this time, but it is displaced in the body, entire and absolute: the body of Christ and those of the allegorical women who conceal themselves by exposing themselves in a subtle displacement, a veritable revolution of thought.

Antonio Corradini and Giuseppe Sammartino seem to me to illustrate perfectly the problematics of presence and absence already contained in an inquiry of representation itself. With them began the modern conviction that culture is a resorption and displacement of the cult: culture will only be the veiling or unveiling, beyond the phallus, of the entire body of representation itself; culture is a representation that unfolds representation. As such, culture is a mystery, though I prefer to say that as a veiling and unveiling it is an exquisite revolt. Perhaps mystery and revolt are the same thing, if you admit the capital place of real presence and its absence, which found and structure our desires as well as the major themes of our civilization. If revolt/transgression is impossible or exhausted today, the baroque sculptor's exquisite gesture invites us to seek ways to veil/unveil the key values of a culture in crisis and to transmute them.

FIGURE 4.1

Veiled Christ by Giuseppe Sammartino, Sansevero chapel, Naples. © Scala.

FIGURE 4.2

Modesty by Antonio Corradini, Sansevero chapel, Naples.
© Scala.

FIGURE 4.3

Purity by Antonio Corradini, Correr Museum, Venice.
© Scala.

5

On the Extraneousness of the Phallus; or, the Feminine Between Illusion and Disillusion

From the perspective of psychoanalysis as a theory of sexuality and thought, I will now deal with the question of female sexuality, or rather bisexuality, and in particular the girl's relationship to the Oedipus, the law, and the phallus. This is of interest, of course, insofar as the question of revolt is also situated in relation to the law. To comment on Freud's statement in *Female Sexuality* that "bisexuality . . . comes to the fore much more clearly in women than in men,"[1] which I would like to highlight in this chapter, I will refer to several of Freud's texts: "Some Psychical Consequences of the Anatomical Distinction Between the Sexes" (1925), "Female Sexuality" (1931), "Femininity" (1933), and *An Outline of Psychoanalysis* (1938; published in 1940), particularly chapter 7 (this last does not directly concern female sexuality, but it nevertheless offers the final state of Freud's thought on the question).

The Phallic *Kairos*

I want to emphasize the copresence of sexuality and thought in order to dissociate myself from two currents of thought that investigate the psyche: cognitivism, on the one hand, which considers the mind solely from the point of view of consciousness, and a pre-Lacanian psychoanalysis, on the other, or at least a psychoanalysis that circumvents the Lacanian contribution and heads off into either a sort of organicism or an analytical approach that accentuates only the fantasmatic aspect of the psychical experience without taking thought into account. Instead of psychoanalysis as a matheme of the signifier, or a theory of "the mind," or the transaction of organs and drives, I will try to show that the originality of the Freudian discovery resides in this: psychoanalysis is a clinic and a theory of the copresence of the development of thought *and* of sexuality. This two-sided (thought/sexuality) approach to the speaking being, which I see at the heart of the analytical experience, is an original variant of the age-old notion of dualism, and far from biologizing the essence of man, it centers the study of the psychical apparatus, its deployment, and its obstacles, in the biunivocal dependency of thought-sexuality/sexuality-thought. As language is the domain of this interaction, it is here that Freud found the "other scene," that of the unconscious, with its components (representatives of the drive) and its logic (primary processes) irreducible to conscious linguistic communication. I will therefore present my reflections on female bisexuality by trying to define it from the angle of women's specific relationship to the phallus.

The Unbearable and the Mystery

To make this difficult question more concrete, I will give a few paroxysmal examples of feminine positions that demonstrate a somewhat dramatic adherence to the phallic, a structural adherence, but at the price of often traumatic suffering.

> Armelle had a high-powered position in an international organization. A wife, mother, mistress, and author, she had everything except personal satisfaction ("It's not sexual," she insisted, "I'm not frigid"). This was accompanied by the feeling of being a little girl, never taken seriously, never operating at her true capacities. She took on all tasks, chores, and obligations, regardless of their difficulty. Armelle was fixed at the pivotal scene that I situate between her Oedipus[1] and her Oedipus[2] (remember these terms; I will use them again). She had a bed of nails made and would lie on the spiked surface, pressing her back or stomach into it until she bled. The martyrology of saints, transmitted by familial tradition, was added to the structural jouissance of "A Child Is Being Beaten":[2] Armelle is being beaten, Armelle beats Armelle, Armelle punctures Armelle until she bleeds; the entire body is a penis-phallus that takes pleasure in sadomasochism to punish itself for clitoral pleasure and to avoid acknowledging itself as a punctured/castrated body. Armelle achieved her professional excellence, her phallicism in the symbolic order, at the price of the denial of her bisexuality: she wanted to be all phallus. Her perverse jouissance was paid for by the physical and mental exhaustion of the superwoman.

> Dominique had a boy's slender body and an allusive way of speaking. Her computer skills were not enough to explain this reserve. She reluctantly revealed that she had had erotic encounters with women but preferred a man, whose masochistic partner she was. Much later, Dominique revealed to me that this man was her hierarchical superior and, later still, that he was black. Dominique had greatly admired her brother, who was a year older, a sort of twin; a younger sister was born five years later. The idyll of Dominique-as-a-

boy ended in adolescence when her brother was hit by a car. "I don't think women have a sex. After my brother's death, I noticed I was smooth between my legs, like a plastic doll." Without a penis, without a clitoris, without a vagina, Dominique lived out the failure of her psychical bisexuality by offering her anus as a hollow penis to her sadistic partner. Another configuration of phallic monism.

Florence alternated between anorexia and bulimia, trying to vomit up an abandoned and abandoning mother, whom she protected and suffered for with her entire body. Too early Florence had taken the place of her divorced father for her loved-hated mother. This maternal score-settling led to Russian roulette. A dream: "I'm playing Russian roulette, which is actually Belgian roulette: you lose every time, meaning you win death. There is no empty slot in the cartridge. You won't believe this, but I pulled the trigger, and I won a sort of big phallus, only it meant that I was dead. It was an absurd dream. Gambling doesn't interest me. My brother is the one who gambles; it's disastrous, he's pathological, he's destroying his family." Florence swallows-vomits the penis (the brother's, the father's) and wins her big phallus, but these creative performances that signal her gain are paid for by a putting-to-death of the entire body, which has become an imaginary phallus that she prefers to erect as well as abolish in anorexia rather than pay the price of the lack through the recognition of bisexuality.

I will come back to this unbearable phallicism in women. For now, I would like to emphasize once again the universality of the phallic reference, which is manifested in both sexes, although in different ways, well before the phallic phase and the oedipal phase it announces and thus before the child locates the importance of the "third." This, as I have already mentioned, is what psychoanalysis calls "phallic monism," which emerged with the clinic and refers to the universality of the phallic reference in the girl as well as the boy, although again in different ways. It appears because of language, because of the paternal function, and because of the maternal desire for the father (her own and the child's). What we call phallic is the conjunction, encounter, intersection between the importance of the symbol—of thought—on the one hand, and genital excitation, on the other. Lacan points out this "*trace* of the phallus" and speaks of "a phallus without incarnation"[3] that always already organizes the subject's psychosexuality. Primary identification, narcissism, sublimation, idealization, the imposition of the ego ideal and the superego are only a few of the well-known stages of the positioning of the future subject vis-à-vis this phallic reference, in other words, this unity of sense and law.

Desire and Meaning

Let us return to what Freud calls the phallic stage, which he situates between ages three and six and which, structurally, is the central organizer of what I have called the sexuality-thought copresence in both sexes. This is the age at which the child discovers his/her sexual organs and their excitability, invests them at the same time as thought, which is related to both language and the third and placed, so to speak, above the sensorial mother-child relationship. Numerous authors have pointed out the particularities that destine the penis to be invested by both sexes and to become the phallus, that is, the signifier of privation, of lack of being, but also of desire, the desire to signify, which consequently makes it the signifier of symbolic law. Remember what I said earlier: the penis, visible and narcissistically recognized, erectile and invested with erogenous sensibility, detachable and thus cuttable, susceptible to loss, is suited to becoming the basis of difference, the favored actor in the 0-1 binarism that founds all (marked/unmarked) systems of meaning, the organic factor (real and imaginary) of our psychosexual network.

Here, I want to examine briefly the *kairos*,[4] this subtle and in a sense miraculous encounter between desire and meaning during the phallic phase that henceforth seals the fate of the human being as desiring and speaking being. Whether anatomically male or female, the subject who desires and speaks is formed by this phallic *kairos*. This is what psychoanalysis reveals to us, after the mysteries; the essence of our psychical destiny bears this mystery's (admittedly dramatic) consequences.

In effect, the phallicism of both sexes thus structured and under the threat of castration (it may be encountered as well as cut) will succumb to latency and repression. The primacy of the phallic remains only an *infantile* genital organization for this phallic primacy is precisely what differentiates infantile genitality from adult genitality, which in principle recognizes *both* sexes and does not remain under the primacy of the phallus.[5] A single sex (the penis), a single libido (male), a single symbol for the activity of thought (the phallus): this phallic experience common to both sexes will remain a basic given of the unconscious for both sexes. Adult sexuality, however, will dissociate itself from it by acceding to the discovery of the second sex (in the optimal hypothesis). Phallic monism is thus an infantile illusion that nevertheless remains an unconscious organizing reality of the psyche. An illusion that has become unconscious reality: isn't this an illusion promised a certain future? This is the foundation of what Freud would call "the future of an illusion," because all religion may be traced back to the phallic cult.

Note in passing that this Freudian theory that the clinic confirms brings with it two consequences that have not been sufficiently considered. First, the phallic *kairos* is proper to infantile genitality, which means that phallic monism is a vestige of this infantile phallocentrism that conditions the Oedipus phase. Second, because this phallicism is repressed and becomes unconscious, the unconscious is phallic. In other words, the unconscious lacks genitality in the sense of a recognition of sexual difference, or, to put it more bluntly, *there is no unconscious psychical genitality* (there is the biological instinct of procreation and the pubescent desire for the opposite sex, but nothing in Freudian theory suggests that there is an unconscious psychical representative of the opposite sex as such).

Keep in mind as well that man undergoes a crisis of the Oedipus complex, which is conditioned by the phallic *kairos*: this crisis is the abandonment of incest and murder and the institution of the conscience and morality that Freud interprets as a "victory of the race over the individual."[6] The agencies of the psychical apparatus (id, ego, and superego) replace the libidinal investments through desexualization and sublimation, and only neurosis—in trying continually to return to the infantile and oedipal or preoedipal pleasures—betrays a rebellion of the ego against the pretensions of the sexual function. What are we to think of this other form of rebellion, which for the subject is no longer represented by neurosis but by the creation of thought and language, the aesthetic creation often parallel to neurosis and even to psychosis but irreducible to it? This inquiry into (female) bisexuality will perhaps make it possible to sketch out an answer to this question that Freud did not raise.

The fate that Freud accords the primacy of the phallic can be summed up this way: it is the central organizer (as is the Oedipus); it is illusory (peculiar to infantile phallic organization); and it shatters under the threat of castration and when the individual is effaced in favor of the race.

We know the revenge and the overinvestment of the phallic to which Lacan devoted himself in order to restore the function of the father and language in the speaking being: a lacking, evanescent phallic, common place of anxiety and, for this very reason, the first symbol that determines sexuation. I emphasize the fact that this is not simply a matter of the erected organ; the penis becomes a *symbol* susceptible to lacking, to not being. "[Man] is not without having it . . . , woman is without having it."[7] I would like to compare this statement with Winnicott's proposition of a driveless maternal that quite simply *is* (the self *is* the breast, the breast *is* the self) and does not "do."[8]

To be, to have, to do: are the differences so clear? I propose the following as an extension and counterpoint to these two propositions by Lacan and Winnicott.

The Two-Sided Oedipus Phase of the Girl

In the little girl, too, a decisive encounter fuses her being as thinking and de-siring subject: the encounter (*kairos*) between the mastery of signs (cold ab-stractions and evanescent frustrations but so many sources of new benefits and powers) and genital sexual excitation (no longer oral or anal). Whether the vagina is or is not perceived, it is essentially the clitoris that concentrates this phallic assumption, at once felt (real), imaginary (fantasized in power/power-lessness), and symbolic (investment and efflorescence of thought). Masturba-tion, incestuous desire for the mother: here is the first aspect of the Oedipus complex (I will call it Oedipus[1]) that structurally defines the girl, as well as the boy, before she arrives at Oedipus[2], which causes her to change objects (the fa-ther instead of the mother). Yet, starting with this structuring (Oedipus[1]), there are differences between the girl's phallicism and the boy's, which perhaps have not been sufficiently underscored.

Sensory Versus Signifying: The Extraneousness of the Phallus and the Illusory

The emphasis placed on language as the organizer of psychical life, though judicious, has too often prevented us from fully appreciating the sensory (prelinguistic or translinguistic) experience. Now, sensoriality, strongly stimu-lated in the little girl in the preoedipal phases by the symbiotic link to the mother (through primary homosexuality), allows her to appreciate the differ-ence of the boy's organic sexual performances as well as the narcissistic over-investment of which he is the object. Of course, individual variations in exci-tation or clitoral pleasure, on the one hand, and the singular variants in the girl's valorization by the father, on the other, considerably influence the mod-ulations of feminine phallicism: a little girl may be as satisfied or valorized as a little boy in the phallic phase, if not more so. Nevertheless, a dissociation is structurally inscribed between the sensory and the signifying in the phallicism of the girl.[9] The phallus as signifier of the lack as well as of the law, supported in the imaginary by the penis, is immediately perceived/thought of by the girl as extraneous, radically other. Invisible and almost impossible to locate, the real and imaginary basis of phallic pleasure in the girl (the clitoris) immedi-ately dissociates the female subject from the phallus in the sense of a privileged signifier in the logos/desire conjunction that I have called a phallic *kairos*, to which the girl nevertheless accedes with as much ease as the boy, if not more. This symbolic ease (of thought), however, is not accompanied by sensorial ex-perience (distinct from the phallic drive), in light of the disappointment of the perception of being less visible and less remarkable: less appreciated, although pleasure is not necessarily less intensely felt. Lesser valorization of the girl by her father and mother, in comparison to the boy, traditionally played out in families or as a result of specific psychosocial configurations, contributes to consolidating this disappointment with regard to the symbolic link. From then on, with the sensory/signifying dissociation, the belief is established that the phallic-symbolic order is illusory.

The perception (contemporaneous with the phallic phase), unfavorable to the girl (she does not have a "remarkable" penis, she is not the phallus), reactivates the hallucination of earlier sensorial experiences (satisfaction and/or frustration in the daughter-mother reduplication and Minoan-Mycenean sameness) preceding or concealed from the appearance of language.[10] From then on, with this gap between the current perception dominated by the phallic *kairos* and the earlier perception/hallucination, phallic monism, referred to the other (the man) that "I am not," immediately strikes the female subject with a negation ("I am not what is," "I am, nevertheless, because of *not*"). The *extraneous* or *illusory* nature of the phallus may be another name for this doubled negativity of "nevertheless" and "not."

It is not a delirium that heals the perception/hallucination gap in the woman but precisely the belief that the phallus, as well as language and the symbolic order, are illusory yet indispensable. On the other hand, one may interpret as a form of delirium the refusal to accept the difference and the illusory aspect of the phallus that this entails, as well as the female subject's desperate attempts to maintain equality with the boy's phallicism through sadomasochism (recall the three examples cited above).

By "belief" I mean conscious and unconscious adherence, without proof, to an obvious fact: here, the obvious fact that the phallus, because of the perception/signification dissociation, always already appears to the woman as illusory. "Illusory"[11] basically means that this law, this pleasure, this phallic power and, simultaneously, their lack, to which I accede through the phallus—that of the stranger—is a game. It is not that it is nothing, but it is not everything either or even a veiled everything, as in the phallic mysteries. The phallus that "I" invest is what makes me a subject of language and of law; there "I" am. There is something else, however, a *je ne sais quoi*. Nonetheless, "I" enter the game, "I" want some, too, "I" play along. It's only a game (*jeu*), it's only an "I" (*je*), "I" am pretending, and this, for the female subject, is indeed the so-called truth of the signifier or the speaking being. I am not saying that women are necessarily mocking or ludic, though some may be. But when they are not under an illusion, they are disillusioned. Women's apparent realism is based on this illusion: women continue to do everything because they do not believe in it; they believe that it is an illusion.

This belief in the illusoriness of the phallus may have some benefits. For example, I cultivate a secret sensoriality, which may be furtive but spares me the boy's difficult experience of making my erotic pleasure coincide with my symbolic performance. Such a dissociation may present the advantage of easing and facilitating the girl's logical abilities, extraneous to eroticism, thereby favoring the well-known intellectual successes of little girls, precocious geniuses who excel at everything. Still, this experience of the extraneousness of the phallus entails its opposite, which is the opposite of facility and may push the girl into a paroxysmal phallic ambition bordering on martyrology, as the clinical examples cited above show. In women, the extraneousness of the phallus may sustain an aspect of what we too summarily call female masochism, namely, the sadomasochistic phallic competition not compensated by Oedipus[2] or by reconciliation with preoedipal femininity. In struggling against the extraneousness of the phallus, the phallic girl—who wants to "have one," like the boy—makes herself more Catholic than the pope, becoming saint, martyr, and militant of a signifier whose illusory aspect all her erogenous zones are mobilized to deny and that she would like to persuade herself she believes in, with rock-hard certainty.

The belief in the phallus as illusory seems to me an immediate indication of female psychical bisexuality, insofar as the illusoriness (or the extraneousness) relies on the dehiscence between the sensory and the signifiable resulting from an always-present adherence in the girl to the preoedipal daughter-mother osmosis and to the code in which this osmosis occurs: sensorial exchanges and prelanguage (the "semiotic" modality in my terminology: rhythms, alliterations anterior to signs and syntax). The abandon of this semiotic modality of *signifiance* in favor of linguistic signs during the depressive position characterizes the boy as well as the girl, though again, there are no doubt differences between the sexes that have barely been explored. Later, the phallic structuring of the subject is added to the acquisition of language and consolidates it. But because of the experience of the extraneousness of the phallus in the little girl, the phallic *kairos* reactivates the depressive position and thereby accentuates in the woman the belief in the illusory nature of the phallus and of language.

A clarification, which is also a warning, is in order: the particularity that I am bringing to the fore is a manifestation of the woman's psychical bisexuality and does not necessarily lead to "as-if" personalities or false selves, the etiology of which requires traumatic splittings. I did not mention splittings but games, extraneousness, the illusory, the illusory aspect of the phallic being the trace of two continents: the phallic continent and the Minoan-Mycenean continent in the female psychical experience. I think that the illusory phallic in the woman may lead her to inscribe herself in the social order with an aloof efficiency; Hegel referred to this in speaking of women as the irony in the life of the community. Moreover, this illusory position of the phallus may also favor the woman's depressive regressions when the attraction to the shadow of the preoedipal object (the Minoan-Mycenean mother) becomes inexorable and the female subject abandons the extraneousness of the symbolic in favor of an unnamable sensoriality, becoming sullen, silent, and suicidal. On the other hand, in the maniacal investment of this illusory phallicism, one can see the logic of ostentation that mobilizes the beautiful seductress: constantly made up, provocative, on parade and just as constantly not fooled and disappointed. This is the well-known case of the female illusionist who knows herself to be such, the "girl-phallus" that Fenichel, and Lacan after him, spoke of.

Inversely, while psychical bisexuality imposes the belief in the illusoriness of the phallus in the woman, the denial of bisexuality presents itself as a denial of the illusory. Such a denial implies identification with the phallus as such, which amounts to an identification with the man's phallic position and scotomization, the quashing of the primary semiotic link with the mother (which some call primary female homosexuality). The result of this is the female paranoiac: the boss, director, or virile lesbian, partisans of power in all its more or less dictatorial forms. As you can see, these different articulations of the phallus offer privileges but also set traps, like every psychical structuring.

Oedipus[2]

But the illusoriness of the phallus does not exhaust the complexity of the strange configuration that is female bisexuality. It was sufficient for Freud to posit the Oedipus phase to see that the girl does not conform to it. "We have an impression here that what we have said about the Oedipus complex applies with complete strictness to the male child only."[12] You have already noted that I am not among those who reject phallic monism and thus the phallic structuring of the girl subject based on this remark of Freud's. I would add however to Oedipus[1] (indispensable for the boy and girl, which phallicism sets in motion) an Oedipus[2], and therefore I propose the notion of an *oedipal dyad* in the woman. Let me explain.

As a result of the threat of castration, to which the experience of the extraneousness of the phallus can be added, the little girl renounces clitoral masturbation, is disgusted by it, rejects it, and turns away from her phallicism, which is as real (the belief that "*I have* the organ") as it is imaginary (the belief that "*I am* male power/powerlessness"). While cultivating her place as subject of the phallic signifier, subject of the symbolic (with the extraneousness and illusoriness she accords it), the girl changes objects in Oedipus[2]. She starts by hating the mother who was the object of her phallic desire, becoming hostile to this mother responsible for castration and illusion, as illusion entails disappointment. The girl, however, still identifies with the same mother who was the object of her phallic desire during Oedipus[1] and moreover identifies with the preoedipal mother of Minoan-Mycenean perfumed paradises. It is from this place of identification beyond hate that she changes objects and from now on no longer desires the mother but what the mother desires: the love of the father. More precisely, the girl wants the father to give her his own penis/phallus, in the form of children that the girl would have as if she were . . . the mother. The renewal of phallic aspiration therefore continues in this Oedipus[2]—which we could say is interminable—and we see how Freud postulates that, unlike the boy whose Oedipus complex dissolves as a result of the castration complex, the Oedipus of the girl—which I call Oedipus[2]—not only does not dissolve but is only beginning, specifically speaking, as female Oedipus. It is *introduced* by the castration complex.[13]

The integration of this feminine position vis-à-vis the father is not free of ambiguity. Indeed, it results from an identification with the castrating/castrated mother, at first abhorred and then accepted, and is accompanied by "a lowering of the active sexual impulses," and a repression of masculinity; "a considerable portion of her sexual trends in general is permanently injured too."[14] Does passivation follow the illusory? Whatever the answer, parallel to this passivation, or depression, penis envy persists as a variant of phallicism— which would suggest that the active sexual trends are far from abolished—as either a behavioral or a professional masculine claim or, more "naturally," in the desire for a child and maternity. This is perhaps where the world as illusory stops for the woman and where that of real presence begins.

Motherhood: Fulfillment and Void

A child, as the real presence of the phallus, is invested by its mother quite differently from any sign or symbol, even a phallic one. This is what the last religion, Christianity, clearly understood, in making its god a child and thereby definitively endearing itself to women, so given to disillusion,[15] so incredulous when presented with an ideal or disembodied superego, that Freud himself was struck by it and severely criticized women's incapacity for morality. Rather than incapacity, I would say "estrangement," a critical and ironic capacity.

If it is true that the desire for a child incarnates the permanent feminine Oedipus, the last and therefore interminable phallic revolt in the woman's

Oedipus[2] ("I want a penis = real presence"), it is no less true that the woman finds another variant of her bisexuality here. Why? Because the child is her penis, she does not renounce masculinity. But at the same time, and still through the child, she accedes to the quality of being the other of the man, that is, a woman who has *given* her child, *emptied* herself of it, *separated* from it. Yet, maternity is most often perceived or experienced not as a disequilibrium of identity and even less as an open structure but as fulfillment, to which the term "androgyny" would be better suited than "bisexuality." When the symbolic order is incarnated in real presence (the child-phallus), the woman finds in it the conjunction of her symbolic essence (phallic thinking subject) and her carnal essence (preoedipal sensuality, mother-daughter sensual duality, reduplication of female parents). As a result, achieving her bisexuality in androgyny in an Oedipus phase that is never completed and always renewed, the woman-mother may appear to be the guarantor of both the social order and the continuation of the species.

Freud's observation of women as social beings culminates in maternal omnipotence,[16] which, following directly from the mother as guarantor of the social and the biological, strives today with the aid of the gynecologist and the geneticist to restore real presence. The maternal woman, served by science and technology, has the fantasy of being able to do everything and often does do everything to bring the real presence of the phallus into existence, and to improve it, through her child.

Hypersocial and Vulnerable

Yet this tableau of a hypersocial, ultrabiological, and ferociously restorative femininity, though not entirely false, seems to me not to take into account two weaknesses. The first is the permanence of illusion/disillusion with regard to all signifiers, law or desire. The other is the vulnerability of the woman who delegates her real presence to that of her child (i.e., to another) and who, at each attack on her child's integrity, relives the throes of castration, if not a brutal identity crisis. What we call female sadomasochism is perhaps the experience of this structural extraneousness of the phallus in these two forms: disillusion (based on Oedipus[1]) or an attack on the real presence relayed by the other of the self, the child (based on Oedipus[2]).

If it is not fixed in omnipotence, female bisexuality tends toward the trials of sadomasochism. Then, still estranged in her latent desire to have the phallus or be it (a desire that nevertheless sustains her being a subject), the woman turns away from the desiring and phallic assumption; she renounces her psychical bisexuality and takes pleasure in a painful sensoriality, which is the carrier wave of *hysterical depressivity* before it topples into melancholia. Inversely, *hysterical indifference* may reveal an option for the phallus erected as superego, disgusted by clitoral pleasure, and deprived of any possible recollection of the link to the preoedipal mother. These configurations of female psychical bisexuality (among others) appear, in sum, as variants of the position of the female subject with regard to phallic monism. The structural difficulties of this positioning—more than the historical conditions that must inevitably be added to it—perhaps explain the difficult fate of women throughout history.

Remember the phallic adherence in Armelle, Dominique and Florence, mentioned at the beginning of this chapter, whose suffering now appears as a denial of bisexuality in favor of a fantasy of androgynous totality. I gave you these brief sketches of a few dramatic aspects of the difficult female condition to emphasize that by avoiding these (ever-so-frequent) impasses, the mystery of female bisexuality may shine forth. Like all successes, female psychical bisexuality is certainly a fantasy. It supposes the inscription of the female subject in the phallic-signifying order, with the procession of symbolic pleasures and gratifications (Oedipus[1]) that this strange and illusory order provides; it also supposes the displacement of castration, depression, and sexual diminishment in a revalorization of the maternal, and consequently feminine, role, which goes through a reconciliation with primary homosexuality; finally it implies the investment of the real presence of the child-phallus, trial of glory and castration, which is finally less illusory, although "always already" somewhat extraneous. In this veritable vortex of adherence and nonadherence to the phallus (to the signifier, to desire), female bisexuality is nothing more or less than an experience of meaning *and* its gestation, language *and* its erosion, being *and* its reserve.

These are the true stakes of the aesthetic experience, this contemporary and lucid variant of the sacred. I am hoping you will meditate on the reason why, in searching for lost time, it is the bisexuality of the Gomorrahan libertine that Proust made the focus of the narrator's fantasy. Might female bisexuality be the object par excellence of literature and art? This is what many writers seem to suggest to us, caught in the vortex of meaning's position and deposition.[17]

But Albertine dies falling from a horse, unless she committed suicide. And beyond the uncomfortable feminine position that many of us are familiar with, the psychical bisexuality of the woman remains a promised land that we must attain, particularly in psychoanalysis, by curving the pleasure that our professional, clinical, theoretical, and clearly phallic accomplishments give us toward the barely expressible and highly sensitive territory of our silent mothers. Transphallic, and in this sense not less phallic but more-than-phallic, this bisexual jouissance would then be, strictly speaking, mysterious, in the etymological sense that I have already pointed out. Is pain the ultimate mystery? If there is a resolution of female masochism, it perhaps involves the resolution of what I have called Oedipus[2]: assumption of the phallic and its traverse in the real presence of the child and reconciliation with the unrepresentable antephallic of the preoedipal maternal and prelanguage. The immense psychical work that such a trajectory requires, though never entirely complete, can be measured in the strange, disillusioned, and yet lively and reliable air of certain women.

To Suffer the Androgynous Fantasy or Explore Illusion?

With bisexuality understood as the resolution of female masochism, I am convinced we are touching on the psychical spring of atheism, were the speaking being able accede to it without militant antireligious counterinvestment. For I see in the psychical bisexuality of the woman not a cult of the phallus or something beyond it, much less beneath it, but a maintenance and an estrangement of illusion as illusion.

The future of an illusion? Necessarily! Freud the rationalist was right: everyone wants an illusion and insists on not knowing that it is one. Structurally, however, a woman is better placed than anyone to explore illusion. I am not sure "atheism" means anything more than taking the other and exploring it. The few guiding lights left to us by eighteenth-century French women may one day lead us in this direction—toward women and atheism— though the current international climate suggests this may be highly perilous.

A discussion of that question must wait. For now, I will conclude by pointing up the incommensurable psychical effort required in acceding to this psychically bisexual being that is woman, a being, one might even say, that never adheres to the illusion of being, any more than to the being of this illusion itself. And I admit that what I have said may only be illusion as well.

6

Aragon, Defiance, and Deception: A Precursor?

The name Louis Aragon is linked to two movements that shook the century: surrealism and Stalinism. I will discuss Stalinism in passing, but Aragon's so-called surrealist period will draw the most of my attention.

You may think you know everything about surrealism: provocation, scandal, rejection of bourgeois conformism, automatic writing, adulated and repressed women, tender passions between men, painting devoted to dreams and shopkeepers: we're all familiar with the leaders, "popes," gurus, schisms, excommunications, epigoni, international dissemination, political-esoteric-sexometaphysical contamination, and so on. The legend has been made; it is impressive, and it sells. And yet, what if there were something left unsaid in the surrealist revolt? What if it were still possible to take it literally, as a revolt in the sense I gave this word at the beginning of this book? Let us try to move humbly forward along this path, though it has been closely watched.

To simplify things, consider this: for a century, perhaps a bit more, an event profoundly marked the European literary experience: *literature's encounter with the impossible*. Beginning with German romanticism, marked by the Schlegel brothers, Schelling, Hegel, Schopenhauer, and Nietzsche and up to Hölderlin's dramatic lucidity, clearly documented by the review *Athenäum* (Berlin, 1798), literature's encounter with the impossible took its most radical form in the French language. Literature renounced its role as purveyor of beautiful language and seductive beauty, religion's little sister. By exploring the resources of the *word*—what to say? how to say it? what does "say" mean? to make and unmake sense?—it first entered a radical debate, or face-to-face confrontation, with religion and philosophy (similarity and then dissociation). It explored the impasses of consciousness and associated itself with madness. Finally, it came up against the resistance of social reality in order not to disavow it but to reflect it no longer and, more, to disavow the imaginary, and thus literature, in favor of social reality (we know the drama of the poet who becomes a businessman as well as the poet who "engages").

In France, literature's encounter with the impossible has three periods: the first is that of Rimbaud, Lautréamont, and Mallarmé; the second is surrealism; the third, *Tel Quel*.[1]

Here are Rimbaud's verses from *A Season in Hell*, "Second Delirium: The Alchemy of the Word" (1870): "Never any hopes; / No *orietur*. / Science and patience, / The suffering is sure."[2] And this is from "Farewell" (1873), also in *A Season in Hell*:

> I who called myself magus or angel, exempt from all morality, I am thrown
> back to the earth, with a duty to find, and rough reality to embrace! Peasant!
>   Was I wrong? Could charity be the sister of death for me?
> At least I will ask forgiveness for having fed on lies. Let us go now.
> But not a friendly hand! Where can I find help?
> Yes, at least the new hour is very harsh. . . .
> We must be absolutely modern. . . .
> I saw the hell of women down there . . .   (p. 209)

And finally, in *Illuminations*, "Morning of Drunkenness" (1871): "Elegance, science, violence! . . . We assert you, method! . . . Behold the age of Murderers" (p. 233). Method, you understand, is violently rebellious.

We must be absolutely modern, in this age of Murderers, for I saw the hell of women down there: a possible montage of Rimbaud's texts. We could assemble others. This one resonates with my reading of the surrealists: the blunt observation of an antinomy between society and poetry, and particularly between a certain spirituality (which the family and Paul Claudel would find in him, or rather impose on him, in the most appropriate forms)[3] and the assertion of an elegant and cruel "method," which is nothing other than a way of thinking beyond judgment, with one's body and tongue. We know that this experience of rupture eventually led Rimbaud to abandon poetic writing; in Abyssinia, the traveler finds an activity as exotic and apparently insignificant, and we are free to believe he gave up the search for a "rough reality" to embrace or, on the contrary, that he pursued it silently. However, before the poetic statement confronts that impossible — the renunciation of the imaginary formulation — another impossible magnificently unfolds in *Illuminations*: the sounding out of the border state where thought is sustained by sensation. Unlike the "good sense" that some believe sums up the sensory, the "derangement of all the senses" (p. 307) — the sign of thinking humanity — moves toward the clarity of a dazzling, dense, unusual language, certainly worthy of being called "illumination." It is the *fold* where a "mind" (or, a subject who has touched his own contours in sense and sensation) escapes in an exteriority that one may call a "voyage," a "path" or a "being." But Rimbaud is too wary of "lies" to content himself with these soothing clichés designating what appears to him, strictly speaking, to be "madness." Listen to him; surrealism would not exist without these verses, an extract of *Illuminations* entitled "Lives":

I am a far more deserving inventor than all those who went before me; a musician, in fact, who found something resembling the key of love. [The conjunction between music and the key of love will also be found in the surrealist project.] At present, a noble from a meager countryside with a dark sky,
I try to feel emotion over the memory of a mendicant childhood, over my
apprenticeship when I arrived wearing wooden shoes, polemics, five or six
widowings, and a few wild escapades when my strong head kept me from ris-
ing to the same pitch as my comrades. I don't miss what I once possessed of
divine happiness: the calm of this despondent countryside gives a new vigor
to my terrible scepticism. But since this scepticism can no longer be put into
effect, and since I am now given over to a new worry—I expect to become
very wicked fool.   (p. 229)

We are at the limit of silence here, but Rimbaud does not cease to compose
with it. Consider these words from "Morning of Drunkenness," also in *Illuminations*: "And now that I am so worthy of this torture, let me fervently gather
in the superhuman promise made to my created body and soul. This promise,
this madness!" The possibility of changing style in a new illumination, if it exists, is linked to madness. "Elegance, science, violence! They promised me
they would bury in the darkness the tree of good and evil, and deport tyranni-
cal codes of honesty so that I may bring forward my very pure love. It all began
with feelings of disgust . . . it ended in a riot of perfumes." The crisis of the relationship to the other, the crisis of the self, its finitude, its purity, explode in a
pulverization of sensation. How does one translate pulverized sensation in language? "Brief night of intoxication, holy night! even if it was only for the mask
you bequeathed to us." The experience is summoned, at once conjured and
cast aside but assumed. Yet the holy intoxication is a mask.

We assert you, method! I am not forgetting that yesterday you glorified each
of our ages. I believe in that poison. I can give all of my existence each day.
Behold the age of Murderers   (p. 233).

Exhortation, exaltation, madness, elegance, science, and violence give access
to the new style.
   The last extract of *Illuminations* I would like to cite is entitled "War." Extreme suffering is close to toppling into warlike refusal, yet music is still invoked as a possible language of love within natural language:

Child, certain skies have sharpened my eyesight. Their characters cast shad-
ows on my face. The Phenomena grew excited.—And now, the everlasting
inflection of moments and the infinity of mathematics hunt me throughout

the world where I experience civic popularity and am respected by strange children and overpowering affections. I dream of a War, of justice or power, of unsuspected logic.

It is as simple as a musical phrase.   (p. 221)

The paradox of this simplicity is clear: the "musical phrase" is the only possible "war."

And from Lautréamont, at about the same time: "It is time to curb my inspiration, and to pause a while along the way, as when one looks at a woman's vagina"; "I shall write down my thoughts in order, to a plan without confusion."[4] Might the logic of the sensitive body and musicality open another scene at the very heart of the judgment that banalizes us in our social lives, another humanity ("poetic," if you like) that would in fact be another logic?

Lautréamont is the explorer of this path, another precursor of the surrealists. You may be familiar with my reflections on Lautréamont in *Revolution in Poetic Language*, and I admit that I am pleased to come across this old acquaintance again. *Les Chants de Maldoror* and *Poésies*, from which I will cite other passages, date from around the same period as Rimbaud's texts. They express the same necessity to escape decorative poetry, to battle romanticism, Parnassus, symbolism, empty rhetoric, the blissful embellishment of pleasure or pain and to compare the literary experience with philosophy and science. In Lautréamont's *Poésies*, this will lead to somewhat formulaic writing: formulas, in effect, that aspire to a scientific and positivist rigor influenced by Auguste Comte—though in a blasphemous and ironic sense—and that reference classical philosophy, insofar as the poet skews the maxims of La Rochefoucauld, Pascal, and Vauvenargues to give a more radical, more diabolical, more rebellious sense to the classical utterance.

The confrontation with the other occurs on two levels: a rewriting of classicism and rationalism in order to unfold the fabric of the thought and experience of the other sex as such. It is not only violence, the intolerable, disgust, but also fascination and, with that, the mobilization of language to acknowledge these states of ambivalent passion.

Here are some extracts from *Poésies*:

"Great thoughts spring from reason! . . . Abandon all despair, ye who enter here. . . . Each time I read Shakespeare it seems to me that I cut to shreds the brain of a jaguar" (II, p. 234). Lautréamont invites us to enter the conflict, to locate the irreconcilable, to manifest the logic of violence and ferocity that is the underside of beautiful language, the literary beauty attached to the name of Shakespeare; this is a violent act: to cut thought, the supreme power, to shreds, to penetrate this tyranny of the intellect whose force Kant indicated and Lautréamont presents in the redoubtable and derisory image of "the brain of a jaguar."

And consider this passage, part of which I have already quoted: "I shall write down my thoughts in order, to a plan without confusion. If they are correct, the first will be the consequence of the others. It is the true order. It characterizes my object by calligraphic disorder."[5] Some thought therefore, while it does not in any way disavow reason, rebels against ossified rationalism and classical "poeticity," on which the poet nevertheless relies because it rises up against the chiaroscuro, the "artistic blur." "I should disgrace my subject too much were I not to treat it with order. I want to show that it is capable of this" (pp. 234–35).

This demand for radical *thought* goes hand in hand with the penetration of the mystery of the norm: the taboo of sexuality and the embellishment of the sexual act. Lautréamont joins his logical revolt to a descent, through the feminine and the vagina, into the derisory hell of the species, our animality:

> It is time to curb my inspiration and to pause a while along the way, as when one looks at a woman's vagina. It is good to inspect the course already run, and then, limbs rested, to dart forward with an impetuous bound. To complete a stage of the journey in a single breath is not easy, and the wings become very weary during a high flight without hope and without remorse. No . . . let us lead the haggard mattock-and-trench mob no deeper through the explosible mines of this impious canto! The crocodile will change not a word of the vomit that gushed from his cranium. It can't be helped if some furtive shadow, roused by the laudable aim of avenging the humanity I have unjustly attacked, surreptitiously opens the door of my room and, brushing against the wall like a gull's wing, plunges a dagger into the ribs of the wrecker, the plunderer of celestial flotsam! Clay may just as well dissolve its atoms in this manner as in another. (pp. 105–6)

I propose that fans of Courbet and *Les Origines du monde* consider this "impious trench" that Lautréamont has traced.[6]

I am citing Rimbaud and Lautréamont in order to point out two elements of literature's encounter with the impossible, which *Tel Quel* took up: on the one hand, literature faced with a classical, and ultimately classicist, philosophical plan; on the other, the comparison of literary utterance and poetic statement with the feminine aspects of both man and woman, which in fact goes back to a transsubjective real, increasingly impossible to define. We would seek it in a way that seemed oneiric to some but was perhaps the root of things: through the prism of the Chinese ideogram and its battle between gesture and sign, reality and sense.

Literature's second encounter with the impossible was that of surrealism. By taking up the message of these two authors, it knew antilyrical rage and the concern for objective discourse—which would exasperate the bourgeois—as well as the journey toward the impossible that I mentioned earlier, with its two variants: the feminine and the real. This voyage however would be mired in the cult of the providential Woman ("the future of man is woman" was one of the most religious impasses of this mistake) and in the adherence to a providential institution: the Communist Party, for Aragon.

What interests me in the experience of *Tel Quel* is the third—still invisible—variant of this encounter between literature and the impossible, a variant that is still invisible for almost the entire media-saturated planet. Why? Perhaps because it was too radical. And because it was not taken up by any institution (religious, partisan, secular, communist, academic, etc.), given that these are precisely the takeovers that make an experience visible, that make visible defiant experiences that otherwise continue to work on the fringes. Why was it radical? Because it assumed the legacy of the predecessors: the exhaustion of beautiful language, the desire to irradiate "universal journalistic style" (Mallarmé), storytelling, literature as distraction. But, in addition, it compared this experience more specifically with the history of philosophy, religion, and psychoanalysis. Hegel, Husserl, Heidegger, and Freud—as well as Saint Augustine, Saint Bernard, Saint Thomas, Duns Scot, and others—became favored references in the same way as Joyce, Proust, Mallarmé, Artaud, and Céline. *Tel Quel* was perceived as a laboratory of reading and interpretation. Academics! some cried. Terrorists! others accused, recoiling. The aim of the comparisons with these philosophers, theologians, and writers was to see how far literature could go as a journey to the end of the night, the end of the night as limit of the absolute, limit of meaning, limit of (conscious/unconscious) being, limit of seduction and delirium. And all without the romantic hope of once again establishing a community extolling the cult of ancient Greece, for example, or the cult of cathedrals, or of "singing tomorrows" and instead confronting today's men and women with their solitude and disillusions, perhaps never before suffered to such an extent in human history.

The paradox—hence the accusation of terrorism—was that this confrontation with the impossible was not cloaked in complacent despair but took the form of irony and vitality. Because it was beyond the impossible, the imaginary was rehabilitated and asserted, whereas before it had been put aside, rejected, particularly by certain currents of surrealism and existentialism. A book such as Philippe Sollers's *Femmes* (Gallimard, 1983) is proof of this assertion of the imaginary beyond the analysis of its imposture, offering the condensation of ironic lucidity and philosophical concern, as well as the paradise of poetry and the affirmation of an imaginary romantic vein. There may have been a crisis of love, values, meaning, men, women, history, but I am not going to Abyssinia, I do not belong to the Communist Party, and if I venture to China or into structuralism, I come back. I pursue the journey to the end of the night. This might be called thought-as-writing. It isn't much, but without it, there is perhaps nothing. This is the path of the samurais.

Breton: Revolt Against Art

I return now to several key points in the surrealist adventure, which I will discuss in light of what I have just said about literature as thought of the impossible or, perhaps, literature as a-thought. Remember what I said about the thought-sexuality copresence, the phallic *kairos* during the oedipal phase. This complex dynamic is laid bare, its heterogeneity and its difficulties brought to the fore, when writing dissolves the apparent coherence of reasoning and deploys the dynamic of thought, a-thought, to show that thought-as-writing exhibits repressed logic, in contrast with the calm of metaphysical thought.

French literature has been too accustomed to beautiful language and too afraid of reason for anyone to advance with impunity the notion that writing can be an act of thought; bookstores are full of examples to the contrary. The surrealist revolt seems radical to me precisely insofar as it tried to specify the unbearable aspects of the variant of thought that the human being carries out by writing. When Aragon continually asserts what he calls the "will of the novel," it is important not to forget the profession of faith in *Paris Peasant* (1924–1926): "My concern is with metaphysics."[7] The "will of the novel" is a continuation—and, as we will see, a mutation—of metaphysics when metaphysics starts to listen to poetry and the senses. By paying too much attention to the new world prophesied as a social world by the surrealists—and this was in fact an aspect of the project—we underestimate the philosophical subversion represented by writing opposed to both action and art. Yet the modernity of this project is incontestable and striking. At this fin de siècle even more than in the surrealist era, we know that the rationality of action does not exhaust the potentialities of being.

The surrealist revolt would first be unleashed on "a world where action is no kin to dreams," as Baudelaire put it.[8] Given that all society, bourgeois society above all, is a society of doers—from noble workers to less noble shareholders— the *Homo faber* has difficulty not thinking of thought as thought-action. Yet the entire history of philosophy shows, if in vain, that philosophy—the love of thought—demands solitude, inaction, contemplation, until the metaphor of not-acting that is death is identified metaphorically with the experience of thinking ("to philosophize is to learn to die"). It was not wise metaphysical contemplation, as opposed to the pragmatic activism of the worker always already on the road to robotization, that André Breton invoked when he repudiated a world where action was asserted against the dream.[9] He was simultaneously opposed to contemplative thought and to pragmatic reason in order to explore the other scene that Freud (a participant, in the eyes of these poets, but personally reticent, given his doctrine, and unresponsive to the insistent and naive calls of the Parisians) had been exploring since the end of the preceding century. There was thought at the limits of the thinkable: a practice of language liberated from the harness of the judging consciousness gave access to it and evidence of it. Perhaps another world (of thought) would change the (real) world.

To this impugnment of the world that bustled about instead of writing, Breton added another. In November 1922, in a lecture to art students in Barcelona, he said: "These days there are several individuals prowling over the world for whom art, for example, has ceased to be an end in itself."[10] Read: the incompatibility between the search for a form of writing that would embody the logic of the dream and the world in which we live led to a rejection of the very possibility of art. It was a violent rejection not only of outmoded or conformist art but of all art. In effect, what the surrealists demanded was no longer art but a revolution of thought. Breton made reference to Rimbaud whose work "revolutionized poetry" (p. 109), adding that one had to manifest "an awareness of that terrifying duality that is the marvelous wound on which he put his finger" (p. 110). Baudelaire was the first to explore the fertile sorrow of this terrifying duality that had already rendered poetry and social action incompatible. In 1919 Tristan Tzara asserted: "Art is putting itself to sleep to bring about the birth of a new world."[11] Another world was coming to lay waste to outdated art. The dadaist movement execrated the fossilized forms of bourgeois civilization. The revolution of poets had no relationship with the ancient figures of poetry, the incoherence of the world was its objective, as well as man's unacceptable condition. However, a shift was occurring between the observation of the difficulty of pursuing the poetic experience—seeking the logic of the impossible, the logic of the dream, the logic of contradiction, the logic of the limits of the thinkable—and the utopia of a realization in the world of this extravagant logic liberated from the constraints of action and judgment. A progressive utopia was built against this vertiginous exploration of a-thought, a utopia that drew from Marxism and prophetic Hegelianism well before the actual apocalypse of an "end of History." The illuminated poet forgot his Rimbaud and set out to produce this antinomy in the world of action that could only be a counterbalance to it or the thorn in its side.

The great hypothesis, which would also be a trap, could then be formulated in these terms: when one is faced with stylistic difficulty, the difficulty of poetic illumination, when one is confronted with silence, one may believe that it is possible to escape it by investing real action. With the breakdown of the imaginary, one stops making poetry and opts for revolution; form will not be changed but society. Of course, to most contemporaries, this second option would not only appear logical but eminently preferable, in spite of the inevitable ideological missteps of politicized writers. Why confine oneself to art and old style, knowing its obstacles? Why confine oneself to a dissident art, by definition elitist and isolationist? Why labor away in the imaginary when one could opt for action, for "engagement," as Sartre would say?

In the meantime, however, before some repudiated the literary experience as amoral futility, the surrealist revolt reclaimed a new thought that overturned the essence of thought. The refusal of insignificant poetry, decorative poetry, the refusal of the "pohème" was confirmed in the writing of the surrealists: "Beware . . . rhyme, syntax, grotesque meaning,"[12] wrote Breton and Eluard who, along with Apollinaire, wanted to tamper with "the essence of the Word."[13] They refused the decorative poem, poetic lace, in order to invent the poem event, from the perspective of the scientific or experimental ambition of their precursors. In subsequent years, this would develop in the form of the happening, which involved the audience, participants, readers, like so many subjects, bodies, atoms of meaning, in play in a given place. "Lyricism is the development of a protest against the sentiment of reality," Breton says in *Notes sur la poésie*.[14] We should be realistic and take what surrounds us into account, but only to wring the neck of a reality that has become banal! Surrealism would not relinquish the razor's edge between poetry and reality.

The Marvelous and Women

"To transubstantiate each thing into a miracle" was the objective of the new poetry.[15] Aragon proposed this in *Treatise on Style*, in accord with both Rimbaud's *Illuminations*, which sought to traverse everyday life and attain the miraculous, itself amalgamated to Catholicism, and with Proust's desire for the written word to become flesh through "transubstantiation," the novel becoming a physical experience.[16] Initially, of course, the issue was to attain a type of illumination or magic through the cult of writing: writing as favored, if not exclusive, access to a-thought. Then, when this cult of writing was in distress or in danger, a double pitfall lay in wait for the new poets—as we see with Aragon—the temptation either to abandon one's work, burn it, or to pursue a political path (some, as we know, having perilously attempted both).

I should underscore that it was the social and political lure (which has since become mediatized) that constituted the tragic dimension of this encounter of poetry with the impossible, and that manifested it much more radically than the depressive symptoms or even the suicides. I will come back to this specifically in my discussion of Aragon and his *Défense de l'infini*,[17] which adjoins the burning of his manuscript and Stalinian engagement. Do not forget this tragic dimension — it extends to the spectacular posturing in which some take pleasure today — when we flush out this or that cynicism or manipulation by the media. This tragic dimension is on the same scale as the cult of writing as radical source of a-thought: "I thus belonged from the earliest age to this zoological species of writers for whom thought is formed in writing," Aragon asserted in the second 1964 preface to *The Libertine* (1924),[18] recognizing that there were no other solutions to thought or living but writing, that only writing could legitimately rise up against watered-down opinion and art, that writing alone was a revolt in favor of the miraculous and the seizure of thought without utilitarian compromise.

Note the ambiguity of the project and its outrageous ambition: to create magic with logic! In this rebellion against calculating and pragmatic reason, against prefabricated arguments and well-worn signs, surrealism — and Aragon along with it — started a veritable cult of mysterious signs, signs that eluded judgments, that concealed an enchanted reality. This search would lead the surrealist group in two opposite directions, with some turning toward occultism — as was the case of Breton — and others toward an explicitly more sexualized, erotic direction (at least initially); these last would seek enchantment in scandalous libido, whether that of female prostitution or, subsequently, male homosexuality, insofar as these were nonconformist. In any case, from the start, these two quests for the marvelous — for the occult or the erotic — stimulated a new style, achieved by destabilizing values and their protagonists, finding signs in them that eluded commentary.

A paroxysmal sexuality was called on to support the language of enchantment so that it revolted against that French language — obviously imaginary — perceived as rational, flat, resistant to enchantment. The French language was "a cashier's language . . . , precise and inhuman," Aragon complained in *Treatise on Style*,[19] before proposing the creation of another with the help of automatic writing, dream narratives, collages, and fragments. Happily, some escaped the Frenchness of precise cashiers, among them Rimbaud, "illuminated" and an "assassin." La Fontaine, on the other hand, was considered "very French" and utilitarian, although another reading would show he was neither inhuman nor a cashier; still, this was Aragon's position when he wrote his treatise. And if you look at his insurrection against pragmatic rationality, which was accompanied by a rejection of an already-there, prepackaged poetics, a harness to the imaginary, it becomes clear that he mobilized eroticism to provoke the unusual and to breathe new life into the imaginary. Indeed, this would be the ambition of *La Défense de l'infini* (1923–1927).

I want to point out other themes in Aragon and the surrealists, part of the debate internal to all European culture of the first half of the twentieth century, in the face of the crisis of pragmatic rationality. Among them is the theme of the *ephemeral*, which was at the very core of the romantic encounter: a delight with no tomorrow that devalorized the bourgeois relationship, marriage, and familial conformism; and *humor*, particularly through the inconstancy of the *visible*: the visible was facetious in its various facets. In this domain, the surrealists were the precursors of the confrontation we are currently experiencing between the rhetoric of the word and the rhetoric of the image that television, for example, imposes on us. In *Paris Peasant*, Aragon emphasizes the pregnancy—which is also an inconstancy—of the image and points out the competition of word and image: "Each image . . . forces you to revise the entire Universe," he writes.[20] Each image forces you to redeploy the word in order to allow yourself to translate the world in a lighter, more playful way.

Thus we arrive at the cascading definition of images of verbal style for which the writer is only an "occasion": "I call style the accent adopted by the flow of the symbolic ocean, reflected by a given man, that universally mines the earth with metaphors."[21] Style opens language in such a way that each individual, any given man, is the representative of the symbolic ocean, of the infiniteness of language, to which we are led if we truly acknowledge the confrontation with the ephemeral, humor, and the image; for the poet, these phenomena are only pretexts for "perpetual revolution" (p. 37), conveyed in turn through metaphors. And the accent, the music, what I call the "semiotic," must be emphasized: the singular experience that insufflates an irreducible sensibility into the communal use of language (the universal "flow" that mines the "earth").

As you see, the surrealist Aragon rehabilitated metaphor, whose transubstantiational profusion we see in Proust. But Proust was a shameful reference for the surrealists, the novel having been rejected as an insufficiently miraculous genre. It was poetry and its impact as event, violence, and act that were prized by the surrealist group over the novel. Aragon's reaction, however, was to vindicate the novel against poetry, not solely in order to return to utilitarian reason, though he did that as well, but also and above all to drown in the symbolic ocean (*Blanche ou l'oubli* [1967] will suffice to convince you of this).[22]

The Libertine reveals a complex vision of the poetic art that I think it is important to underscore before tackling the other texts. Besides the poet's implication in the infiniteness of language, Aragon's experience involved a parallel engagement in the plenitude of the world and real history, defined in the second preface of 1964 as the lifelong attempt "to wed this full thought, which is my own, to the outside world."[23] In the conjunction of the infiniteness of the symbolic ocean, the solicitation of the outside world in its instability or banality, and the promises of change offered by technology and revolutionary movements, the external event that attracted dadaist as well as surrealist poets, and in particular Aragon, was *scandal*. The surrealists always sought out unbearable, provocative, or erotic events to repel the bourgeois. We see this obsession with scandal starting in the nineteenth century with dandyism and then, for example, in Mallarmé's fascination with anarchy, but these were relatively tame, socialized forms of scandal. At the dawn of surrealism, scandal (provocative, childish, but not devoid of risk) was a favorite and violently adopted term, and although in 1922 Breton distanced himself from the dadaist taste for scandal for scandal's sake, Aragon wrote, in 1924 in the first preface to *The Libertine*, "I've never looked for anything but scandal."[24] Scandal was now to be seen as the association of a lifestyle with the insolent themes of a kind of writing whose very logic was raving mad. The choice of characters in surrealist poetic and prose texts was itself dictated by the notion of the scandalous event. Characters were frequently criminals or prostitutes; the criminal woman appeared as a particularly auspicious conjunction of the flow of the "internal ocean" and the instability of the external world.

The rejection of watered-down poetics, of decor, of literary and artistic fetishism went hand in hand with the two themes of the marvelous and the feminine. I have already situated the marvelous in the wake of Rimbaud's *Illuminations*, the interior externalized in the explosion of being, the sacred desacralization of the religious experience ("no *orietur*"). The surrealists and Aragon in particular set this illumination—defiance, façade, audacity?—in the modern landscape of the city. With the young Aragon, ecstasy was urban. The city was seen as the modern, urban marvelous. In *Paris Peasant*, for example, we read about walks through the city, written with a vertiginous search for the magical and the unexpected, which Aragon called "the metaphysics of place" or "circumstantial magic," the desire to discover strange meaning in every recess. Urban reality was apprehended through the prism of the imaginary; it was sustained by a paradoxical, oneiric imaginary, "surrealist" in the fullest sense. Unexpected circumstances, irrational visions and encounters, formed the geography of the surrealist fascination. Hence another recurrent theme in surrealist texts: that of the passageway, the garden, the unexpected place considered not only in terms of its architectural reality but also, above all, in terms of its signifying presentation, the language that expressed it, the "fiction"—in Mallarmé's sense of the term[25]—in which they were likely to be cloaked.

The outside world was not forgotten, but the trick was to shift the accent of this circumstantial reality to signifying reality, to discourse: the sometimes absurd game one allows oneself to play with language to embellish this logic of the marvelous. The peasant must return to dull reality in order to give it new meaning, hence an epiphany of the city and of the feminine, whose circumstance is its core.[26] Here the essential was circumstance; possibility was provided not by reality but by the fluidity of language that referred to this reality. An apparently delirious logic could be deployed in the imaginary starting with a language made of references: "the vertigo of the modern," "the legend of modernity" "an essentially modern tragic symbol."[27] The writer was attracted by the exterior—landscapes, cities, women, bordellos, scandalous situations— and at the same time, still, by the "symbolic ocean": by the signifying possibilities of language that would lead him beyond the dream and the marvelous, not to dementia but to a way to revitalize life. Breton defined the encounter with the miraculous as a chance accorded to beings of goodwill: this notion of chance would be greatly accentuated by the surrealists. It involved above all seizing its rhetorical value. Mallarmé figures among the precursors of this chance, the real chance of the rhetorical find, as in "the flower . . . absent from all bouquets," or when he writes, "A verse must not be composed of words, but of intentions; all words must yield to sensation,"[28] before Proust dreamed of the transubstantiation of Madeleine into madeleine, and vice versa, in the shadow of cathedrals.

Writing transmuted into chance/jouissance that also, at the outset, sustains it: this would be the argument of a text entitled *La Défense de l'infini* that Aragon destroyed. Only a few fragments are left, among which, most significantly, *Irene's Cunt.*[29] The notions of chance and the infiniteness of meaning and writing were constructed through a trivial and yet scandalous reality, the erotic experience, which is clearly not as extraordinary as all that (either for the narrator or, to be perfectly frank, for most of us, despite what people say and what credulous libertines still claim) but to which verbal revelation accords the marvelous, imparts the miraculous. It was with the feminine, the translation of the feminine, as I said, that the poetic revolt against the old style and the encounter with the impossible would take on all their meaning.

Let us consider the surrealist feminine before encountering it again—on the verge of suicide and the Communist Party—in *Irene's Cunt.* October 4, 1926, is often underscored as a determining date in the history of the surrealist movement. On that day, André Breton met a young woman called Nadja on the rue Lafayette in Paris.[30] A conjunction of the ephemeral, scandal, and the feminine, this encounter was in effect essential: the slight reality of this woman would be incorporated into the fiction of the feminine that the poet would develop. It was this somnambulant character of the so-called real woman that would allow the poet to deploy his own infinite "symbolic ocean." It was neither a specific woman nor women as social individuals who were in question here but what I referred to in the last chapter as the *feminine*, a part of every subject's psychical life, represented with difficulty for both sexes. It so happens that in order to speak of the feminine—and moreover in order to write it—one is obliged go through the visible, through the plastic, sometimes even through feminine reality (some venture that far!) and thus to take into account feminine bodies such as one encounters them. Here, feminism cries encroachment, for real women—we are told with staunch reason—are taken over in order to create a myth of the universal feminine that is revealed to be above all the feminine of the man. Indeed. But beyond the scandalous sociological aspects of this undertaking, it seems to me that something important is revealed: what are the conditions for the alchemy of the verb or, as I called it earlier, a-thought, to occur? How does the imaginary come to be? How does one create fiction, whether one is a man or a woman? By relying on a certain exploration of bisexuality, in this case by creating a fiction of the feminine starting with a particular erotic experience, whose secrets *Irene's Cunt* reveals.

The graphic anomaly—a-thought—that I propose requires that one not forget the negative charge that this writing deploys against what we call "thought" and that we too often compare to knowledge and action. Neither knowledge nor action but with them and through them, a-thought deploys the polyvalence of metaphors, the semantic resources of sounds, and even the pulse of sensations in the flesh of language; a constellation of meanings then unfolds the secrets of the speaking being and links him to the indeterminable pulsations of the world. The reduction of thought to knowledge makes us forget this dimension of the experience that I called *significance* and that a-thought discovers with provocation but that perhaps constitutes the veritable dynamic of thought. The a-thought pulse, the a-thought unveiling of meaning: recall the folds and veils of *Christ, Modesty*, and *Purity*.

As a modern echo of the baroque sculptor, the writing of a-thought covers and denudes the substance of language in order to allow one to imagine not a personal symptom but beyond that: the germination of meaning in sensorial desire as well as the threat of their mutual eclipse. The sentences in *Irène* from *La Défense de l'infini*, for example, veil and unveil the flesh of the self and the other in a-thought, the flesh of the overturned world, hidden yet namable. Ultimately we are persuaded that there is no flesh more arousing than that of writing, just as the folds of the veil emerge as more mysterious and truer than the faces they are supposed to hide or reveal. You will note however that with the a-thought of writing in *Irène*, it is not Modesty or Purity that is seized but the violence of desire and the marvelous of erotic annihilation. This is because for two centuries, thanks to Freud and men's freedom, a-thought has pursued its path in language: it seems to have recognized in genitality the condition that makes the desacralization of meaning, its investigation and its renewal, possible. *Irène*, or genitality as source and trial of a-thought? On the other side of the phallic cult, a-thought scandalizes our phallic aptitude for knowledge, which I spoke of in chapter 4. If it desacralizes knowledge-as-thought, if it desacralizes the phallus, a-thought involves the risk of identity collapse. On the other hand, if it sacralizes feminine jouissance, it runs the risk of erecting a new religion: the prospect of occultism and political utopias. The true scandal of the surrealists, cast in the face of culture, was to remain between the two, in the crucible of a-thought.

Let us return to *Nadja* and to the cult of the feminine that the surrealist movement developed: the exaltation of the goddess-woman, the fairy, and a series of highly valorized characters (often bitterly denigrated in the surrealists' personal lives) accompanies the development of this rhetoric of the paradoxical, the marvelous, the oneiric, the incompatible that will remain characteristic of surrealist poetics. The phenomenon is also found in other literary currents, in France as well as abroad, with the aspiration to the spiritual sustained by the identification with the feminine and its repression. Still, Breton's exaltation of Nadja—which has the advantage of acknowledging esotericism's debt to the devouring passion for a feminine of slight reality—has been compared to the far more institutional ecstasy of Claudel during the illuminated moment of his conversion to Catholicism behind a pillar of the Notre Dame forty years earlier.

We will first look at this strange cult of the feminine in Breton. It begins by highlighting the mechanical aspect of the human body in general, and the feminine body in particular, emphasizing the body as a desiring machine. All Paris was talking about a mediocre play entitled *Les Détraquées* [Roughly, "Unhinged Women."—Trans.] at the Théâtre des Deux-Masques. In the style of Grand-Guignol, this play was inspired by a foul crime committed in a boarding school for girls; the murder was finally attributed to a woman, a close friend of the headmistress. This was a universe of women: a headmistress, her friend the criminal, Solange, a nymphomaniac and sadist but a great beauty, who, as incarnated by the actress Blanche Derval, fascinated Breton; he painted the actress's portrait in *Nadja*. The female character of Nadja is thus a mixture of several sources forming the diabolical, mechanical, and sadistic vision of a feminine at once powerful and dethroned.

In 1921 Breton went to Vienna to meet Freud, attracted by what he took to be an interest, identical to his own, in the hidden: the hidden meaning of words and behaviors, scandal, and sexuality, holder of all secrets. The encounter was doomed, given that Freud ferociously refused these poetic transactions, which appeared suspect to him. In my eyes, however, this failed encounter had the advantage of dissociating the surrealist erotic from the psychoanalytical investigation to which many are eager to assimilate it and situated it, on the contrary, in the obsession with the feminine that has haunted the decomposition of Catholicism and its esoteric aspects since the nineteenth century. One can link the surrealist cult of the powerful and fallen woman to the decadents of the late nineteenth century (Huysmans, Péladan, etc.) who were fond of the image of the bloodthirsty woman (Salomé, in particular) in blasphemous counterpoint to Christ.

"Love shall be. We shall reduce art to its simplest expression, which is love," Breton wrote in *Soluble Fish*.[31] The place of the other, in this case the woman, was maintained but the meaning of love moved toward something entirely different from an "illumination" (although the "violence" and "assassination" of which Rimbaud spoke was not lacking). The vague treatment of the feminine led straight to moral discourse; as Jean Decottignies observes, love became the topic of such a discourse. Breton not only targeted conventional morality here but asserted his intention to research the logical impulses subjacent to love, in other words, to locate, under the cover of a "moral" intention, the essential movements of thought, the logical imperatives that govern an individual in an amorous encounter.[32] This logic of unbearable love would burn more than one, however, and its path would henceforth be closed by the genteel worship of "mad love" that came to take on all the appearances of national civility.

For the representation of this "unhinged" femininity, Breton referred to Gustave Moreau, and not only to the figure of Salomé but also to Helen, Dalia, and other chimeras, constructing the image of an intractable and entrancing femininity that reemerges in Aragon's *Irene's Cunt*. Another highly curious text inspired the surrealists in the search for this representable impossible or this impossible representability that is the feminine: "L'étonnant couple Moutonnet," by Villiers de L'Isle-Adam.[33] In this story, Villiers depicted the extreme violence of the famous Moutonnet couple, in which the man imagines making love with a headless woman. It was this double aspect — paroxysmal violence against a woman and the preservation of an erotic excitation with this decapitated feminine, "cause [of] real amorous felicity" — that would interest the surrealists: the abysmal connotation of the feminine as the opposite of the representable, the visible, the phallic that psychoanalysis illuminates and that remains a locus of fascination. This, in any case, is an encounter that French writing alone explored and that German idealism, with its daring within the confines of reasoning reason, never elucidated: one cannot advance in the exploration of the encounter between speaking man and a-thought if one does not explore this version of the feminine—the acephalous, wounded, decapitated feminine—because it reveals an eroticized castration, the threatening antithesis of the phallus.

In Breton's *Soluble Fish*, Solange is a medium described as fabulous and simultaneously devalorized: she is clairvoyant yet seedy, "discreet as crime," her hand "clutching a revolver."[34] In Aragon's *Paris Peasant*, the woman is also a theatrical and grandiloquent phantom, presented as the conjunction between the infinite and the eternal: "There rises up an adorable phantom . . . a woman larger than life,"[35] a "boundless woman" (p. 171) who offers "that divine taste that I know so well in every vertigo" (p. 199). The feminine is at once the image of the divine and a profanation of the traditional sacred, glorified yet presented as extremely ambiguous.

Thus courtesans and prostitutes populate *Paris Peasant*, *Anicet ou le Panorama*,[36] and *Irene's Cunt* while maintaining the mystery, the pleasure of the infinite, and the vertigo of the senses and permitting the writer to avoid what he rejects: generalization, idealization, the positivized archetype. The type of the prostitute, necessarily generalizing, and the myth of the courtesan, equally so, take a precise, singular form that brings the archetype down to earth while also degrading it: "Fearsome, charming whores, let others take to generalizing in their arms."[37] The writer, on the contrary, wants to go into detail— great, necessarily sordid, detail—in keeping with "an outlaw principle" (p. 51). *Paris Peasant* tells us that women are "kleptomaniacs of passion" (p. 52). This fantasmatic and monstrous feminine opens the world of instability, transaction, and transgression: "Neither the human face nor the deepest sighs can rediscover the mirror or echo for which they are searching" (p. 110). Inhabited by an acephalous, archaic, and untamable violence, women have chosen "the vagrancy of uncertainty" (p. 52) and a new version of love based on "an outlaw principle, an irrepressible sense of delinquency, contempt for prohibitions and a taste for havoc" (p. 51). They are no one, nothing, if not Rimbaud's "derangement of all the senses": "Woman . . . is contained in fire, in the forceful and the feeble . . . in the flood tide's flux and flow, in the fall and flight of foliage, in the false front of the sun where like a voyager lacking guide or horse I lead my fatigue astray into a far-flung fairyland" (pp. 171–72). The conclusion of *Paris Peasant*, "persons have had their day upon earth" (p. 205), echoes the heroine of "The French Woman" (1923): "After all, loving is not a question of people."[38] This woman's notes, short letters found near her suicided lover, prefigure what *Irene* reveals: it is the woman who formulates the excess of jouissance, the writer placing himself explicitly in the very place of this feminine speech. The theft of identity through jouissance, and particularly the jouissance of women, already a theft in itself, is what the writer seeks to make tangible, to "presentify," first through a character and then through style itself, making this paradoxical feminine jouissance his. The poetics of *Blanche ou l'oubli* is already under way, for in the end, the woman, the "kleptomaniac of passion," is the writer himself, the one who creates writing, and not one of his criminal and vile goddesses.

Would the true "kleptomaniac of passion" be style? I conclude with this surrealist image: "Error with fingers of radium, my melodious mistress, my appealing shadow."[39] This is Aragon's signature in *Paris Peasant*. Like love or the woman who holds you, the absolute is radioactive error: an appealing shadow from which the alter ego of the one tracing style must separate.

A Defense of *Irène*

I have just presented a few of surrealism's antecedents and some problems concerning reality, the fantastic, the feminine, the occult, the rational: all problems that solicited the era's imaginary, and particularly, Aragon's imaginary. I stayed within a general framework, without going into the details of Aragon's life, while pointing out the cross-links between his literary experience and the surrealist imaginary. Now I will deal with a few aspects of Aragon's biography as well as the text *La Défense de l'infini* or rather the fragment that remains of it, *Irene's Cunt*.

The "True Lie"

"At every instant, I betray myself, I refute myself, I contradict myself. I am not someone I trust," the writer proclaims in "Révélations sensationnelles."[40] This will serve as an epigraph to what I have to say about Aragon, whose controversial persona you are certainly familiar with. It expresses the protean, polyphonic aspect of both the personage and the work, which he himself called "le mentir-vrai" (the true lie): the ambition to tell the truth through a thousand disguises, masks, theatricality.[41] There is more than one split in Aragon, who wrote sixty books in sixty years, almost as many as Hugo. He is a true *feu d'artifice*, the artifice no doubt imagined as a reflection of Baudelaire's dandyism, "this simultaneous double postulation" signaling our own distorted, diminished, and mystified identities before the masquerade of society and the media.[42]

Indeed, Aragon's personality, life, and work give the impression—call it subjective, or ontological; in any case, it seems unshakable—of never being univocal, of scattering in pastiche, simulacrum, and approximation, so many

roundabout ways of expressing truth. This is the truth of an impossible identity, not a being in the world or a nonbeing but a continuous variation, both
passionate and disappointed, bipolar, if you want technical terms, that the
writer-seducer sums up prettily by speaking of words that "make love with the
world."[43] This need for immersion/dissolution, taking possession/impotence,
power/passiveness, virilization/feminization—you can change the terms of
this plasticity as you like—no doubt responds to the incoherence or the impossibility of personal coherence manifested in the exaltation of the amorous
act. This exaltation will take two forms: one, scandalous—*Irene's Cunt*—the
other, institutional—conjugal love and adherence to the French Communist
Party.

A few biographical elements will allow you to situate this writer who is
somewhat forgotten today.[44] They may repel some and compel others, but
they seem to offer, even today (perhaps more so today) a style and/or symptom
(this is Lacan's accolade) that is still valid. He was born October 3, 1897, and
died December 24, 1982. We know about his mother, Marguerite Toucas, a single parent, and her sisters, Marie and Madeleine. In his autobiographical rec-
ollections—which are vague and cautious—Aragon often refers to the maternal configuration formed by his grandmother and her three daughters.
Marguerite belonged to a bourgeois family of aristocratic descent through her
paternal grandmother, who came from a family of Lombard petty nobles, the
Biglione. Marguerite's maternal grandmother was a "demoiselle Massillon," a
descendant of the famous prelate of Hyères. Marguerite used the names of
both lines, Toucas-Massillon: seek there, if you like, the possible indication of
a split that will reach its peak in the writer. Her maternal grandfather, François
Toucas, had become a subprefect in Algeria and had abandoned the family
when Marguerite was sixteen years old, in 1899, the year of the World Fair. He
was an adventurer, a dashing figure who resurfaced in Constantinople at the
end of the century as Monsieur de Biglione, reclaiming the noble maternal genealogy. All these details are not extraneous to the imaginary construction of
a fascinating feminine saga or to the impact of filiation and maternal characters found in *Irene's Cunt*.

Here then, in the real life of Louis the child, was a tribe of women, illustri-
ous ancestors, an absent globe-trotting grandfather, and only one man, Uncle
Edmond, the brother of the three sisters, who was rarely present. I would underline that, although not unusual, single motherhood was nevertheless note-
worthy at the time, especially in a bourgeois family. Not only did Marguerite
conceal her pregnancy, she pretended not to have the child: the infant disappeared for thirteen months in Brittany, in the care of a wet nurse. He was not
supposed to have been born in the Toucas family (or Toucas-Massillon, to

complicate the genealogy), so when he returned to his mother, he was passed off as her young brother, and the grandmother was presented as the mother. The "true lie," the term Aragon would use to refer to the imaginary adventure, was already inscribed in his personal history. Caught in this system of social deception and half-truths, his novels and biographies would also be peppered with oddities, imaginary confessions, inaccuracies, discrepancies, and variations. In 1965 the writer would say, for example, that he was "given as a child to deceased friends" and adopted by a couple of dead friends.[45]

As you may have guessed, the father of the future writer seems to have been totally absent, unknown. Apparently he presented himself as the child's godfather and became his tutor: Louis Andrieu, his initials identical to those of Louis Aragon, a geographical name vaguely homophonic to Andrieu. In *Feu de joie*, his first collection of poems, written in 1919, Aragon recounts his life through an imaginary character called Jean-Baptiste A., who bears the first name of a distant maternal uncle, Jean-Baptiste Massillon, and whose last name is indicated only by the initial "A," which would become his own.[46]

Various accounts report violent scenes between the godfather and Aragon's mother in Neuilly. Andrieu was anticlerical and a friend of Clemenceau. In one of his novels, Aragon alludes to a Louis Andrieu, a deputy of the Third Republic engaged in battle during the separation of church and state, who drives nuns from their convents, a character at once conventional and rebellious from the viewpoint of an established bourgeois.[47]

Aragon's mother's clandestine pregnancy and maternity make her an afflicted woman, though her valiant character, which her son admired, should not be overlooked. She made a living painting fans and plates, as Aragon recounted in the first volume of *Oeuvres croisées* ("Et comme de toute mort renaît la vie" [And how from all death life is reborn]).[48] She also managed a boardinghouse on avenue Carnot, which appears in *Les Voyageurs de l'impériale* as "Etoile-famille"; she would sell it in 1904 to move to 12, rue Saint-Pierre in Neuilly.[49]

This was Aragon's childhood, at once sheltered and dramatic, subject to the "true lie" from the start. A poem called "Le mot" published during World War II, after his mother's death, in a collection of texts on the Resistance, evokes for the one and only time, to my knowledge, a lyrical and shattering image of this mother, immediately associated with the uncertain birth of speech ("the word") on the verge of "the lie":

> The word did not pass my lips
> The word did not touch her heart
> Is it a milk from which death weans us
> Is it a drug an alcohol

I said it only in my dreams
This heavy secret weighs between us
You swore me to concealment
    At your knees

. . . .

To call you my sister disarms me

. . . .

If I feigned it was for you alone
To the end played innocent
For you alone until the shroud
    Hid my blood

I will go to the end of my errors
Born, my error was living.[50]

Note the lyrical, tragic, and emotional elements as well as the restraint and discretion.

From Anicet to Nancy Cunard

World War I brought mobilization and disaster. In 1917–1918, Aragon was a medical auxiliary. He met André Breton at Val-de-Grâce, formed friendships with future members of the surrealist group, founded the dadaist group to which he remained faithful for fourteen years and the review *Littérature* with André Breton and Philippe Soupault. "To step on the throat of your own song," as Mayakovsky wrote in 1930, was also the project of surrealism and dada from their inception. It was a project with social and moral connotations but above all a poetic and rhetorical project, inscribed in and against the poetic tradition. The idea was to assassinate prettiness, the beatific lyricism of earlier poetry, to wring the neck of the propensity toward embellishment, toward incantation, all for far more than rhetorical ambition, for the program aimed at nothing less than "a new declaration of human rights."[51] Radical nihilism or a panorama of the novel, already?

In March 1919 Aragon signed a secret pact with Breton, the nihilistic rage of which you may appreciate:

The one who renounces, ruin him, discredit him, by any means necessary. There is only one morality at this level of "incapability": that of bandits. A law that does not tolerate the slightest weakness, which is the *refusal of the written law*. . . . We will shatter the others. Until the day it is necessary for us to go even further, one or the other will abandon one or the other in turn. . . . *To know that the other will run you down. To know. Therein lies the condition for action.*[52]

Beyond the psychological "clairvoyance" regarding the fate of this friendship, the violence of this pact raises a question: when the "refusal of the written law" is so implacable, what is left to support a-thought if not the mirage of senses that will be incarnated by feminine jouissance and the tyranny of historical reason revealed by the people's revolution? I will return to this soon.

If Aragon's first published collection—*Feu de joie* (1919)—is an attempt to reconstruct the self through the imaginary character of Jean-Baptiste A., the following writings are texts of rage, which will culminate in *La Défense de l'in-fini*, where we find *Irene*. Before looking at this largely destroyed text, however, one should consult what precedes it. In 1921, in *Anicet ou le Panorama*, there is an ironic chronicle of an apprenticeship of revolt in a group of conspirators to which the artist is opposed. At once in league and in conflict with them, the narrator measures the contradictions and traps of this confrontation.

Note that Aragon's first novel, written in 1918 immediately following the young medical auxiliary's war experience and often praised by critics for its "virtuosity" and "jauntiness," is a truly stunning agenda—a panorama?—of the writer's entire trajectory, as Philippe Forest's study shows.[53] By settling his scores with Rimbaud (Arthur is the central character until he gives way to An-icet) and by borrowing from Voltaire (*Candide* seems a favored intertext), Aragon continually double-deals and gives the slip to the very people who give him inspiration. Baptiste Ajamais (André Breton) "subjugates" Anicet with his "authoritarian being"; although grateful to be "under his influence," the young victim "divines fascination." Nevertheless Anicet, a prototype of the Camus antihero, will be condemned for a crime he did not commit, which has been hatched by Ajamais. This failure of artistic strategies (Breton's as well as Rimbaud's) does not prevent the novelist from deploying the vertiginous skill of a puppet master and iconoclast that is far from simple virtuosity. For the gravity of the disappearance of the self already emerges in this text, resonating with Vaché's suicide, and attributes to *writing alone* (and not to the pathos-ridden act) the mission of revealing the being-for-death of the one who speaks. "Don't you see that I am wresting words from myself, like teeth, so as to lose any intelligence, any subtlety, any reason, any judgment, and to reduce myself to being only a will?"[54] says Anicet, a puppet, no doubt, but a radical one. Ex-istence is useless, Anicet's and even more Baptiste's, who has conquered beauty only to be swallowed up by a banal existence. Mirabelle herself, the very emblem of fascinating Beauty, is reduced to sordidness. But talking about failure is different from failing: this is double-dealing. The 1924 preface to *The Libertine* makes it clear:

> I realize that . . . you force me to a conclusion, and that now at least I should shut up, even if some people shrink from this conclusion as if it were death, while others easily find it morally satisfying, like the enjoyment of well-wrought verses. No sacrifice, no drama: no flowers, no wreaths. What is important is to think for one moment that you'll stop writing. . . . I don't propose to do anything . . . I am simply loath to imitate the action of dogs who cover over their excrement with sand.[55]

Not a romantic tomb, therefore, but the insolent project of furthering freedom through scandal: "I've never looked for anything but scandal, and I sought it for its own sake" (p. 18).

To stop writing or not: the dilemma is posited at the outset, continually, until *La Défense de l'infini*, where the encounter with the feminine imposes an unbearable demand; the renouncement of life and work then become actuality, attempted suicide as well as auto-da-fé. If Aragon has a resurgence, thanks to the party and Elsa, is this only a sinister compromise, or a cynical masquerade, or more of the double-dealing ushered in by *Anicet* as a means to evade nihilism, the quashing of the self and writing? Those who hold Aragon's compromise in contempt may not have sufficiently considered surrealism's confrontation with the impossible values that the writer brought to the bottleneck where history was strangling. "Which will strangle the other / hand in hand / Let's pull the victim's name from a hat / Aggression a slipknot / The one who spoke departs this life / The murderer gets up and says / Suicide / End of the world," Aragon writes in *Feu de joie*.[56]

In 1922 Aragon published another novel, *The Adventures of Telemachus*, a rewriting of Fénelon's *Telemachus*.[57] Here, there is a doubling of the dadaist negation of the interior in the name of imprescriptible sentiments. Fénelon's *Telemachus* deals with education, feeling, nothing less than the defense of a young man's psychical life as he is coming of age. Aragon's text is a sort of dialogue between the dadaist project and this classic *Telemachus*, where paradoxical emotions exist rather than the coded feelings of classical psychology. "If you know what love is, make allowances for whatever follows," Aragon tells the reader, warning him that his *Telemachus* reinvents love, true love.[58]

In 1924 *The Libertine* is also presented as a debate with another text, a sort of mask, a critical imitation, highly mimetic and subtly detached. Aragon finds his way through a series of dedications; he dedicates fragments to different authors and places himself in rhetorical competition with them; he mimics them, distinguishes himself from them.

Then in 1924–26 comes *Paris Peasant*, in which Aragon explores the marvelous of the city, the night, and the feminine, a masterpiece of the surrealist assertion that provoked an enormous scandal and that Drieu La Rochelle defended. Later, the two writers would have a falling out for political and social reasons, but at the time, Drieu revealed himself to be an advocate of this prose and its lofty elegance, which he referred to as the Sturm und Drang of the twentieth century.

In 1925 the Moroccan war shook the young generation of the period, including, of course, the writers. Some, such as Naville, asserted that it was imperative to break with the literary experience and engage in the world, particularly in the Communist Party. The review *Clarté* documented the debates between Communists and writers.[59] Surrealism asked: do we aim for revolution/revolt on the level of ideas, language, and style, or start an actual revolution? Breton emphasized the possible transformation through art, the necessity to pursue the inner experience. Aragon, on the other hand, stigmatized literary activity as "vanity," and although he published Artaud's *The Nerve Meter* in 1927 with Doucet's money,[60] he sought a solution to the contradiction between social efficacy and redeemable literary activity in politics.

In sum, Aragon suffered a crisis of confidence in the imaginary. The simultaneity of the adherence to the Communist Party and the writing of *La Défense de l'infini* suggests that the political choice might have served as an unconscious counterbalance to the risks of the imaginary. In 1927 Aragon joined the party and went through a tumultuous period in his romantic life. It was as if political adherence brought balance to the ravaging disorder of his affective and passionate experiences. This was the period of his intense relationship with Nancy Cunard, which took place in an elegant, cosmopolitan circle in Paris and in various European countries (England, Holland, Germany, Spain, and Italy). Then came the split. The writer went through a period of depression,[61] destroyed the manuscript of his novel *La Défense de l'infini* in Venice in September 1928, and attempted suicide in the fall of 1927 (biographers hesitate over the chronological order of the suicide attempt and the auto-da-fé).

Nancy Cunard, born in 1896, was the granddaughter of the founder of the Cunard Line, the shipping company, and the daughter of Lady Emerald, a friend of the queen of England and often mistaken for her at receptions. She belonged to a wealthy and worldly set and in 1920 moved to Paris, where she associated with such great literary and artistic figures as Ezra Pound, Oskar Kokoschka (who painted her portrait in 1924), and Tristan Tzara, with whom she wrote a play entitled *Le Mouchoir de nuages*, performed at the Boeuf sur le toit. In 1916 she wrote a collection of poetry in English, *Outlaws*, and later produced two subsequent collections, though she was never recognized as a poet.

In 1926 Cocteau wrote to Picabia: "Breton preaches, Aragon lives at the Boeuf sur le toit with Nancy Cunard." Aragon himself, however, situated the beginning of his relationship with the young woman in 1927.[62] Aragon saw in her a beautiful, extravagant, and insolent foreigner, who inspired passion and had several passions of her own, one of which was African sculpture. During his wife Elsa's lifetime, Aragon only spoke of Nancy Cunard allusively; however, he spoke of the affair at length in *Le Roman inachevé*.[63]

Burdened by his financial dependence on the wealthy heiress as well as by social humiliation and jealousy, the liaison between Nancy Cunard and Aragon constantly threatened to fall apart. Captivated as he was by the American girl's worldly milieu, Aragon probably was not the anarchist described in the insolent *Paris Peasant* around her. Nancy was violent, alcoholic, unburdened by moral constraint, and tomboyish, characteristics that gave Aragon occasion to develop a rhetoric of the antiphrase in order to talk about love. Consider two poems on the subject. The first is called "Très tard que jamais":

Sexual things
An odd way to talk about
Sexual things
I was ready for everything
But definitely not that.[64]

The second, "Maladroit," reads:

Firstly I love you
Secondly I love you
Thirdly I love you
I love you enormously
I do what I can to say it
With the desirable elegance
I never had the slightest idea
How to incite desire
When I would have wanted to incite it
A naive exhibitionism in matters of sentiment
A character mentally and physically
God all of this is hardly amusing
As an attraction it's zero.[65]

You know enough about literature not to reduce *Irene* to a prototype. Nevertheless, if I tell you that the *text* is an experience, the biographical experience is imperative, not as a cliché but as something to be investigated. In this perspective, let us look at other encounters with women that Aragon had at the same time. At Giverny, there was Clotilde Vail, a young American girl (another one!) whose brother, Lawrence, had just married Peggy Guggenheim. Aragon would dedicate the play "In a Tight Spot" in *The Libertine* to Vail. Now, Giverny is near Vernon, where the narrator situates *Irene*. There is a mysterious lady from Buttes-Chaumont, and another who appears as Blanche in *Le Cahier noir* (and again in *Blanche ou l'oubli*, in 1967).[66] "It is to ourselves that the novel is the key,"[67] Aragon writes, but "ourselves" is protean in the sadomasochistic experience of the amorous link that *Irene* reveals.

In this context dominated by the conflictual relationship with Nancy Cunard, the writer attempts suicide and destroys the great novel he apparently spent a great deal of time writing (it was thousands of pages long). A collection that Gallimard published in 1986 reprinted the pages Aragon himself saved from destruction, which he entitled *Irene's Cunt*. These pages were saved from the fire to be sold to a collector and alleviate the writer's financial difficulties, he explained, as though to excuse himself. (The first edition dates from 1928;[68] it was republished in 1948, 1953, and 1962, anonymously, and under the pseudonym Albert Routisie in the 1968 Régine Deforges edition.)

If we compare the tone of *Irene's Cunt* with that of the novels already mentioned—rebellious, a bit mocking, scandalous, provocative—we might conclude, like Pierre Daix, whose opinion I share, that not only does this novel surpass *Paris Peasant*, it is also the first novel the author wrote without constraint, without an agenda, spontaneously. And it gives the reader the ineluctable and rare sense of a masterpiece. Two things motivate it. The first is explicitly rhetorical and literary: it presents itself as a rejection of bourgeois ennui and the nausea provoked by the fact that "all this will end up in a story . . . for stupid cunts," as the narrator bluntly describes them.[69] Nevertheless, this anger is still expressed in a novelistic style: the writer maintains the necessity of the novelistic imagination as a way to explore reality and truth, counter to the pronouncements of the surrealists, who felt that poetry, and poetry alone, could meet this objective. While there is narration, however, it is subordinate to the act of writing at its most singular, solitary, and oneiric, as well as to the ascendancy of words that, like a simulacrum of automatic writing, generates the characters and the fragmentary structure of a narrative made of collages.

> It was a novel one entered through as many doors as there were different characters. I didn't know anything about the history of each of the characters, each was determined starting with one of these constellations of words

I was talking about, its peculiarities, improbability, by which I mean the improbable character of its development. . . . This whole crowd of characters was to find themselves, through the logic or rather the illogic of each one's destiny, in a sort of enormous mess [Aragon says "immense bordel," literally, an immense bordello.—Trans.] where there would be criticism or confusion, which is to say the undoing of all morals in a sort of immense orgy.[70]

This is how Aragon described his project for the destroyed, unfinished novel *La Défense de l'infini*. Thus revolt against conventional morality leads to an exaltation of the orgiastic and heralds a paradoxical novelistic rhetoric: the plurality of narrative paths, confusion, and entanglements as in *Blanche ou l'oubli* (these elements recur in the postwar novels). The poetic project is in this sense surrealistic: it is the logic of signifiers that programs the characters; there is no psychological or realistic necessity preceding the a-thought of writing. Nevertheless, the novelistic project remains, even if it must end in an *"immense bordel"* (also to be understood in its first, sexual meaning). "I never learned how to write," Aragon points out, to underscore the paradoxical nature of his project.

The second motivation concerns the appropriation of the feminine as a revolt against the degeneration of man (or, if you prefer, Man).

"Writing Is My Method of Thinking"

The history of this text, once again, is like a rebellious burst of the imaginary in a complex process that, at the same time, led Aragon to the gesture of revolt that was adherence to the French Communist Party (before the defensive, deluded, and delusional aspects of this adherence become apparent). And, though he never gave up writing novels, he lessened—when he didn't suspend—the beautiful destructive rage at work in *La Défense de l'infini*. The *infini* in question is the narrative of an excessive jouissance that will be transferred from the woman in the story to the writing of the narrator.

A young man who is bored in a provincial town (a dadaist, surrealist theme but also the basis of countless coming-of-age novels) "curses, bites, and sees red" when he is unbearably awoken, before going off to a brothel to drown his boredom in an orgiastic scene. What follows is an eroticism at once exalted and failed: the young man will remain frustrated by the erotic experience, perhaps because of his own impotence. What saves him is a story in the rudimentary sense of a family history and beyond this, the adventure of language as the only possible salvation. This story is that of Irene, a country girl who lives with her mother and a powerless grandfather. In counterpoint to the virile female image of Victoire, the lesbian mother-boss who governs her world of country peasants, the male image of Victoire's father, Irene's grandfather, is a devalued one.

Let me emphasize this modern tragic form that tends to present the man as the opposite of a hero. Maladies contracted through less than glorious sexual experiences have brought the old man to his invalid state. The active man (remember Breton's attack against the world of action), the thinking-working-acting man, the man with "his little virile reason" (Mallarmé) can no longer be the hero. Exit the Hero. In the sorrowful place of this exit, the bitter taste of disappointment remains: castration, impotence, early signs of depression. The One is annulled; hysterical excitability is left. Who can say anything about this evil spell? A person? A poem? No, a polymorphous narrative, the vertigo assigned to the place of one girl who comes without knowing it. As the impotent Hero exits, a collage of narration devoted to female jouissance follows, the equivalent in words of the shattered mirror reflecting Irene's magnificent spasms and groans.

"Rimbaud and Lautréamont, on the one hand, Zola, on the other, *Irene's Cunt* is in fact an observation of the failure of eroticism," Philippe Sollers writes, referring to this position as "female identification" and offering this blunt description: "What he likes is being the voyeur, watching a woman with her lovers. Being the dog who submits to a woman, or else this woman herself—that's his dream."[71] Aragon, like Breton and other surrealists, glorified the feminine as a new divinity—I have pointed this out often enough—but Aragon inflected this perspective in a particular direction. Irene is an ambiguous character, the narrator's double, a libertine, an idealized echo of the prostitute; in addition, however, she exercises a power over others—and over the narrator—thanks to words: an infinite power, a power against the finiteness of love. This love, exalted in the beginning, is later devalorized in favor of the infiniteness of Irene's words. Does she create the words herself, or does she inspire them in the narrator? This remains ambiguous; the writer and the muse are almost assimilated; he is a woman and she is him. A split projects the libertine into the role of female creator and assigns the writer to the feminine role, thereby acknowledging the creator's bisexual nature. In counterpoint to the narrator whom eroticism disappoints, Irene remains in a place where she observes the failure of love not through repression but excess. Writing becomes imperative when love (that of God, the troubadours, the romantics, a love unifying values and egos) is powerless. The young man at the brothel whom we follow at the beginning of the novel—as in *Paris Peasant*—devotes himself in the second part to this more intimate *bordel* that is the stylistic experience: the depths of language on fire, the narrative in flames. Only Joyce in

Ulysses, through a polyphony that rivals la *Somme théologique*, attempted such an orphic appropriation of the jouissance of Eurydice/Molly, transfusing her incantations into the peerless artist's unprecedented style.

The devalorization of the erotic experience is rather specifically Aragonian; the "ignoble fiasco" of which the narrator speaks no doubt translates his own amorous or erotic impossibilities, indeed, the profound motivations for his attempted suicide. But he exhibits it with complacency through the character of the invalid man or when he writes: "What bloody sadness there is in all erotic achievements!"[72] Like the character of the man, the narrator may no longer be able to make love, but he can write the novel through which the ennui of erotic scenes is transformed into the pleasure of writing. It is no longer a matter of a "novel/story" just good enough for "stupid cunts"; by shattering the story, it becomes what the author has elsewhere called "rather scientific writing": an X ray of the pulverized identity, laid bare and laid to rest in Irene's jouissance. This is the form that the confrontation of literature and the impossible takes in Aragon: in the biographical difficulty of the unbearable lived experience, he burns his novel, in the literal and figurative sense, keeping only a few pages.

"What I am thinking naturally expresses itself. Everyone's language differs from each to each. I for example do not think without writing, which is to say that writing is my method of thinking" (p. 36), Aragon explains. Doesn't this evoke the Lautréamont of *Poésies*? For Aragon, too, there is no thinking prior to the act of writing: "The rest of the time, not writing, I have only a reflection of thought, a sort of grimace of myself, like a memory of what is. Others rely on diverse procedures. Thus I greatly envy the eroticists, whose eroticism is their expression" (p. 36).

The disenchantment of eroticism is rather rare in French literature, which, having placed eighteenth-century libertinage at the zenith of the experience of freedom, continually vies to glorify sexual exploit. This Aragonian admission of weakness, impotence, disgust does not mesh with the style of sexual liberation, the exaltation of the erotic act extolled by other writers during the same period and that continued to pervade anarchist literature and art until recently (we have only just started to question the basis of this freedom, since the mass media has made hard sex a conventional norm). Jouissance in *Irene's* narrator is transposed to another level. Faced with the sadness of eroticism, he valorizes the magic of the word, "the prodigious metaphorical value that I attribute to words alone" (p. 36). And again: "That words impose on me, I mean. I probably do not appreciate this particular and immense poetry. I understand that. Hence the terrible *finiteness* of my sensations, and worse, of my life" (pp. 36–37).

> Eroticism . . . has often led me into a field of bitter reflections. I'm consid-
> ered an arrogant man. Let that pass. During the time I'm referring to, I'd let
> my mind wander at some length, in the solitude of my room, faced with a
> distressing flowered wallpaper, over things erotic and their importance in
> my eyes. The erotic idea is the worst mirror. What one glimpses of oneself
> in it makes one shudder. Any old pervert, how I'd like to be just any old per-
> vert. This wish spoke volumes about my underlying idea of all truth. I don't
> much like thinking about a person's sex life, yet I must acknowledge that
> mine is over.   (p. 37)

Don't be too quick to accept this rejection of all sexuality as a rule. It is the
"I" that speaks and no doubt it speaks for the narrator at a given moment in his
trajectory. "The terrible *finiteness* of my sensations" will be contradicted by
Irene's sensorial whirlwind of jouissance, and it is precisely this nonfiniteness
of the feminine senses, Irene's infiniteness, that the writer wishes to translate
in the entirely verbal *Défense de l'infini*. Consequently, the attack on sexuality
aims beyond the brothels and other manifestations (highly prized before) to reveal the crisis state of "my life." Aren't we very close to depression here? The
comparison of the erotic state and the state of writing reveals a melancholic
gap and announces another jouissance: that of metaphor, a transport, an ecstasy, that passes through the contemplation in solitude of a sorrow, a nothingness, bitterly recognized.

From then on, we find Aragon again, who has not abandoned surrealist
wordplay but works it into the structure of the novel: "Fish fish it is I, I am calling you: pretty hands agile in the water. Fish you resemble mythology" (p. 58).
The illogicalities that follow can be understood as allusions to the mythological value of the fish, to Christ and the Gospels as well as to the penal and mas-
turbatory symbolism of these aquatic creatures.

> Your loves are perfect and your ardours inexplicable. You do not approach
> your females and here you are with enthusiasm for the mere idea of the seed
> that follows you like a thread, for the idea of the mysterious deposit made in
> the shadow of the shining waters by another mute, anonymous exaltation.
> Fish you do not exchange love-letters, you find your desires in your own el-
> egance. Supple masturbators of both sexes, fish I bow to the dizziness of your
> senses. . . . [Note the irony in relation to the solitude, the coldness, and the
> masturbation as well as the nutritive and sacred image of fish.] Your trans-
> parent transports, Christ's death ah how I envy them. Dear divinities of the
> depths, I stretch and thrash about if I think for a moment of the moment in
> your wits in which develops the beauteous marine plant of sensual delight

whose branches spread throughout your subtle beings, while the water vibrates around your solitudes and makes a song of ripples heard toward the
shores.   (p. 58)

The play of paralogism, metaphor, opposition, and connotation recalls Breton's *Soluble Fish*. While, in his *Fish*, Breton declares his desire to reduce art
"to its simplest expression, which is love," Aragon's text, which is certainly in
the surrealist style, enters a violent polemic with *Mad Love*, André Breton
style. In this passage, a concentrate of autoeroticism appears as a transition between the depressive moment and the subject's "taking things in hand"—certainly the case here—through and in a rhetorical jubilation, mingling the
anger against norms and the pleasure of free moments.

I would like to return to the character of Irene's mother, significantly
named Victoire [Victory], who assumes the role of the criminal. "A strange
family in which two generations of males have been subjugated by their wives.
Irene's father died soon after his marriage. It was said locally that Victoire had
got rid of him, not liking to support a man she'd be obliged to treat as an equal.
Victoire's father is still there in his invalid chair after forty years of contemplating the women's triumph and their rude health" (pp. 75–76). This impotent old man, this castrated man, is the quintessential antihero: remember
the decapitated woman of the "Moutonnet Couple" who fascinated the surrealists; here it is the man who is figuratively decapitated and the powerful
magic of women, at the antipodes of classical tragedy, that casts a spell on the
narrator. The a-thought of writing produces a new configuration of the tragic,
expressing female jouissance alongside male impotence. Though varied, feminine powers exert an absolute domination. Thus: "What does rather distinguish Irene from Victoire, and has, furthermore, considerably estranged the
latter from her daughter, is that Irene has never had that taste for women
which possessed her mother very strongly and still does, so much so that since
she's run the farm not one maidservant has stayed on there without being or
turning lesbian. This peculiarity has partly contributed to Victoire's success.
She has gained the affections of a flock of women" (p. 76). While the mother
is a sapphist, the daughter

> thinks quite frankly that love is no different from its object, that there's noth-
> ing to look for elsewhere. She says so, if need be, in direct and very dis-
> agreeable fashion. She knows how to be crude and personal. *She's no more
> scared of words than men*, and from time to time relishes using both. She's
> by no means verbally reticent during lovemaking. Words spill from her ef-
> fortlessly then, in all their violence. Ah, what a filthy bitch she can be. She

excites herself, and her lover along with her, with a vile and scorching vo-
cabulary. She wallows in words as in a lather of sweat. She lashes out, she
raves. No matter, Irene's love is really something.   (p. 81; emphasis mine)

Jouissance Can Say Itself, Entirely

Here lies the sense of the chiasma between the all-powerful erotic woman ex-
ercising her sexuality and what the writer would like to steal from her: the same
violence, the same sexual force, but shifted to words. It is not a matter of creating poetry in the decorous sense of the word but of creating an obscene poetry, an enraged literature, of which the aroused and foul-mouthed Irene is not
only the product but, above all, the metaphor. The unbearable image of literature that results is neither to be sanctified nor sold; it is a literature of scandal.
The a-thought that seeks to formulate the power of desire and excitation comes
up against the fantasy of the phallic mother, which is also one of a woman
"without a love object," self-satisfied and aloof. To steal this indifference from
her is another jouissance, equally irascible, "Irene-like." The poet learns this
in an androgynous osmosis in the body of Irene, who comes and transfers her
pleasure into words proffered in the sexual act: decentered, overturned, obscene, poetic words. The articulation of scandalous eroticism and scandalized
literature is clear in the passage I have just quoted. The abjection and horror
of amorous states and imaginary states are present and assimilated. And female
jouissance can henceforth be described in one of the most beautiful passages
in French literature on the subject. Consider this description full of physiological detail, sensation, emotion, and desire:

> So small and so large! It is here that you are at ease, man finally worthy of
> your name, it is here that you are back on the scale of your desires. Don't be
> afraid of moving your face closer to this place—and already your tongue, the
> chatterer, is restless—this place of delight and darkness, this patio of ardour,
> in its pearly limits, the fine image of pessimism. O cleft, moist and soft cleft,
> dear dizzying abyss. . . . Touch that voluptuous smile, trace the ravishing gap
> with your finger. There: let your two motionless palms, your love-smitten
> mitts with that prominent curve, join up towards the hardest, best point
> which raises the holy ogive to its peak, o my church. Don't budge, stay, and
> now with two caressing thumbs take advantage of this tired child's goodwill,
> press with your caressing thumbs gently, more gently, part the beautiful lips
> with your two caressing thumbs, your two thumbs. And now, all hail to thee,
> pink palace, pale casket, alcove a little disordered by the grave joy of love,
> vulva appearing for a moment in its fullness. Under the designer-label satin

of the dawn, the colour of summer when one closes one's eyes. . . . The mirage is sitting stark naked in the pure wind. Beautiful mirage built like a pile-
driver. Beautiful mirage of man entering the cunt. Beautiful mirage of a
spring and heavy melting fruit. Here are the travellers crazy to rub their lips.
Irene is like an arch above the sea. I have not drunk for a hundred days, and
sighs quench my thirst. Oof, oof. Irene is calling her lover. . . . Oof, oof. Irene
is about to die and contorts herself. He's stiff-pricked as a god above the
abyss. She thrusts, he eludes her, she thrusts and strains. Oof. The oasis leans
down with its tall palms. Travellers your burnouses rotate in the abrasive
sand. Irene is panting fit to burst. He contemplates her. The cunt is steamed
up awaiting the prick. On the illusory chott, the shadow of a gazelle. . . .
Hell, let your damned toss off, Irene has come.   (pp. 65–66)

The violence of the surrealist rhetoric here echoes the libertine literature of
the eighteenth century and attains one of the summits of French prose. Defy-
ing norms and pragmatic thought, literature confronts the sensorial experience at its most excessive, the example of which is taken in feminine jouissance. For the risk of this revolt must certainly be measured against Reason as
Norm: it confronts the unnamable, psychosis, aphasia; this is the reverse of the
absolute that Irene incarnates at the borders of the human.

Before reaching this limit of annihilation and death, a few pages in *Irene*
formulate this challenge to bourgeois conformism as a revolt against narrative
rhetoric: the writer would like words—their dynamic, their metaphorical/
metonymical play, the mythological evocations in which they are connoted,
their alliterations—to be one with what he perceives as female pleasure. The
difficulty or impossibility of this transposition can only lead him to pursue the
literary experience or burn everything. Note the "collage" composition of this
fragment saved from the fire. There is no stylistic continuity: the narrative passage alternates with a poetic writing, "automatic writing" (the passage on the
fish); the enraged narrative yields before the folkloric and ironic vein of the
tableau of the farm where Victoire, Irene, and the old, impotent father are outlined, pathetic, against a background of misery, before a style of polemical treatise—a sort of sociology of the novel compared to journalism—temporarily
closes this scathing attack. This patchwork does not seem to be merely the result of a text under construction, saved from disaster and then polished and ho-
mogenized. The stylistic fragmentation reflects the hurricane unleashed on
the one who is writing,[73] this rage that seizes a ductile body whose feverish and
disillusioned eroticism traverses the fiasco and transmutes its rage first into
feminine jouissance and then into writing, which will become its confirma-
tion, its accomplishment and apogee. There is no focus, no center that fixes:

the gaze, the pen, the style change place and mode, accommodation is sought but not made, all the images are destabilized, sparkling stylistic jouissance is doubled by the woman coming. I do not know of any text—not even Joyce's more ironic and refined text on Molly—that flows with as much complicity, precision, and admirative tenderness into the feminine marvelous. Aragon invents it as though within his own flesh and creates it in his own unappropriated language.

"Arranging everything into a story is a bourgeois mania." "There are people who tell other people's life-stories. Or their own. From which end do they start? . . . Unknown melancholy . . . , an immense physical despair. . . . The same issue of *Paris-Soir*. I give way to discouragement when I consider the multiplicity of facts."[74] One thinks of Mallarmé criticizing literature as "universal journalistic style."[75] In sum, against the rationalism of the lived experience, the a-thought of *La Défense de l'infini* is placed in a situation of scandal, sets fire to the manuscript, and keeps only part for publication. To put it plainly, the imaginary is in a state of collapse faced with the immensity of the project that the translation of feminine jouissance, not the "multiplicity of facts," represents: fantasmatic, certainly, but maintained as the incarnate variant of the divine.

The senselessness of the revolt consists in the absolute ambition to translate into language this *semiosis*—the "semiotic," as I said earlier[76]—that exceeds the speaking subject and of which feminine jouissance is the fantasmatic representation. The suicide attempt and auto-da-fé put an end to this senselessness. In counterpoint, meeting Elsa in the fall of 1928 and adherence to the Communist Party in 1927 stabilize and reassure. The adherence will be effective in 1930 and will in fact consolidate the identity of the writer. The social realization of a political future will supplant the impossible mission of vying with fantasmatic feminine jouissance. Is this adherence a true lie, a sham, a mask, an artifact? Aragon's last years might suggest this, given that by then he had rid himself of his respectability. Nevertheless he occupied this role for a very long time and drew criticism from those—staunch bourgeois or liberal anarchists—who accused him of cynicism and conformism. Adherence to the party as well as conjugal "mad love" were no doubt his lifeline after burning the manuscript, the mirror necessary for identity assurance: "I" belong, because "I" do not know who "I" am and "I" do not want to be struck down by the jouissance of the other, "I" adhere, "I" stabilize myself, if only temporarily, "I" take advantage of this in order to continue writing. The alternation between revolt and adherence structures the surrealist period itself, with the group assuming the role of identity support before the party takes its place and seals off the intransigence of revolt in social protest. With Stalinism, Aragon abandons revolt in the name of a sometimes critical, sometimes servile engagement, always wanting everything ("always the whole rainbow," Breton said of him), without absolutely embracing any identity, any precise truth. This is what some of Aragon's critics have called his successive and permanent "betrayals," betrayals that also allowed him to pursue his path as a writer. After burning *L'Infini*, writing could only be a permanent betrayal/translation of styles, genres, postures, tones.

Stalinism Against the Sensorial Infinite

"When I Do Not Know Who I Am, There I Am": Adhering Replaces Being

I ended the last section by mentioning the adherence to Stalinism, the great affair of the century. As you may well imagine, I certainly won't exhaust the question here! Nevertheless, we have to start somewhere, and my point of view is not one of social utility (to defend the "damned of the Earth" against the bourgeois) or political necessity (to counterbalance one totalitarianism with another), although these views are defensible. I say this unblushingly and as a victim myself (a modest victim but a victim nonetheless) of those who promised "singing tomorrows."

Adhering to Stalinism was revealed to be a passion with much more devious roots. Take the invalid man in *Irene*. One might imagine such a man restoring himself by adhering to something strong: there is no longer a reason for being, but there is a group that incarnates the reason of History. The reason of History is the counterweight to depression, and the party of the masses becomes the manic version of melancholia. He forgets about poetry's insurgence against the world of action; he thinks this revolt is "trop con" [slang for "stupid" but also "cunt." —Trans.]; he wants action in the name of reason and History. He sees Communism as "consciousness incarnate," the absolute mind "back on its feet." Hegel warned that terror was Kant put into practice, but he is no longer wary of the terror imposed by the dialectic put into practice. Who is "he"? In the case that interests us, "he" is an adherent to the dialectic incarnated in the people: "he" has battled against the law and the norm of an oppressive consciousness to the point of undoing its stability as well as his own. Identity in disarray is restabilized by the erection of the dogma of reason incarnate.

I would add that a certain French materialist tradition does not repugn the cult of the incarnation of historical reason that the party represents. That a human group can materialize the absolute power that German idealism attributed to the idea does not fail to seduce the descendants of those who claim filiation with sensualism and who hold in contempt the obscurantism of cathedrals. The cult of the irrational marvelous given substance by a woman borders on the inconstancy and the plurality of the baroque, as we have seen. But the cult of the rational marvelous that dialectical materialism represents, in counterpoint to the preceding, reassures, solidifies, and fills one with enthusiasm all at once.

The fantasy of a popular power becomes the social place of this sensorial magic that the female enchantress holds in the private realm. Here the imaginary power of the phallic matron has command over the males' sadomasochism. That homosexuality is the open secret of this alchemy does not take long to understand, and Aragon himself played it out for us, though late in life and not without a certain derision, which, after all, kept the symptom at a distance.

Yet in this logic where the motivations of the unconscious communicate with political options—Breton's *Communicating Vessels* might be evoked again here—ideological credos take on the intense changeability that also characterizes the sadomasochism of amorous states and the polysemy of poetic language. And beneath the appearance of the political canker—patriot, communist, and ideologue—one finds the salubrious provocation of a ham actor. But is this really only amoral manipulation on the part of an impostor? Or a borderline state of the unbearable identity: that of the self, that of groups? Or a critical period in Western consciousness where the refusal of this pair formed by consciousness and the norm is ossified in an antinorm and an anticonsciousness more constraining and more lethal than their traditional targets, revolt thus failing in radical oppression, unable to follow in thought alone, in lone thought, this archeology of the sensory and the sensible, this debate in metaphysics, against metaphysics, that Aragon announced in *Paris Peasant*? One thing is sure: while we have gone beyond this critical period and see its impasses today (which do not solely concern Aragon's compromises), we may have also lost its unsettling vitality. And an opening to a-thought may be temporarily closed.

At the point we have reached, 1928, the impasses of Stalinism are only beginning. Still to come are 1930 and the congress of Kharkov with its redoubtable adherence to socialist realism and then 1932 and the break with surrealism. *Le Monde réel* is started in 1933 and lasts until *Les Communistes* of 1949.[77] Next comes the conjugal and patriotic pathos of the Resistance poems (but didn't they have to be written? who will cast the first stone at the alexandrines?), then *Aurélien* in 1945, and finally (I say "finally" because for me it was a relief to see that the writing had caught its breath again) *La Semaine sainte* in 1958.[78] But we hear nothing more about *La Défense de l'infini*, which would not be republished until 1986. In 1969, in *Je n'ai jamais appris à écrire*, Aragon still does not mention *Irene* though he describes the style of the novel he set on fire.

The Sensorial Infinite or A-thought in Danger

What is the meaning of this "infinity" in flames? In distinguishing between thinking and judging, intellect and reason, understanding and meaning, Kant accords judgment and the quest for meaning unlimited power. This relentlessness, a component of thought itself, which led the Greeks to consider the infinite as the source of all evil,[79] is manifested fearsomely in the unlimited power of modern pragmatic reason: the technological reason that turns away from the search for truth in order to dominate the sensory. This debate, which Hannah Arendt conducts in *The Life of the Mind*, leaves open the question of the sensory infinite: the domain of the soul and the passions in classical philosophy, this universe—favored terrain not only of art and literature but also psychoanalysis—is far from passive and uniform but teems with infinite singularities that classical aesthetics, because it is classical, does not manifest. This sensorial infinite doubled by infinite reason, although founded on and in the sensory world, drowns any evidence of it in an excess that only metaphors of the infinite can approach; here the polyphonic stylistics of language shatter the traps of unity (unity of word, syllable, rhythm, sentence, narrative, character, etc.), which is nevertheless used, summoned, and pulverized. It is this sensorial infinite that jouissance reveals and by which writing is measured and that inspires—the age-old word—the mystic as much as the writer. We must note that the apparently formal and passionate revolt of writing in *La Défense de l'infini*, as in other avant-garde experiments, takes place in a world dominated by the infinite violence of technological reason and affixes to it the resistance of the sensorial infinite, insofar as this is the reserve of a human truth. This truth is itself internal to language, provided it can be wrested from the calculus and brought nearer to the pulse of thought, its infinitesimal germination, anterior to One, to the subject, and to meaning. We can then measure the risk to identity—melancholic, psychotic—of this excess that is another way of referring to freedom.

The Impossible of Revolt

I would like to link these remarks concerning Aragon's text, life, and engagement in the surrealist movement to the theme of revolt. No doubt you can see the connection just beneath the surface and also hear echoes of it in the partition of the right and left discussed during political campaigns. At a moment when the speeches of the candidates to the presidency of the Republic of France—speeches rallying us to go to the polls—seek demagogically to erase cleavages and differences, the term "revolt" incites fear. It does this precisely because it entails questioning present contradictions and new forms of revolt in our postindustrial society. To speak of revolt does not immediately call to mind the rallying that might make a candidate win; on the contrary, it incites auscultation, displacement, dissimilarity, analysis, and dissolution. To speak of revolt does not call to mind integration, inclusion, an unchanging social idyll but underscores that economic, psychological, and spiritual contradictions exist and also that these contradictions are permanent: they are not solvable. When one recognizes that the contradictions of thought and society are not soluble, then revolt—with its risks—appears as a continuous necessity for keeping alive the psyche, thought, and the social link itself. Of course, the political landscape is not necessarily the place to raise the question of revolt; perhaps it will be if the left can be reestablished, as some claim it can be. But it will take time for this necessary party to do so, after a time of not having power.

Our question here is rather one of psychical revolt, personal revolt, and consequently revolt as a form of aesthetic expression. Do Aragon's political and aesthetic revolt, the lack of a father in his life, the worship of the feminine in the form I described, the adherence to the Communist Party constitute elements of the revolt that I situated in the framework of Freudian thought as a revolt against the father and against the law? In part, yes, as is revealed at the beginning of *Irene* by the narrator and his adolescent rage against the conformism of provincial society, where he is restless. But beyond this conflict with the father and the law, and especially when the place of the father is vacant and the son is illegitimate, another variant of the tragic appears, beyond the oedipal tragic: it is the confrontation with what must be called the impossible.

I have mentioned this word on several occasions. It is the word Lacan uses when he speaks of the real, asserting that it is impossible.[80] The impossible, according to *Irene's Cunt*, is presented in Aragon's imaginary as a confrontation with the maternal and the feminine, insofar as these represent the fantasy of unrepresentable excitability: the diabolical *mater*-matter. We are thus above and beyond paternal law and the identity of signs that this law guarantees. In surrealist writing, the signs of language—of identity and identifying—come unhinged, without undergoing total alienation as in Joyce's portmanteau words or Artaud's glossolalia.

Nevertheless, surrealism is characterized by these paradoxical metaphors, examples of which occur in the fish passage quoted above, and by these reveries, realized in automatic writing, that destroy logic. Sacralization and fetishism of the woman will lead the surrealists to an image of the feminine that is both abject and fascinating. This ambivalent war against the feminine is to be understood in counterpoint to the war that the subject wages with himself: with his superego and paternal identity. In order to protect himself from the abjection of the other (starting with the other sex) and the other itself, the woman is made sacred, fetishized: this is what the two sides of surrealist feminine imagery (ambivalence-rejection, marvelous-magic) make apparent. The fascinating criminal woman or the wild Irene are the writer's alter egos, in which both the imaginary feminine roles and facets of the subject himself are found, deliciously and horribly confused with this feminine at once oedipal, because desirable, and preoedipal, because a narcissistic reflection of the self.

Irene is the character invented by Aragon who best demonstrates this particular interweaving of three images: the hypostatized woman, idealized as desirable oedipal mother; the negativized woman, abysmal, filthy, base, and devouring; and a third component: the identification of this split with the very dynamic of representation, of a-thought, which the writer, the enunciator, the speaking subject attributes to himself. Neither Victoire nor Irene is a real woman, of course, in the social sense of the term. I stress this to underscore that this is a fantasy, a prosopopoeia of the narrator's and the writer's unconscious, in that a prosopopoeia is a representation of an absent, dead, supernatural, or inanimate being who speaks and acts, while the fantasy creates this scenography with the products of our own unconscious, products that are not dead at all.

In this mise-en-scène of a new tragic form where the man-narrator is confronted with the impossible (the other, the feminine, the sensory), we are led, through Aragonian poetic language, to the heart of a double tragedy, which is feminine this time and no longer oedipal. On the one hand, the poet is unaware of the woman's real, psychological, and social existence: all one needs to do is think of the dramatic biographies of a number of women who trailed in the wake of the surrealists, and of the crushing of their autonomy along with their desire, which drove some of them to suicide. On the other hand, he identifies with a feminine hypostasis, he absorbs it, he is she: he is Irene and writes the impossible of femininity, assimilates it, sucks its blood. In doing this, he manages however to bear witness to the impossible as well as to jouissance, which, without this tragic ambivalence, would no doubt remain unspoken.

Isn't (Political, Mass-Media) Engagement Always a Deception?

After this tragic period, starting in the thirties, Aragon's adherence to the Stalinist party, his cult worship of Elsa, and finally his homosexual activity can be

read in retrospect (beyond the unquestionable psychological, moral, and political uses they might have) as an immense display of the burlesque. In effect,
Aragon did not cease to playact and to make himself look ridiculous through
masquerade, fakery, and various tricks at the core of his most serious opinions.
His life offers paroxysmal testimony, in our century, to a pathetic and
grotesque variant of the tragic, to what at the beginning of this introduction to
Aragon I called the "impossible hero." Deleuze and Guattari's *Anti-Oedipus*
has suggested that certain "poetic" experiences, such as that of Artaud, ignore
oedipal stabilization and work in psychosis.[81] Among the surrealists, the institutional isolation that Artaud experienced does not occur. On the contrary,
however marginal and antiestablishment it might have been, the position of
the surrealists was seductive and integrated, framed within the context of esotericism for Breton and the apparatus of the party for Aragon, whose writing remained eminently socialized. In the nonoedipal tonality of an impossible
heroism, however, the polymorphous instability of a modern Narcissus is dis-
played. This representative of baroque inconstancy—henceforth deprived of
God, however—is a bard of the feminine, which he traverses and appropriates
the better to play his subtle role within political apparatuses, before these bequeath their power to television. If he doesn't arrive at the integration that
makes him an impossible hero or the hero of the impossible, this chameleon
risks annihilation. Explorer of the unrepresentable, he dedicates himself to
being a ham.

Alongside the personal tragic element, the story of Aragon has the advantage, so to speak, of showing political engagement as a relay and link of tragic
revolt. For Aragon, political engagement took place at a moment of great subjective malaise. He approached the party in 1926 or 1927 and, after a long
process, became a member. What does this engagement mean in the context
of what we have learned of his life and work, in view of the fluidity and instability that take on aspects of sexual ambiguity and a game with signs? Well, one
can interpret it as a sort of repudiation of the imaginary: my revolt will no
longer take place in the imaginary or in writing; it will be an act that will assure true revolt insofar as it is both psychical life and social engagement. The
adoration of the social group will replace the adoration of the feminine for
Aragon. I am not questioning the many good reasons that one may find to justify adherence to a political party. But if one seeks to understand in depth the
psychical significance of adherence, it is not uncommon to find at its root a
will to restore the father and the law, in order to struggle against the disappointment of depression, against invasion by the feminine, against the plunge
into a-thought of which *Irene's Cunt* is such a perfect example.

I know that some of you will be unsatisfied by this conclusion, not having found your preferred myth of Aragon in my analysis: the cult of the couple and the people, of Elsa and the party. You miss all this, not only because these myths are part of France's history but also because your imaginary is eager for them. I must tell you that I have not lost sight of this mythology of fidelity, or your desire for it. It is based on this mythology that I have discussed what precedes it and how the unbearable excess to which *Irene* testifies made the recourse to certainty imperative. Adherence, starting with adhering to a relationship, involves an assurance of identity that guarantees our survival. We all want it, and some of us manage to get it, with certain of our illusions intact. The grandeur and misery of illusion? So be it. The man who was "mad about Elsa" knew, although he forgot, that the mad love he celebrated counterbalanced another madness, that adherence (to Elsa, to the party) was satiating and calming another infinite delirium: Irene's. Some have implied that the consecration of the couple's relationship was used to struggle against homosexuality. More than that: it was used to struggle against the quashing of the self in confusion with the primary feminine, in menacing genitality. The myth of faithfulness and adherence were all the more necessary and real—a hypnotic reality for both the protagonists and the public—in that they helped to stabilize the turmoil. From then on, forgery and disguise, even if they were perceived as such by some, inspired discomfort more than rejection in even the most intransigent critic.

If we can now make out the historical and social causes of totalitarianism, it is not certain that we have dismantled the psychical motivations for it nor that we are safe from the need for identity, which too often and without Stalinist monstrosity, causes our revolts to alternate with our impostures. Here, we are no doubt at the heart of what underlies membership: "I" do not know *who* "I" am, "I" do not know *if* "I" am (a man or a woman); but "I" am part of adherence. The post–cold war thaw, revisionism, the critique of totalitarianism, the fall of the Berlin Wall represent so many mutations of history that reactivate the events of a more personal, more subjective revolt and show that the confrontations with the sacred maternal, on the one hand, and the safety belt of language, on the other, are the true secret doubles of political engagement, its *mise en abîme*. Political engagement is a marker and a mask; Aragon's life is proof of that.

As practical reason takes over for a-thought, activism is renewed: resistance, the defense of the oppressed, struggle against the imperialist plutocracy. But practical reason excels in dialectical strategies, before falling prey to egotism and the critical justification of totalitarianism. I say this to you with all the more gravity having lived in a Stalinist country. I am among those who appreciated Aragon's opposition to dogmatism and count his contribution to the thaw as part of the process that led to the fall of the Berlin Wall. The enthusiasm of adherence, and what it implies in terms of the choice of civilization and subjective choice, nevertheless remains problematic.

Traitor, clown, opportunist, profiteer, impostor, liar, all these epithets have stuck to the writer in spite of the fact that he was an alchemist of the Word. A true actor, he acted out the spectacle of adherence without ever abandoning the dimension of the unfathomable that he confronted in writing, in a rhetorical and subjective experience that one may or may not appreciate but that nevertheless remains singular.

Is it legitimate to speak in this context of an impasse of revolt, an impasse of the imaginary, in favor of the practical reason of which Stalinism would be the sinister apotheosis? One could pose the question another way: is the imaginary experience of Aragon audible, readable without the political backdrop, without the mass media visibility that Communist popularity procured for him and that gave him one of his reasons for being? Aragon is not read much today. Is this imaginary that ventured to the limits of the sensory and the feminine, which I described as specific to him, impossible to save under the pretext that he died with ideological membership associated with him? There is in fact a non-sense of revolt in the way Aragon used it that makes it impossible to practice today. Sartre will offer another example of this, and Barthes a completely different approach.

There remains nonetheless the question of thought. When it is deployed as psychical life, when it has the ambition of being psychical life in the sense of the revitalization and resurrection of identity — in the sense of a-thought — it inevitably confronts the maternal, on the one hand, and signs on the other. Is this experience inseparable from the sort of safety belt that institutional membership can offer? If so, what is it today? If not, what solitude! In either case, perhaps no one can assume its risks at the price of the paroxysm that Aragon exhibited, though it is structural when the strongest prohibition is associated with the archaic or the sensory. Which means that, beyond freedom, it is a-thought itself, along with this revolt, that is in peril. Perhaps other links can be built that are not the partisan links of practical reason. Right now, we are a long way off.

7

Sartre; or, "We Are Right to Revolt"

"I Am Free"

Around 458 B.C.—about forty years before Sophocles' *Oedipus the King* (420 B.C.)—Aeschylus wrote his *Oresteia.*[1] In 1943 a modern rebel, Jean-Paul Sartre, would refashion it as *The Flies*: "I'm free as air, thank God! My mind's my own, gloriously aloof. . . . I shall not come back to Nature, . . . in it are a thousand beaten paths all leading up to you—but I must blaze my trail. For I, Zeus, am a man, and every man must find out his own way. Nature abhors man, and you too, god of gods, abhor mankind."[2] The speaker is a curious matricidal humanist, a remorseless atheist who represents the absolute stranger, that is, the free man Sartre will ceaselessly champion in an intellectual and political career that proved one of the most turbulent and controversial.

To examine revolt in the contemporary world, in contemporary literature, Sartre's experience cannot be ignored. I am all the more delighted to present his work here because a sort of weak consensus has reigned for some time that disparages Sartre, unfairly in my opinion. Like that of Barthes, which I will discuss soon, it is impossible to reconstruct Sartre's experience in the pages at my disposal here, but I hope nevertheless to give you an introduction of some depth in this time of oblivion. I will not tackle the Sartre-Beauvoir question—a scandal to some, a fascination for others—but I bring it up here to mention two things in passing: it has never been easy for a woman to gain recognition in the closely guarded pantheon of letters without a certain conventional complacency and complicity—it is not any easier today; it has even become increasingly impossible—and Beauvoir in her various writings has deftly articulated the effort and struggle this cost her. Nor is it easy for a man to be the companion of a woman of Beauvoir's intelligence. I will come back some day to this confrontation called "a relationship" precisely in light of what I plan to say about Sartre's trajectory.

Sartre was born in Paris on June 21, 1905, and died on April 15, 1980. For him as with Aragon and Barthes, though differently for each, the biographer is immediately faced with a question regarding the paternal function. Aragon was illegitimate, as you recall. This was not the case for Sartre, whose father died in 1907, when the child was two years old. He was raised by Karl Schweitzer, his maternal grandfather, the focus of both his adoration and his desire for autonomy. He expresses this in *The Words*,[3] an autobiographical book in which he retraces his childhood and expresses his need to confront his grandfather and put in his place not the authority of the father or even the refusal of this function but what he calls "the mind." This term sums up the intellectual experience or that of sublimation, the investment in ideas and words that will characterize his entire life. His mother remarried in 1916, and Sartre left the family circle, sent off to a lycée in La Rochelle between 1916 and 1919. As a student, he began to assert his autonomy. Accepted at the Ecole Normale in 1924, he passed the *agrégation* [exam for teachers] in 1929 and began his military service in the meteorology department in Tours. Later, he became a philosophy teacher in Le Havre, in Laon, and, in 1937, at the lycée Pasteur in Paris. Then war broke out, which he discussed in his *Diaries*.[4] He was taken prisoner on June 21, 1940, in Lorraine and led to Stalag 12D in Trier. Freed on April 1, 1941, he returned as a civilian to the lycée Pasteur before teaching at the lycée Condorcet. He went on an unlimited leave of absence in 1945 and would never teach again, devoting himself entirely to the work of writing and philosophy. Around the same time, he took his first trip to the United States.

Among the many events that mark Sartre's postwar itinerary, I will speak only of those that, in my eyes, sum up what I call the sense and non-sense of revolt. In 1964 Sartre refused the Nobel Prize; in 1966 he participated in the Russell tribunal, which opposed the Vietnam War and "American imperialism"; in 1968 he appeared at the Sorbonne to support the student movement (from this *La Cause du peuple* was born, which he would head); between 1970 and 1973 came his break with the Communists and in particular with the Soviet Union, following revelations of the existence of the gulag and under the pressure of Solzhenitsyn. Sartre was then a leftist. In 1973, fatigued by intense intellectual work, the use of strong stimulants, and age, Sartre went partially blind. This did not prevent him from pursuing his vocation as a rebel, with the help of his friends. His death, on April 15, 1980, provoked acute emotion among leftists, youth, and a great number of intellectuals, despite the violent reactions that his political activities never failed to incite.

The Nobel Prize Affair

Sartre's refusal of the Nobel Prize constitutes a good example of the ambiguity of his positions, and the Nobel Prize affair appears to me to be emblematic of the sense and non-sense of revolt.[5]

On October 4, 1964, a rumor circulated that the Nobel Prize jury was planning to award its prize for literature to Sartre; there was even a small mention of it in the October 4, 1964, issue of *Le Figaro littéraire*. On October 14, Sartre sent the following letter to the Nobel Academy:

> *Mr. Secretary,*
>
> *According to certain information I was made aware of today, I have some chance of obtaining the Nobel Prize this year. Although it may be presumptuous to decide a vote before it has taken place, I am taking the liberty to write you now in order to clear up a misunderstanding. I would like to assure you first, Mr. Secretary, of my deep esteem for the Swedish Academy and the prize with which it has honored so many writers. Nevertheless, for reasons that are personal and for others that are more objective, I do not wish to appear on the list of possible prizewinners, and neither can nor wish, either in 1964 or later, to accept this honorific distinction.*
>
> *Please accept my apologies, Mr. Secretary, and my deepest respect.*

Apparently this letter arrived at its destination on a weekend, the secretary misplaced it, and it was lost: Sartre was therefore announced as the recipient of the prize. Afterward, he gave an interview to the Swedish and international press at the Swedish embassy in Paris.

By refusing the Nobel Prize, Sartre refused 250,000 francs, a substantial sum at the time; his refusal, however, cannot be reduced to moral rigor and financial asceticism. He could have accepted the prize—which in his eyes "bought" the work and the writer—and used it for political causes—for example, Vietnam, tortured and starving children, and so on. More profoundly, he explained his refusal as a desire to show that the writer must remain inalienable, rebellious to any allegiance, even an institution as prestigious as the Nobel.[6] Finally, and this is where ambiguities arise, Sartre felt the writers who had already been honored by the Nobel jury were all part of the capitalist bloc—the bourgeois bloc—and that the prize was only rarely given to writers of the Eastern bloc, which Sartre, despite his circumspection, continued to appreciate. When a Soviet writer was honored, he was sorry it was not the "right one," in his eyes: the Nobel Prize was awarded to Boris Pasternak and not to Mikhaïl Sholokhov.

Sartre's arguments would soon be made obsolete at the very least by events that showed the Eastern bloc in all its horror: Solzhenitsyn's revelations would lead Sartre to move away from Communism and withdraw his critical sympathy; Sholokhov would even be charged with stealing the manuscripts of an unknown writer and publishing them as *And Quiet Flows the Don*, which cast a lugubrious light on the demand for libertarian rigor that Sartre advanced in preferring him to Pasternak. Of course, Sartre had no reason to suspect Sholokhov, but he did have ways of knowing about the existence of the camps and the manipulations in which the Soviet system indulged.

All this applies much more dramatically to Aragon and his long complicity with the Stalinist reality, which I have not emphasized enough and which is not well-known. As for Sartre, his concern to detach himself from Western conformism had blinded him, and he adhered completely, without the spirit of revolt he demanded elsewhere, to a certain leftist propaganda of the time. Total revolt against some, doubts finally erased concerning others: Sartre's position at that moment, with its distinct and dogmatic moralism, similar to that of a good many intellectuals and writers, would gradually become more complex and nuanced with the development of global history and his own thought, but it is striking today in its sectarianism. Consider Sartre's arguments as they were developed in the interview I just mentioned:

> I keenly regret that this affair has taken on an appearance of scandal. A prize was awarded and someone refused it. The fact was, I was not informed early enough about what was being planned. When I saw an article in *Le Figaro littéraire* of October 15 by the paper's Swedish correspondent saying the choice of the Swedish Academy had not yet been established, I imagined that by writing a letter to the Swedish Academy, which I sent the next day, I could clarify things and no one would talk about it anymore.
>
> I was unaware that the Nobel Prize was awarded without asking the opinion of the party in question and I thought it was important to prevent that. But I understand that when the Swedish Academy has made a choice, it cannot retract it. The reasons for which I renounce the prize concern neither the Swedish Academy nor the Nobel Prize itself, as I explained in my letter to the Academy. In it I invoked two sorts of reasons: personal reasons and objective reasons. My personal reasons are the following: my refusal is not a spontaneous act. I have always refused official distinctions. When, after the war, in 1945, I was offered the Legion of Honor, I refused, even though I had friends in the government. Likewise, I have never wished to enter the Collège de France, as some of my friends have suggested. This attitude is based on my conception of a writer's work. A writer who takes political, social, and literary stands must act only with the means that are his own, that is, the written word. All the distinctions he may receive expose his readers to a pressure that I do not consider desirable. It is not the same if I sign my name "Jean-Paul Sartre," or "Jean-Paul Sartre, Nobel Prizewinner."
>
> The writer who accepts a distinction of this sort also engages the associa-

tion or institution that has honored him. My sympathy for the Venezuelan underground engages no one but me, whereas if the Nobel Prizewinner Jean-Paul Sartre supported the Venezuelan resistance he would drag the entire Nobel Prize as an institution with him. The writer must therefore refuse to allow himself to be transformed into an institution, even if this takes place in the most honorable forms, as is the case here.

This attitude is obviously entirely my own: it does not comprise any criticism against those who have already been honored. I have much respect and admiration for several prizewinners whom I have the honor of knowing.

My objective reasons are the following: the sole possible struggle on the cultural front is for the peaceful coexistence of two cultures, that of the East and that of the West. I am not saying we have to embrace each other. I know that the confrontation between these two cultures must necessarily take the form of a conflict. But it must take place between men and between cultures without the intervention of institutions. I feel the contradiction between the two cultures personally, profoundly.

Note the emphasis on the malaise engendered by these contradictions, and the choice nevertheless supported: "I am made of these contradictions. My sympathies lean undeniably toward socialism and what is called the Eastern bloc. But I was born and raised in a bourgeois family. This allows me to collaborate with all those who want to bring the two cultures closer together. Of course, I hope the best one wins." Since the best one, in Sartre's eyes, was socialism, his error has been denounced with the greatest virulence. The victors say Sartre was always mistaken, although most of these righteous sorts never ventured any thought or position whatsoever themselves. (I am not talking here about the perspicacious, such as Raymond Aron, who always denounced totalitarianism, even at the price of the subjective reserve that characterizes liberal rationalists, while the writer-intellectual, on the contrary, shares and assumes the anxieties of individuals and the century.)

This is why I cannot accept any distinction distributed by high cultural authorities, either in the East or the West, even if I fully understand their existence. [As an aside, let me remind you that, unlike Aragon, Sartre never accepted an award from the East either.] Although my sympathies lie with the socialists, I would be just as unable to accept the Lenin Prize, for example, if someone wanted to give it to me, which is not the case. I know that the Nobel Prize in itself is not a literary prize from the Western bloc, but it is what we make of it, and events could arise that the Swedish Academy does not determine. This is why, in the current situation, the Nobel Prize presents itself objectively as a distinction reserved for writers of the West or rebels of the East. [As you can see, Sartre refuses the revolt of the rebels of the East; is he therefore accepting a situation where revolt would be limited, prohibited to some?] Neruda, for example, a great South American poet, has not been honored. Louis Aragon has never been talked about seriously though he certainly deserves it. It is regrettable that the prize has been given to Pasternak before Sholokhov, and that the only Soviet work honored should be a work published abroad and prohibited in its country.

As though samizdat and publishing abroad has not always been necessary to publish dissident works! But in 1964, Sartre was oblivious to this. He rebeled against bourgeois "right-thinking" and contrasted it overall to Soviet "socialism." Consider Michel Contat's commentary on the subject, the sympathetic tone of which does not in any way diminish its critical pertinence:

> You had to be very familiar with Sartre to understand the nastiness beneath the homage to Aragon, who certainly deserved this prize. It only caused laughter in the sixth arrondissement. On the other hand, Sartre quickly noticed that he had committed a serious gaffe by mentioning Sholokhov, a Stalinist writer, and by criticizing the attribution of the prize to Boris Pasternak (who was forced to refuse it, in 1958) without condemning the prohibition of *Doctor Zhivago* in the USSR. As for asserting that no Communist writer had ever received the prize, he was mistaken, since Salvatore Quasimodo had been given the prize in 1959, precisely as a way to reestablish the balance. Was it to prove Sartre wrong that the Swedish Academy awarded the prize to Mikhaïl Sholokhov in 1965? And should it be seen as punishment that no French writer would receive it until Claude Simon in 1985?"[7]

Sartre immediately returned to the French context and to his role as a spoilsport:

> A balance could have established by a similar gesture in the other direction. During the Algerian War, when we signed the "declaration of the 121," I would have accepted the prize gratefully because it would have honored not only me but also the freedom for which we were fighting. But this did not happen. And it was only when the fighting ended that the prize was awarded to me. In the Swedish Academy's motivations, they speak of freedom; this is a word that invites numerous interpretations. In the West, we only under-

stand a general freedom; as for me, I understand a more concrete freedom that consists of the right to have more than one pair of shoes and to eat when hungry. It seems less dangerous to me to decline the prize than to accept it. If I accept it, I lend myself to what I will call "an objective takeover." I read in the *Figaro littéraire* article that my "controversial political past would not be held against me." I know that this article does not express the opinion of the Swedish Academy. But it clearly shows how my acceptance would be interpreted in certain circles on the right.

In advocating concrete individual freedom, Sartre worried that his rebellious past might be erased, especially during the Algerian War:

I consider this "controversial political past" still valid, even if I am prepared to recognize certain past errors among my comrades. By this I do not mean to say that the Nobel Prize is a "bourgeois prize," but that is the bourgeois interpretation the circles I know well would inevitably give it. Finally, I come to the question of money. The Academy places a great weight on the prizewinner's shoulders by accompanying his homage with an enormous sum. And this problem tormented me. . . . [You can hear Sartre's rather Protestant and moralistic tone.] Either one accepts the prize and, with the sum received, supports movements or organizations that one considers important—for my part, I think of the Apartheid Committee in London—or one declines the prize based on general principles and deprives this movement of the support it needs. But I think that this is a false problem. I obviously renounce the 250,000 francs because I do not want to be institutionalized either in the West or in the East. But one cannot be asked, for 250,000 francs, to renounce principles that are not solely your own but that all your comrades share. This is what has made both the attribution of the prize and the refusal that I am obliged to give so difficult for me. I want to end my statement with a message of friendship to the Swedish public. . . .[8]

Sartre's position was clear. His honesty led him to refuse the prize for the reasons he mentioned. Nevertheless, given the events that have followed, particularly the revelations about the East and the fall of the Berlin Wall, an ambiguity persists and taints the whole of his rebellious position in that it did not go so far as to challenge what he called "socialism," a term that cannot be used generically to encompass all of Eastern European Communism, although some have no qualms doing so, in a pejorative sense, tracing totalitarianism back to the Enlightenment! We are presented with a curious symmetry of ap-

parently opposed intellectual parties during the Stalinist era: some (with
Sartre) supported "socialism," which included Communism, in order to posi-
tivize it and to rise up against the injustices of bourgeois societies, using it as a
weapon; others used the same amalgam to reject the "monster" as a whole in
favor of a beatification of liberal democracies. Some—antiauthoritarians, libertarian socialists, indeed, leftists—absolutized revolt without revolting precisely against the revolt itself and limited their critical judgment; others—
democratic liberals—obscured the role of the negative and of revolt in
psychical and social life. Note, however, that Sartre's union with what he
called "socialism" was an attempt at critical proximity not with the socialist
left, whose evasions he did not support, but with the Communist Party, whose
anti-Americanism, critique of bourgeois conformism, and impact on the
"masses"—the "proletariat"—he appreciated and which so strongly seduced
the intellectual, guilty about his scarcely popular refinements. He explained
this himself in On a raison de se révolter. Thus, regarding three articles entitled
"Les Communistes et la paix" published in Les Temps modernes during the
cold war, he said: "When I think about it today, I think I was compelled to
write them out of hatred of bourgeois behavior more than the attraction the
party exercised over me."[9]

   That said, as a result of positions of which the Nobel Prize affair was but a
spectacular emblem, a strong and lasting hatred of Sartre was set into motion
that went well beyond the ambiguity of his position and his so-called mistakes.
I recommend Jean-Jacques Brochier's very topical book, which I have already
cited, which mentions a number of Sartre's most virulent detractors—Jacques
Laurent and Jean Dutourd, among others—who ceaselessly denounce "the
pedantic and barbarous language of this philosopher lost in literature," this
"patent corrupter," and so on.[10] More surprising are criticisms from people
such as Kostas Axelos, philosopher and ex-theoretician of the Greek Communist Party, who found Sartre's leftist positions unacceptable.

   On the other hand, to allow you to persist in the idea that revolt defines free
men, I was struck by two voices which Brochier also mentions and which seem
to me to be very significant: two great intellectuals and writers who do not join
the chorus of detractors, François Mauriac and Gilles Deleuze.

A Free Man, in Touch with Our Difficulties and Enthusiasms

Mauriac's ironic and critical question published in L'Express remains famous:
"O Sartre, why are you so sad?" Fortified by glory and the Catholic resurrection, Mauriac was persuaded to dispense hope beyond Billancourt and to
avoid the negative and caustic tone Sartre adopted when he denounced the

evils of the era and society. He thus falsely inscribed himself against Sartre's positions, but in his weekly "Bloc-notes" in *Figaro littéraire*, he revealed himself to be a man of great decency and underscored Sartre's moral and human force:

> "He only got what he deserved!" Jean-Paul Sartre might have cried when Albert Camus won the Nobel Prize. Camus, if he were still alive, would not be able to respond "Catch!" because Jean-Paul Sartre managed to avoid the golden paving stone that fell on his head and did not in fact catch anything. Let's give him some credit: he gave his reasons to the city and the world without getting turgid, his tone appropriate, like a well-bred bourgeois. But, above all, Sartre was able to avoid ostentation: that was the danger in his gesture. Think what you like of the philosopher, the essayist, the novelist, the dramatist, but in the last analysis *this great writer is a true man, and that is his glory.*

I emphasize this, because if you know how sparing Mauriac was with his compliments, you can appreciate the homage! "I hear myself when I give him this praise," he continued. "A true man doesn't grow on trees, much less in newspaper rooms or the antechambers of publishing houses. Because he is this true man Sartre reaches those who are the most estranged from his thought and *most hostile to his opinions.*"[11] Even Mauriac, as you see, who counted himself among those "most estranged from his thought and most hostile to his opinions," nevertheless considered him "a true man," the likes of which did not "grow on trees."

> *Everything a true man says, everything he writes engages him. This goes without saying for him but is surprising in a world where gestures and words no longer engage anyone.* . . . To get back to Jean-Paul Sartre, he refused what I myself was very surprised to receive, but just as happy to accept, not in order to give millions to the "apartheid" committee in London or some other pious deed, as Sartre, had he accepted the prize, confides he would have done but to redo the bathroom in my house in Seine-et-Oise and repair the fences. The strange thing is that I don't read anything by this true man without at some point in my reading throwing down the book and crying: "No! That isn't true!" Sartre's engagement [is] so singular, this absurdity must be ventured: a disengaged engagement [I would add: disengaged in the sense that it is constantly critical, except perhaps in a certain umbilical attachment, as I pointed out earlier, to the Eastern bloc. You see, we can be more critical than Mauriac with regard to the existentialist philosopher, without losing sight of the profound sense of his rebellious gesture.] . . . with the pro-

letariat and thus with the Communist Party, but without ever consenting on any point to bring his thought to heel. *A true man, for whom to write is to act, and who is entirely in each of his words, a free man . . .* I'll stop here and praise and admire myself for so generously admiring this philosopher who, at the start of his literary life, and right off the bat, sought to wring my neck.[12]

I will leave you to contemplate this critical homage and move on to another, by Gilles Deleuze. I cannot quote the entire text (published the same year as Mauriac's, 1964, in the review *Arts*) in spite of my admiration for it, but I strongly encourage you to take a look at it. In it Deleuze says what one would not necessarily expect from the author of *Anti-Oedipus*: "He was my master," he declares quite simply. And yet, in retrospect, the resonance between the two thinkers is unquestionable, not only in terms of their anticonformism but also and above all in terms of their examination of freedom and evil.

The sadness of generations without "masters." Our masters are not only public teachers, though we have a great need for teachers. As we come of age, our masters are those who strike us with a new radicality, those able to invent an artistic or literary technique and find ways to think that correspond to our modernity, that is, to our difficulties as well as our diffuse enthusiasms. We know that there is only one value of art and even truth, that is to say, the "first hand," the authentic newness of what one is saying, the "little music" with which one says it. Sartre was the one for us, for the generation in their twenties at Liberation. Who then knew how to say something new, if not Sartre? Who taught us new ways to think? As brilliant and profound as it was, the work of Merleau-Ponty was professorial and in many ways depended on Sartre's. . . . Camus, alas, was at times inflated virtuousness, at times secondhand absurdity. Camus claimed filiation with the *penseurs maudits*, but his entire philosophy took him back to Lalande and Meyerson, authors familiar to anyone with a high school diploma. The new themes, a certain new style, a new polemical and aggressive way of posing problems came from Sartre. In the disorder and hopes of the Liberation, we discovered, rediscovered, everything: Kafka, the American novel, Husserl and Heidegger, endless clarifications of Marxism, the impulse toward a new novel. All this happened through Sartre, not only because, as a philosopher, he had a genius for totalization, but because he knew how to invent the new. The first productions of *The Flies*, the publication of *Being and Nothingness*, the "Is Existentialism Humanism?" lecture, were events. One learned, after long nights, about the identity between thought and freedom.[13]

I would like in turn to demonstrate the correspondences Sartre sought to maintain with "our difficulties" and "enthusiasms." First off, there was an identity between thought and freedom, particularly in the Sartrean theater as revealed through the libertarian value of the strange characters in his plays. What is striking in Sartre's theater is the spirit of freedom and revolt, a minor manifestation of which we have just seen, misguided although not without pertinence, in the refusal of the Nobel Prize; this spirit of revolt and freedom that did not retreat from error or even from evil was crystallized in the characters of the criminal, the bastard, the actor, and the intellectual. Following the trajectory from *Nausea* (1938) to *The Flies* (1943) and other plays, it composed a sort of faceted deconstruction of the rebellious hero.

"Foreign to Myself . . . I Am Doomed to Have No Other Law But Mine":
The Flies *under the Occupation and Vichy*

Let's start with *The Flies* and move backward chronologically, for the major themes of Sartrean revolt are present here in an imaginary form, and you do not necessarily need the philosophical apparatus of existentialism to access it.

Imagine *The Flies* during the Occupation and Vichy when Sartre adapted the Greek legend. Orestes, son of Agamemnon and Clytemnestra, is twenty; he arrives with his tutor at Argos from which he was sent away at the age of three after Aegisthus, Clytemnestra's lover, murdered Agamemnon. He is excluded, in the position of the tragic hero, but not just any hero: not Oedipus the King but Orestes the Exile, who will be revealed to be the free Man. The identification of the dramatist—and the spectator—with the excluded is already a position of revolt. Orestes wants to enter the city from which he was exiled to incite revolt among the people protecting themselves from death and evil through the complacency of remorse: the flies represent the Furies. Philebus/Orestes directs the violence of his gesture at the homogeneous and the identical, all the more because Aegisthus, the murderer, feels no remorse. While the entire city is invaded by remorse, a diffuse, persecuting, always sickening remorse that takes the form of flies, none is assumed by the sovereign criminal who is the cause of it.

Given that this play was written during the German Occupation, the insinuation is clear: it is an indictment of a fetid state of mind, of a crowd concealing the crime of leaders and condemning itself to abjection in passiveness, guilt-ridden though complicitous and incapable of resistance and freedom. As André Green remarks, the theater offered Sartre "the chance to exhort an audience by means of the spoken word, under the nose of the Germans, these

Aegisthuses who slept with a collaborating France."[14] How will Orestes lead the city of Argos to rebel?

As you recall, he does not succeed, but he commits an act that shows us the difficulty of revolt and the compromise in which the tragic hero and/or rebel engage: another evil must be committed in order to conquer evil. This, at least, is the path Orestes follows, pushed by his sister, Electra, who disowns her brother once the infamy is committed. What is the new evil? Killing not only Aegisthus but also Clytemnestra, his own mother.

Sartre's mise-en-scène is spectacular and significant: Orestes takes the path of crime, the path that starts on the hill and leads down to the city, there "for the taking" through "an act beyond all remedy." [15] Once the double murder is perpetrated, Orestes is not a victor destined to reign supremely; he is forced to flee, for the path he has chosen is unbearable. This obligation is also a choice: a second choice, for Orestes takes the road outside the city, under the sun, of his own will, well before the persecution of the crowd begins. When Electra calls him a "thief," impugning the horror her brother has committed, Orestes protests that he is free and leaves Argos forever. The path of freedom is an open road that involves temporary implication in evil and crime. Which leads us directly to one of the major themes in existentialism, in Sartre, and above all in his theater, namely, freedom. "I am doomed to freedom," Sartre asserts through Orestes; freedom is not a grace or a good, we are condemned to it as by a moral obligation to the second degree that challenges the conventional morality of the victors, and we must assume it with all the violence it implies for ourselves and others. Moreover, if freedom is an endless path, it can only be reached through the boundary composed of evil and crime: the crossing of this boundary is intrinsically necessary. Freedom is antigood, antinature, anti*physis*: because nature is the mother, the mother must be killed. Man can only attain his free being through the self's conquest of nature, by wresting himself from it, by denying all nature: this is the meaning of the mother's murder. We assert ourselves as free subjects only by asserting ourselves as antinatural. We are a long way from the feminine marvelous here, as you can see!

I would like to emphasize the excessiveness of this freedom that integrates evil. This is not just a matter of recourse to a mythological metaphor to justify the violence of the Resistance fighters or terrorism against the conformism of compromises and foundations. It is, in an echo of Nietzsche, about establishing an Antichrist, an antichristic antihero who wrests himself definitively from divine protection as well as from the aspiration to moral purity and consequent divinization. "A man was to come, to announce my decline" (p. 160), Zeus confesses to Orestes, seeing in this son who kills his mother a radical deicide.

Against the Banality of Evil: Playing Freedom

Let us compare this Sartrean *Oresteia* to the oedipal revolt, the foundation of the Freudian discovery.

Although the photo of Jean-Baptiste Sartre still hung above his bed; although his love for Anne-Marie—his mother, imagined as a sister—was as firm as his animosity toward his stepfather, Joseph Mancey; and although his maternal grandfather, Karl Schweitzer, was an undeniable paternal, super-egolike figure (especially if you go by *The Words*), Sartre, who claimed orphan status, often denied the importance of the Oedipus complex for him. Yet this denial in large part explains the choice of Orestes rather than Oedipus as prototype of the free hero: in *The Words*, the writer pointed out that Orestes was himself as he would have liked to have been. Moreover, we know that while in captivity Sartre reread Sophocles and thus *Electra*, which remains faithful to Aeschylus' *Oresteia*. Even so, the Greek tragedy is greatly modified in *The Flies*: Orestes does not succumb to destiny; he takes responsibility for his act and liberates himself from divine tutelage while he turns tragedy into mocking; moreover, Sartre's Orestes amalgamates certain traits of Oedipus ("plague" for Oedipus, "flies" for Orestes; like Oedipus, Orestes is ready "to do himself the greatest harm").[16]

Yet Orestian revolt is far more radical. To kill his mother and cut the ties with the social group by exiling himself of his own free will makes this man "foreign to himself." He says to Zeus: "Foreign to myself—I know it. Outside nature, against nature, without excuse, beyond remedy except what remedy I find within myself. But I shall not return under your law; I am doomed to have no other law but mine."[17] What does this total refusal of (mother) nature as well as (paternal, civic, divine) law mean? Is it a denial of the oedipal truth? A desire not to know that love draws him to Clytemnestra and rivalry to Agamemnon/Aegisthus/Zeus? In a clinical framework, such a denial opens onto the fragmentation of the subject, and foreignness to oneself turns into psychosis, when it is not sealed off by perversion. From Hitchcock to *A Clockwork Orange*, contemporary art has shown modern Orestes, murderers of their mothers and the law, whose latent or claimed homosexuality is dissimulated in addiction to evil. This interpretive path nevertheless avoids the cruel novelty of Orestes in relation to Oedipus.

The very foundation of identity—that of the social group and its legislation, that of the individual—is challenged here. Whether the critical state of Greek legislation, or the critical state of the European states during World War II, or even the internal crisis of a technological and media-driven society, we are differently and conjointly confronted with a demand. When the symbolic link (political law, as in sated Aegisthus, or divine law, as in mocking Zeus) fails, oedipal revolt is impossible and fails in its dialectical function to construct the subject's autonomy. Condemned henceforth to shatter the most archaic links—those of desire for the mother and even the attachment to natural bio-logical survival—the subject reaches these zones of turbulence that are discord or war: turbulence in oneself, the family, the city, and at the core of being. This radical wretchedness—in counterpoint to Heidegger's "serenity of being"—is what the speaking subject faces. His freedom depends on it, and he assumes its risks, either by compromising himself in crime and its duller variants, corrup-tion and deceit, or by trying to find polyphonic signs of this fragmentation. (This would be the destiny of modern poetry, where, as you may recall, Georges Bataille sought the emblematic figure of Orestes; in painting, Bacon's admira-tion of rotting flesh had the Furies and Orestes in the background). By practic-ing the "disengaged engagement" (as Mauriac said) that Sartre made a new moral code by calling it "freedom," he imparted to it the stigmata of error—or why not say evil?—as its inevitable, if not necessary, condition.

We have no choices other than a beatific moralism or this Orestian path whose risks are atheism and psychosis. But is it really a risk or the necessity of lucid men, which Sartre confronted with pioneering force, conjugating the contemplative life of the philosopher and the active existence of the citizen? The evil is not here, for, you must admit, Sartre's *The Flies* has the advantage of not banalizing evil, or even resorbing it in the reconciliation of an Oedipus who has realized his enigma and soothes himself in order to die in the light of Colonus. It inscribes it ineluctably at the heart of man if he wishes to follow the paths of freedom.

Consider this, from *The War Diaries*: "For example, from the outset I un-doubtedly had a morality without a God—without sin but not without evil."[18] This evil is not even the lesser evil one would use against absolute evil. Instead it is the necessity of evil assumed in total lucidity, the latter being the only thing capable of limiting it and engaging it in the violence of freedom. The other evil, on the contrary, is more pernicious: the kind that stops pointing out evil, evil that suspends the evil that it is, the arrest of the negative. That Sartre did not take this rigor, which he nevertheless posited, to the end could be held against him in hindsight. But who is in a position to do so? Who among us has not stopped at some point or another on a certain path, in certain private labyrinths that today recall the voyages of Oedipus and Orestes? Who has gone to the end, and what does "to the end" mean?

Orestes, in any case, is not a psychoanalytical hero. Oedipal subjects, the subjects of psychoanalysis, are dialecticians who displace the negative, but they do so within the boundaries of identities they wish to be independent, of cities whose laws they cite but whose recognition they seek. However, by exploring border states and social crises, psychoanalysis is henceforth solicited by Orestes: by the strangeness of socialized psychosis, by the art that an excessive fragmentation exhibits, and by the new variants of increasingly unusual, polymorphic, and free intersubjective links. And perhaps by not listening to Orestes, psychoanalysis (always attentive to Oedipus) neglects the modern subjects that we are, the freest among us, the most foreign. Orestes is not an anti-Oedipus; Orestes is the culmination of Oedipus, the completion of his rebellious logic and the announcement of an unthinkable foreignness, "gloriously aloof." I measure my words as I say this, knowing the personal and political risks posed by the destruction of the mind, that is, psychical space: it is not certain that men can develop a civilization of freedom without traversing the danger of this "gloriously aloof mind" that Orestes prefigured, the pinnacles and pitfalls of which Sartre experienced.

Electra is horrified and repudiates her brother, though it was she who suggested the possibility of fighting evil with evil; she feels the same guilt that "the people" feel, while her brother traverses it and opts instead for freedom by loudly claiming responsibility for his act: "I am free, Electra. Freedom has crashed down on me like a thunderbolt. . . . I have done *my* deed, Electra, and that deed was good. I shall bear it on my shoulders as a carrier at a ferry carries the traveler to the farther bank. And when I have brought it to the farther bank I shall take stock of it. The heavier it is to carry, the better pleased I shall be; for that burden is my freedom."[19] He later adds: "I am free. Beyond anguish, beyond remorse. Free. And at one with myself" (p. 149). It is this aspect of existentialist morality that will cause scandal, a radical atheism that was too quickly confused with amoralism. On the contrary, it traverses religious and, more specifically, Christian guilt and proclaims itself an accomplice of violence: "I am no criminal, and you have no power to make me atone for an act I don't regard as a crime" (pp. 150–51). "Suddenly, out of the blue, freedom crashed down on me and swept me off my feet. Nature sprang back. . . . And there was nothing left in heaven, no right or wrong, nor anyone to give me orders" (p. 158), asserts the rebellious hero doomed to freedom. Perhaps now this line from *The War Diaries* will be clearer; it absolutizes the freedom of language rid of clichés and stereotypes—that is, it praises the freedom of literature—at the price of matricide (unless matricide is the price to pay for literature): "I would condemn someone definitively for a linguistic mannerism, but not because I'd seen him murder his mother."[20]

In many of Sartre's plays we find the theme of freedom that entails evil, an evil that is no longer experienced as an evil and even less as a culpable and culpabilizing evil. And yet it is not the "banalization of evil" that Hannah Arendt

deplored when she denounced the Nazis' inaptitude for judgment and freedom. It is the recognition of the necessity of violence, but, more profoundly
still, a recognition of the death drive and the jouissance henceforth called
sadistic that Freud taught us to detect at the boundaries of the psyche and that
Sartre accords a sociological and moral argument.

In *The Respectful Prostitute* (1946), Lizzie encourages the black man to kill
the white man who is threatening to lynch him for a crime he did not commit.
She herself cannot commit, or allow herself to commit, such an disrespectful
act; she remains a slave, a slave of conventional morality, while the black man,
constrained by necessity, assumes his crime in order to obtain his freedom. In
The Devil and the Good Lord, Goetz does evil for evil's sake and claims to be
the devil. To commit evil in its pure state corresponds to the temptation of the
absolute and the refusal of the world that does not want him. When Heinrich
asks him why he betrayed his brother Conrad, he replies: "Because I like
things to be clear-cut. . . . I am a self-made man. I was a bastard by birth, but
the fair title of fratricide I owe to no one but myself."[21] One might say his illegitimacy situates him naturally among the marginal and the excluded, but it
is assuming his fraticidal act, being aware of his antinature, that allows him to
assume his freedom.

The theme of the bastard also appears in Sartre's adaptation of *Kean*, a play
by Alexandre Dumas, named after the English actor born in London in 1787.
An illegitimate child, Kean became one of the great actors of the period, the
best interpreter of Shakespeare. By reflecting on the copresence of illegitimacy
and the condition of the actor, Sartre constructed his conception of the intellectual as one who refuses origins and naturalism and of subjectivity as a permanent conquest of freedom. Thus, for example, through betrayal, deception,
and evil, Jean Genet would become "saint" and "martyr." Illegitimacy, games,
and the actor would be markers in the asceticism of the intellectual such as
Sartre perceived it. "Do you understand that I want to weigh with my real
weight in the world?" Kean asks in a series of monologues that highlight his
conception of the actor as a synthesis, a trompe l'oeil virtuality; he thus reveals
not his presumed outlaw perversion but the secret and essential character of
all consciousness that negativizes facts, acts, and objects and that, by recon-
structing them in the imagination, is asserted as fatally free. True revolt—that
of Kean the bastard and that other bastard/artist, the writer Genet—does not
reside therefore in a particular act targeting a particular object. It lies in the repeated representation of this act, which extracts it from its reality and confers
on it the imaginary power of a re-creation. It draws its ultimately political value
from its nullity, its impersonal nothingness, the actor's paradox that thwarts
the presentation of identity and opens the way to projections and multiple
interpretations.

Do you understand that I want to weigh with my real weight in the world? That I have had enough of being a shadow in a magic lantern? For twenty years I have been acting a part to amuse you all. Can't you understand that I want to live my own life? . . . But why can I be nothing? . . . Between your admiration and your scorn, you are destroying me. . . . Come, sir, you need not be afraid. It was only Kean the actor, acting the part of Kean the man. . . . There was nobody on stage. No one. Or perhaps an actor playing the part of Kean playing the part of Othello. . . . I am not alive—I only pretend.[22]

Truth as Game

The possibility of a putting to death (Orestes), here applied to the self (Kean), thus leads to the polyphonic identity of the actor: inessential, it marginalizes perhaps, but it is the only path of freedom that Sartre sees in the face of political and ideological burdens. "You cannot become an actress," Kean says to Anna. "Do you think you have to act well? Do I act well? Do I look as though I could work hard? You are born an actor as you are born a prince. [Truth is a matter of game playing, not of nature or becoming.] And determination and hard work have nothing to do with that fact. . . . You cannot act to earn your living. You act to lie, to deceive, to deceive yourself, to be what you cannot be, and because you have had enough of being what you are" (p. 199).

Here, in the form of a theatrical dialogue, we have an aspect of Sartre's debate with Heideggerian philosophy. Being, on the horizon of freedom and in relation to the classical subject? But a being uprooted ceaselessly by its confrontation with nonbeing. The bastard/actor/intellectual continuously betrays being and struggles against it relentlessly, through negativity, in nonbeing. The verb "to lie" that Sartre uses in the passage I have just quoted is not to be taken as a moral term; "to lie" means "to play games" in opposition to the identity of being. Sartre called for permanent disidentification, which constitutes the permanent and necessary crime against identity itself.

"You act because you want to forget yourself. You act the hero because you are a coward at heart, and you play the saint because you are a devil by nature. You act a murderer because you long to poison your best friend. You act because you are a born liar and totally unable to speak the truth." No single role is possible in itself. The love of truth as well as the hatred of it are traps in which the intellectual/bastard/actor cannot be caught. The actor succeeds best, for he plays them all against each other unremittingly: morality against antimorality, love against hate, truth against the hatred of truth. "You act because you would go mad if you didn't act. Act! Do I know myself when I am acting? Is there ever a moment when I cease to act? Look at me; do I hate all women or am I acting at hating them? Am I acting to make you afraid?" (pp.

199–200). The thematics of acting will end up replacing that of the criminal, heralded initially, or that of evil, as the optimal way to emerge from the conformism and fixedness of being. In the context of the apotheosis of the game — an unprecedented rehabilitation of the ludic — Sartre would write his impressive *Saint Genet: Actor and Martyr* in 1952, in which he sanctified the myth of the actor or, if you like, the impostor who takes control of the spectacle in order to thwart it.[23]

In these texts, which are insufficiently read today, we find unusual resonances with what history has revealed to us since World War II — Sartre's crucible and that of his generation — but also resonances with analytical investigation. Via completely different paths from philosophical argumentation on morality and authenticity, psychoanalysis — Lacanian breakthroughs in the clinic of "as if," "false self," or "borderline" personalities — has taught us that subjectivity is constructable: that it is formed of projection/identification in mimeticism and "pretending," that pretense is *one* path toward truth, not *the* truth but the necessary accumulation and deflagration on the way to the difficult, impossible truth.

"What about the society of the spectacle?" the well-informed among you will ask, readers of Guy Debord. Sartre was not a man of the spectacle, although the spectacle used him; his thought was concerned with an ideological stage and political choices that the society of the spectacle diminished, when it didn't sweep them aside. But if you reread his writings on the actor and the bastard in the light of your television screens, you will be surprised to find a contemporary in old Sartre. By thwarting the trap of identity, by praising the inauthenticity of the impostor who asserts himself as such in order to unmask the good and bad faith of pretenders to conventional authenticity, Sartre had already launched a message that continues to incite fear: namely, that there is no possible exit from the spectacle, except by traversing it in full awareness and therefore only by thwarting it, surely not by ignoring it or playing it naively or cynically.

Characters as Spokespeople in the Philosophical Novel

The long line of Sartrean characters who rebel against identity and the fixity of the social link seems to me to find its most political expression in the trilogy of *The Roads to Freedom*, in the character of Mathieu.[24] You remember that, taking refuge in a church, he was surrounded by Germans. Surrendering would be the only way to save himself; instead, he starts shooting with an irrepressible and joyous ferocity. We are no longer in the game but in the double of the game.

I do not want you to get the impression, in what I am saying about sem-blance and the game, of a facile superficiality, an artificial lightness that would not truly engage the subject. What Sartre teaches us, on the contrary, with *The Roads to Freedom, Saint Genet*, and *Kean* is that the experience of the game can be extremely violent, for the stakes are nothing other than the death of the other and of the self as condition of independence and sometimes life. If I am writing about Sartre here, it is precisely to allow you to glimpse the imaginary as revolt, in order to restore this violence underlying the game, which has nothing decorative or "spectacular" about it. What emerges in Sartre's work is a proximity, a complicity, between Mathieu and Kean, between the actor and the writer Genet, between the impostor and the actor, between the bastard and the resistance fighter or militant: all play roles continuously in order to show that freedom is an imaginary experience that is a violent experience and that one cannot dissociate these two aspects of the rebellious hero: Orestes/Math-ieu, on the one hand, and Kean/Genet, on the other.

Consider this from *Troubled Sleep*:

[Mathieu] approached the parapet and stood there firing. This was revenge on a big scale; each one of his shots wiped out some ancient scruple. One for Lola, whom I dared not rob, one for Marcelle, whom I ought to have ditched, one for Odette, whom I didn't want to screw. This for the books I never dared to write, this for the journeys I never made. This for everybody in general whom I wanted to hate and tried to understand. He fired, and the tables of the law crashed about him—Thou shalt love thy neighbor as your-self—bang! in that bastard's face—Thou shalt not kill—bang! at that scare-crow opposite. He was firing on his fellow men, on Virtue, on the whole world: Liberty is Terror. The *mairie* was ablaze, his head was ablaze; bullets were whining around him, free as the air. The world is going up in smoke, and me with it. He fired; he looked at his watch: fourteen minutes and thirty seconds. Nothing more to ask of fate now except one half-minute, time enough to fire at that smart officer, at all the Beauty of the Earth, at the street, at the flowers, at the gardens, at everything he had loved. Beauty dived downwards obscenely, and Mathieu went on firing. He fired: he was cleansed, he was all-powerful, he was free. Fifteen minutes.   (p. 256)

This paroxysmal mise-en-scène, whose pathos might offend good taste, has the advantage of allowing the foundation of the imaginary act to come to the sur-face, which in my reading of Proust and in more Freudian terms I have called sadomasochism. Here, in existentialist terms, Sartre speaks of revenge against classical values—Virtue, Christian morals, Beauty—but, at the same time, this is not just vengeance against moralism or the constraints others impose on the self but also a putting to death of the self as a unitary or monovalent conscience. Of the liberation of the self—also to be understood this way: how does one liberate oneself from the self?—that is part and parcel of the annihilation of the self. Read Sartre in this perspective, for apart from him and a few rare psychoanalysts, who today will present you with the annihilation that is the condition for all psychical and practical renewal and resurrection? Transpose Mathieu's scene to *Kean* and *Genet*, and you will understand that this game of masks, which is imaginary freedom, is indissociable from violence against the identity of the self and others and that the risk of this violence may certainly be replastered with the cynicism of imposture but it returns to us beyond this risk as a critical requirement without which humanity loses the sense of its adventure.

To return to the complicity among the bastard, actor, and intellectual, the bastard's temptation, in Sartre's language, is to conquer his being, which is refused him because he has no identity, but to conquer it in evil; that is, he must continue to do evil to others and to himself in order to rise to the level of this being that is refused him and that he will nevertheless reconquer through the negativity of his consciousness. This leads the subject, who is indissolubly bastard/actor/intellectual, to struggle against the morality of others as well as the plenitude of being. Sartrean negativity is doubly oriented: toward others and toward being. Mathieu shoots the Germans, "self-righteousness," and, more fundamentally, serenity of being itself. Yet the morality of the other and of being recaptures him relentlessly and mercilessly. It cannot be escaped. And this is where Sartre's existentialist drama is played out. The Sartrean subject—this antihero—cannot *not* struggle against the other and being, but neither can he escape them. The other and being always recapture us, in a way. They mystify us as they mystify the Sartrean hero just when he thinks he is free to despise them. Pure being does not exist: no one can identify with being and the other, thinking they can master them. To want to be pure (not a bastard, not an actor, not an intellectual) is a new trap of being and of the other as authentic self, as natural identity, as untouchable entity. There is no serene state or entity in Sartrean thought; negativity itself, if it were accidentally crystallized as such, as being "itself," would fall into the trap of being. All it can do is criticize itself permanently. If we follow this logic, if we consider that any stopping, any serenity, any stasis in the process of negativity is already a trap, we understand not only that identity is impossible but that love is impossible, because lucidity leads us to see in all love an interminable comedy and to play tricks on love so as not to be caught in the trap of idyllic amorous repose.

The Sartrean universe is split: on the one hand, there are the idiots and cowards who fall into the trap of identity every time, into the trap of the other, the gaze of the other and, symmetrically, of being, of identity itself; on the other hand, there is refusal and, after this refusal, repeated negativity and solitude. The last hero I will discuss here is the absolute representative of this: Roquentin, the narrator of *Nausea*, an unextraordinary individual who is nevertheless confronted with his own consciousness and with the impossibility of this consciousness. This juxtaposition of the consciousness (insofar as it confers an existence) and the negativization of this consciousness (as permanent and corrosive lucidity) comes up against the sense of existence and by dissolving it in disgust appends to it . . . the beauty of the music shared among the writer, the Negress, and the Jew. Thus the certitude of existing, which might afford some a feeling of grace, happiness, or simply joy, arouses in Roquentin nausea: the Sartrean version of negativized plenitude. Leaving aside any psychoanalytical explication we might obviously attempt (which would take into account Sartre's childhood, his so-called ugliness, his sexuality), Sartre chooses nausea as an emblem of existence. Nausea and not grace is the metaphor of the unfulfilled and the open, of the negative and the impossible, of being and the other. Nausea inscribes the trace of refusal in existence.

Roquentin starts out as an intellectual preparing a book on the marquis Adhémar de Rollebon. As an author of historical novels, he aspires modestly or ambitiously but always very ethically to preserve someone's memory. He goes to the library, which allows him to objectivize the other in History, in the past to which he intends to devote his consciousness and, of course, his critical sense. But gradually, as the plot develops, Roquentin gives up ordering the past of the other and becomes more and more interested in what surrounds him: the quotidian and banal present, objects, and his own body—in short, his personal existence. There is also an acerbic and biting critique of the man engaged in humanistic socialism, the Self-Taught Man, this ridiculous man that each of us more or less is. The Self-Taught Man represents this impassable thing that is adherence to values, limited by definition, to which Sartre/Roquentin will contrast the raw truths of existence: the endless nausea that defies both values and the comprehension of the traditional intellectual, who believed, at the beginning of the novel, that he had to pursue his work as an archaeologist of the past and thought. Instead, it is from the junction between being and negative consciousness that nausea is born, nausea that is impossible to resorb and that Roquentin sees as being man's sole reality, as the rebellious man in his solitude perceives it and perpetuates it. In his solitude, he comes up against the unshakable feeling of existence by observing that the human body is a residue in the face of being. Having nevertheless become aware to the point of disgust that these residues of tangible thought are the true roots of his isolation, he makes it a rebellious attitude that, from now on, has nothing pathetic or romantic about it but announces itself as a perseverance in strangeness and refusal: "I want to leave, go to some place where I will be really in my own niche, where I will fit in. . . . But my place is nowhere; I am unwanted, *de trop*," Roquentin says.[25] And starting with this life given to him "for no reason," he casts a caustic glance at the "idiots" around him, reveals the strangeness of the human comedy, and describes nausea as a feeling that is neither pride nor shame but exile.

Novel-as-Philosophy

A "Melancholic" Philosopher Reveals the Border States of Nausea

To make theater is certainly a political act: it is a question of acting on the public, mobilizing the presence of living bodies, which the book cannot do. But let us not be too quick to say that the theater of an intellectual like Sartre anticipates the desire to establish his party or media popularity, as it would later be known. To such intentions, which are always possible and more or less unconscious, I would add the challenge represented by the very type of representation Sartre brings into play in his theater. Take the characters, these intellectuals/actors/traitors/bastards. What we see here is a philosophical option embodied in a rhetoric of the spokesperson, which is surprising in itself, for the bourgeois and homogeneous theatrical audience did not recognize in this the psychological density of the realistic characters it was used to applauding. In Sartre, the characters are the spokespeople of a situation that is the true subject; it was a small step from this to the accusation that his theater was "too intellectual." No doubt aware of this criticism, Sartre himself offered if not a justification than at least an explanation in *What Is Literature?*:

> The theater was formerly a theater of "characters." More or less complex, but complete, figures appeared on the stage, and the situation had no other function but to put these characters into conflict and to show how each of them was modified by the action of the others. I have elsewhere shown how important changes have taken place in this domain; many authors are returning to the theater of situation. [Sartre was not alone in bringing about this change, which was also occurring in modern theater in the works of Pirandello and Brecht.] No more characters; the heroes are freedoms caught in a trap like all of us. [They are disembodied in order to show the inconsistency

of the pretension to identity, History, and being.] What are the issues? Each character will be nothing but the choice of an issue and will equal no more than the chosen issue. [Also, the absence of psychological density is itself a revolt against the lie of a global, social, or metaphysical solution.] In a sense, each situation is a trap—there are walls everywhere. [And in this trap a path will emerge, necessarily forced but the only one.] I've expressed myself poorly: there are no issues to *choose*. An issue is invented. And each one, by inventing his own issue, invents himself. Man must be invented each day.[26]

This forced path and this rage of permanent invention that may appear schematic are signs—within the dramatic construction itself—of the philosophical and political necessity of ceaselessly inventing freedom.

Sartre's plays come after *Nausea* chronologically, but I thought it wise to begin with the theater, for it seems to me to introduce more directly—more dramatically and more schematically in the sense I have just mentioned—what is addressed in *Nausea*, this novel whose thunderous impact has yet to be fully measured in the realm of French literature. *Being and Nothingness* can only be understood in light of this novelistic, imaginary experience of an analogous problematic that these two books deal with in different ways: the copresence of being and nothingness in the existence of the subject.

Sartre borrows the epigraph of *Nausea* from Céline, whose work and the importance of abjection in it I have had occasion to comment on.[27] The sentence that Sartre takes from the Célinean "opera of the flood" simply emphasizes, instead, the solitude of the individual who no longer has anything in common with any collectivity: "He is a boy without collective importance, barely an individual." [This epigraph, which does not appear in the U.S. edition of *Nausea*, reads in French: "C'est un garçon sans importance collective, c'est tout juste un individu."—Trans.] His links with the collectivity are broken, whether by him or by others is of no importance. The philosopher seized the subject in this state of absolute desolation that is as much a freedom as the mediocrity of anyone at all. I emphasize this vision of the subject that Sartre would later describe as "individuality," which is the vision of a certain metaphysics of freedom whose limitations nonetheless reveal truths. In this case, it is the truth of depression for psychoanalysis, this copresence of being and nothingness, that Roquentin's existence unveils. Roquentin sends us back to the depressive solitude of the contemporary individual. It is rooted in the personal experience of the impossible link to the other that is ultimately the maternal object, although the dissolution of all other social links follows from this microuniverse. Naturally, this depressivity may also refer to social history: national crisis, ideological and political conflicts, World War II. It is not surprising that Dürer's *Melancholia* was used for the cover of the first edition of the book. Indeed, the author had initially chosen "Melancholia" as the title; it was Gaston Gallimard who proposed the repulsive "Nausea." The logic of repulsion, which underlies the melancholic appearance, prevailed: the public followed, not at all disgusted to know more about what disgusts it. As for Sartre, he was haunted by this negativity, which he would develop in *Being and Nothingness*: being inhabited by nothingness is accessible only in nausea.

The Rejection of Being as "Other" or "Past"

The novel begins, as I said, with the story of the intellectual Roquentin grappling with his work. He wants to write the history of Rollebon, a marquis involved a number of intrigues and implicated in the "necklace affair," who disappeared in 1790 before turning up in Russia. There, Sartre explains, he "attempts to assassinate Paul I. . . . In 1813, he returns to Paris. By 1816, he has become all-powerful. . . . In 1820, . . . he is at the height of distinction. . . . Seven months later, accused of treason, . . . he is thrown into a cell, where he dies after five years of imprisonment, without ever being brought to trial."[28]

At first, the intellectual tries to apprehend being in the form of the past: a perfectly commendable practice (anyone planning to write a thesis on a personage of the *past*, a writer, preferably, is in the same situation as Sartre's narrator; in short, all scholars are Roquentins at their beginnings). In effect, however, Sartre challenged this cliché of the solitary person grappling with being as past. How? By showing that Roquentin's existential experiences (take "existential" in its simplest sense: his daily existence, his love affairs with women, walking down the street, encounters with nature, and particularly his encounter with the Self-Taught Man) gradually cause him to become detached from his initial objective and give up wanting to write. He will no longer apprehend being in the form of the other or the past but will confront the implication of nothingness in raw existence that nausea reveals to him. Roquentin will start by feeling "unwanted": "My place is nowhere," he says, "I am unwanted, *de trop*." He will experience the ontological solitude described in *Being and Nothingness*: no links, nothing in common with others. This will lead him in a grimacing, caricatured way to unveil the dissatisfaction and falsity at the heart of his own adventures as well as in those of others: the falsehood of the amorous link. Moreover, the pathos of the "humanist" reaches its peak in the character of the Self-Taught Man: humble before knowledge, registered with the Socialist Party to spread good in the world, ashamed of his homosexuality, taken to task by the Corsican supervisor for approaching young boys in the library where he works. Faced with this definitive collapse of good intentions, whether political or erotic, Roquentin is confronted with the same nausea that the roots of the chestnut trees summon in him, the roots that revealed to him the inaccessible residue of an existence that is unthinkable and yet felt in its nothingness. Submerged in nausea, he betrays the society of men, withdraws into his solitude, and ends up considering his life, Life, a harsh, unjustifiable phenomenon, "a contingency . . . given for no reason." If it is true that he is still part of humanity, "he is foreign," the author writes. When all is said and done, nausea does not quash being but reveals the strangeness of being as well as of the self. Like Roquentin coming up against his radically intransmissible and unjustifiable existence, being is radically foreign: connection and communication are of no help in the face of the unassimilated foreignness of existence, the border state experienced by someone who ultimately frees himself of contingencies. Nausea bears witness not only to the human comedy but also, in the end, to the irremediableness of existence that resists intellection and exchange.

Consider this: "M. de Rollebon was my partner; he needed me in order to exist and I needed him so as not to feel my existence." By escaping in the other, "I" hide what is unbearable about my existence from myself. But Roquentin resists this flight that would mean occupying himself with Rollebon so as not to be occupied with his own nonexistence or his own difficulty with existence. "I furnished the raw material, this material I had to re-sell, which I didn't know what to do with: existence, *my* existence." He continues to seek the opaque remnant that is not transmitted in communication with the other. "His part was to have an imposing appearance. He stood in front of me, took up my life to *lay bare* his own to me" (p. 98).

Take your own situation: You are interested in certain matters concerning existence while at the same time occupied here with literary representation. Now, existence is what resists representation, is concealed from it. This remnant that eludes representation persists precisely as existence. But those who have access to it are few, those who are not caught up and taken in by the net of representation. Roquentin, too, is caught up in the artifices of his work as an archivist, enclosed within stories and missing out on existence outside of representation; he is nevertheless plagued by doubt—the negative lies in wait!— which will lead him to nausea. "He [the Marquis] stood in front of me, took up my life to *lay bare* his own to me. I did not notice that I existed any more, I no longer existed in myself, but in him." In this mirror game, the "I" of the narrator delegates himself in Rollebon, as a graduate student delegates himself in the author who might be the subject of his thesis: and the graduate student no longer exists; the thesis subject exists in his place. "I ate for him, breathed for him, each of my movements had its sense outside, there, just in front of me, in him; I no longer saw my hand writing letters on the paper, not even the sentence I had written — but behind, beyond the paper, I saw the Marquis, who had claimed this gesture as his own, the gesture which prolonged, consolidated his existence. I was only a means of making him live" (p. 98).

Sartre questions the human being's becoming a "tool" (a "means") in action, insofar as all action is based on projection and comprises alienation. As soon you start preparing something, a thesis or anything else, you are instrumentalized, you are only there *for* this action, *for* someone or something else, be it an object, a thesis, or an act that may even be very commendable, very humanistic. However extraordinary a good intention may be, an obstacle arises concerning the complexity of the subject and his relation to existence: "I was only a means of making him [Rollebon] live, he was my reason for living, he had delivered me from myself."

But who does this self think it is? you might ask. Does it take itself for an absolute sovereign by detaching itself from others and from being as if wanting to dominate them? You would be right to express this objection. Yet before becoming negativized in nausea, the rebellious self must posit itself precisely in its excessive sovereignty. In effect, given the state of alienation one arrives at in social exchanges, one might raise the question of the value of the self and restore to it unrepresentable logics that elude representation as well as alienating links with the other. Here is what Roquentin says: "He [Rollebon, the other, the past] had delivered me from myself. What shall I do now? Above all, not move, not move. . . . Ah! I could not prevent this movement of the shoulders. . . . The thing which was waiting was on the alert, it has pounced on me, it flows through me, I am filled with it. It's nothing." Thus, all of a sudden, having rejected what he was there for, what he was working on (that is, Rollebon or any other project), Roquentin is filled with another dynamic that at first sweeps away his ego but ultimately liberates it and allows him to attain the "thing" that he *is* and that is *nothing*: this plenitude of nausea that cannot be objectified. "It's nothing: I am the Thing. Existence, liberated, detached, floods over me. I exist." One could call this negative ecstasy a hollow narcissism, a melancholic jouissance in the withdrawal into the self emptied of objects, as well as a moment of rupture with alienating links. It is, however, simultaneously a moment of revalorization. Based on what? Based on creativity unbound and unalienated: melancholic nausea may start a psychical, physical, and creative rebirth. "I exist. It's sweet, so sweet, so slow. And light: you'd think it floated all by itself. It stirs. It brushes by me, melts and vanishes. Gently, gently. There is bubbling water in my mouth. I swallow. It slides down my throat, it caresses me — and now it comes up again into my mouth. For ever I shall have a little pool of whitish water in my mouth—lying low—grazing my tongue. And this pool is still me. And the tongue. And the throat is me" (p. 98).

In the mouth that tastes but also vomits, Roquentin is—we are—at the borders of valorization/devalorization: "I" has extricated itself from the other, "I" has found "me," and this "me" is sweet but repulsive; "I" seize it in its very ambiguity.

> I see my hand spread out on the table. It lives—it is me. It opens, the fingers open and point. It is lying on its back. It shows me its fat belly. It looks like an animal turned upside down. The fingers are the paws. I amuse myself by moving them, very rapidly, like the claws of a crab which has fallen on its back. The crab is dead [The theme of repulsion becomes clear.]: The claws draw up and close over the belly of my hand. I see the nails—the only part of me that doesn't live. . . . I draw back my hand and put it in my pocket; but immediately I feel the warmth of my thigh through the stuff. . . . I jump up: it would be much better if I could only stop thinking. Thoughts are the dullest things.   (pp. 98–99)

It is not just the mouth or even the body: thought itself is shaped by these ambiguities and this insipidness that provokes both adhesion and disadhesion, which is nothing other than nausea.

> Duller than flesh. They stretch out and there's no end to them and they leave a funny taste in the mouth. Then there are words, inside the thoughts, unfinished words, a sketchy sentence which constantly returns: "I have to fi . . . I ex . . . Dead . . . M. de Roll is dead . . . I am not . . . I ex . . ." . . . For example, this sort of painful rumination: I *exist*, I am the one who keeps it up. I. The body lives by itself once it has begun. But thought—I am the one who continues it, unrolls it. I exist. . . . If only I could keep myself from thinking! I try, and succeed: my head seems to fill with smoke . . . *I am the one* who pulls myself from the nothingness to which I aspire: the hatred, the disgust of existing, there are as many ways to *make* myself exist, to submerge myself in existence.   (p. 99)

At the Border of Being and Nonbeing

Nausea, the border between being and nonbeing, colors the flesh and thought of the speaker but also the cosmos that shelters him: the chestnut trees, their absurdity, and the gratuitousness of existence as a whole.

The roots of the chestnut tree were sunk in the ground just under my bench. I couldn't remember it was a root any more. The words had vanished and with them the significance of things, their methods of use. . . . I was sitting, stooping forward, head bowed, alone in front of this black, knotty mass, entirely beastly, which frightened me. Then I had this vision. . . . The chestnut tree pressed itself against my eyes. Green rust covered it half-way up; the bark, black and swollen, looked like boiled leather. The sound of the water in the Masqueret Fountain sounded in my ears, made a nest there, filled them with sighs; my nostrils overflowed with a green, putrid odour. . . . *In the way*, the chestnut tree there, opposite me, a little to the left. . . . The word absurdity is coming to life under my pen; a little while ago, in the garden, I couldn't find it, but neither was I looking for it, I didn't need it: I thought without words, *on* things, *with* things. Absurdity was not an idea in my head, or the sound of a voice, only this long serpent dead at my feet, this wooden serpent. Serpent or claw or root or vulture's talon, what difference does it make. . . . I made an experiment with the absolute or the absurd. This root—there was nothing in relation to which it was absurd. . . . I had not seen the seeds sprout, or the tree grow. But faced with this great wrinkled paw, neither ignorance nor knowledge was important: the world of explanations and reasons is not the world of existence. . . . This root, on the other hand, existed in such a way that I could not explain it. Knotty, inert, nameless, it fascinated me, filled my eyes, brought me back unceasingly to its own existence. In vain to repeat: "This is a root"—it didn't work any more. I saw clearly that you could not pass from its function as a root, as a breathing pump, *to that*, to this hard and compact skin of a sea lion, to this oily, callous, headstrong look. . . . This moment was extraordinary. I was there, motionless and icy, plunged in a horrible ecstasy. But something fresh had just appeared in the very heart of this ecstasy; I understood the Nausea, I possessed it. To tell the truth, I did not formulate my discoveries myself. But I think it would be easy for me to put them in words now. The essential thing is contingency. I mean that one cannot define existence as necessity. To exist is simply to be there; those who exist let themselves be encountered, but you can never deduce anything from them. I believe there are people who have understood this. Only they tried to overcome this contingency by inventing a necessary, casual being. But no necessary being can explain existence: contingency is not a delusion, a probability which can be dissipated; it is the absolute, consequently, the perfect free gift. All is free, this park, this city and myself. When you realize that, it turns your heart upside down and everything begins to float, as the other evening at the "Railwaymen's Rendezvous": here is Nausea; here there is what those bastards— the ones on the Côteau Vert and others—try to hide from themselves with their idea of their rights.   (pp. 126–129, 131)

I will conclude by emphasizing the brilliant return that Sartre makes us undergo at the melancholic state by transforming nausea, which is the "gustatory" perception of it, into a position of revolt. Aristotle diagnosed melancholia as the malady of genius or geniuses. If there is a reason to establish such a link, it is not the spleen of romantic states of mind that demonstrates it but indeed this Sartrean nausea that leads subjectivity to a melancholia in the Freudian sense of the term: that is, to the subject/object, language/affect, sense/non-sense *borders*.[29] To write a novel with *that* was quite something!

I am not sure we are still capable of reading the masterpiece that is *Nausea* in all its implications. Because of the minimalism that reigns in the French market, the philosophical novel—which was once a prestigious national tradition—is no longer French: there are no more French philosophical novels. Apart from Sollers, who still writes philosophical novels, and who can read them?

In Search of an Authentic Practice

Being-as-Other

I would now like to take up certain aspects of *Being and Nothingness*. Let me remind you of the date: 1943. As you might imagine, it is a difficult work for students of literature but indispensable in pinpointing the problematic of revolt that I am trying to explore here. We often come across notions like "being," "the other," or "the negative" used wantonly under the pretense of borrowing from Lacan, when a solid genealogy traces them back to Hegel or Heidegger—it is to them that Sartre mainly refers—and the Sartre-Lacan proximity has not yet been thought out in postwar France. Don't we often have a tendency to psychologize the notion of the other, for example? This even happens to analysts. Now, it is not a matter of placing the psychoanalytical dimension over psychological functioning. It is a matter of salvaging the notions of being and the other in their transmetaphysical dimension in order to situate them later in treatment and also to understand the stakes of writing, which is my primary concern here.

From Husserl to Hegel; or, From "Knowledge" to "Consciousness"

I will therefore present to you Sartre's definition of being and the negative, in which the relationship to the other is inscribed. But to arrive at Sartrean definitions, one cannot avoid a few encounters with Husserl and Hegel. The voyage through Husserl and Hegel allowed Sartre to establish a difference between the dimension of being and that of knowledge, which is correlative to it but distinct from it. Thus he went back to Descartes's *Cogito*, from which and in which knowledge is deployed, but he distinguished being as it appears in *ergo sum* to say that the being of this "I am" of *consciousness* is not necessarily that of logical or cognitive *knowledge*, although all positivist philosophy has been able to articulate "thought" and the "world" in logical formulas (which is also what cognitivism does today). Sartre first pointed out Husserl's failure, which, he told us, was to take being for knowledge, to telescope the two sides of this fundamental enunciation of philosophical modernity that the Cartesian formula is. Sartre's reasoning is more radical still in his debate with Hegel. Sartre revealed what he saw as Hegel's failure, although he recognized that Hegel placed the debate on its true plane, namely, that he was the first to differentiate between "consciousness" and "knowledge" (it is one of his major contributions). "Consciousness is a concrete being *sui generis*. . . . It is selfness and not the seat of an opaque, useless Ego. The very *being* of consciousness, since it is independent of knowledge, pre-exists its truth. . . . Consciousness *was there* before being known."[30]

Sartre then becomes interested in conflict, in the famous Hegelian negativity (follow the thread of revolt that I never quite abandon even while leading you down the very abstract paths of this philosophical argumentation!), particularly the equally famous dialectic of the master and the slave. Sartre retains the essential "moment" that Hegel calls being-for-the-Other, which is a fundamental stage of self-consciousness: "The road of interiority passes through the Other," an other, however, that is an other for me, that is, another Me, subjected to the ego in this dialectic of recognition that links master to slave and vice versa. "The Other appears along with myself since self-consciousness is identical with itself by means of the exclusion of every Other. . . . It is only insofar as each man is opposed to the Other that he is absolutely for himself" (p. 236). I have no representation/knowledge of my interiority except through the other who mirrors it. This supposes that at the end of these reflections we observe a common measure between us. The master is contrasted to the slave, the slave is contrasted to the master, but they are both linked in a pact, the possible comparison between the same and the other; they exist through each other; they *are* insofar as they are united, a permanent provocation, an insoluble dialectic. We come to the idea that, beyond the apparent opposition between the same and the other, even in the paroxysmal forms of bloody war between master and slave, we are obliged to recognize a common link so that the comparison can occur, a common measure that constitutes the dialectical link between me and him. If being is being for the other, it is a permanent revolt, which Sartre formulates this way: "The very being of self-consciousness is such that in its being, its being is in question." This "pure interiority" does not cease to question itself; "it is perpetually a reference to a *self* which it has to be" (p. 241). As for the consciousness of the other, it is opaque to self-consciousness: the Other's consciousness is that which I can only contemplate. The Other is forged in a "pure given" instead of being "what has to be me." Because the only consciousness that appears to me in its own temporalization is mine, where it loses objectivity, we will say along with Sartre that "the *for-itself* as for-itself cannot be known by the Other" (p. 242). Consciousness thus comes up against two major obstacles: the separation of consciousnesses (their plurality) and the conflict of consciousnesses.

Here is the essential solitude that *Nausea* echoes and that, in the philosophical text, leads to the observation of an ontological solitude of being in the world. I will examine this reasoning a bit more closely.

The Inaccessible Other: The Scandal of the Plurality of Consciousnesses

In order to apprehend the other as subject, "I" must apprehend it in its interiority, while, on the contrary, the "Other-as-a-mirror" never appears to me in its own interiority but only in the Time of the World. The common measure envisaged by Hegel between me and the other is revealed to be an "ontological optimism" and according to Sartre ends in failure: "*Between the Other-as-object and Me-as-subject, there is no common measure.*" It is not through *knowledge* but through *transcendent consciousness* that "this apprehension of myself by myself" occurs. But this "ekstatic self-consciousness" apprehends the other only "as an object pointing to me." There is no common measure, therefore, but a separation between the "other-as-object" and "me-as-subject." Sartre concludes: "No universal knowledge can be derived from the relation of consciousnesses. This is what we shall call their ontological separation" (p. 243).

There is a more fundamental optimism in Hegel, however. The identicalness of consciousnesses is established in the Whole: there is a global force that posits a Whole outside consciousnesses, considering them from the point of view of this absolute Whole that has become a "mediator" among consciousnesses but also between consciousnesses and the world. If Hegel can posit this Whole, however, it is because it already *is* at the outset. It is therefore not in consciousness but in being that I can posit the problem of the other. We are back at the *Cogito*. The being of the other cannot be found through knowledge but solely as transcendence: "If . . . the being of my consciousness is strictly irreducible to knowledge, then *I cannot transcend my being toward a re-*

ciprocal and universal relation in which I could see my being and that of others as equivalent. On the contrary, I must establish myself *in my being* and posit the problem of the Other in terms of my being" (pp. 243–44; emphasis mine). In other words, I can transcend myself toward a Whole, but I cannot establish myself in this Whole; we are henceforth dealing with the multiplicity or separation of consciousnesses: "The separation and conflict of consciousnesses will remain" (p. 244).

From now on, my relationship to the other is not one of knowledge to knowledge but being to being. "My relation to the Other is first and fundamentally a relation of being to being, not of knowledge to knowledge" (p. 244). I ask you to contemplate this: who has drawn the consequences of this? Surely not the cognitivists, who return at best to Husserl and who assault us with strategies of cognition that are refinements of *cogitation*, not analyses of consciousness. The *analysis* of consciousness was done by Freud, who exposed in it the veritable negativity that is that of the unconscious and its "other scene," its heterogeneous logic, including the drive. But Sartre did not want to deal with this, while at the same time being one of the rare writers to refer—obliquely—to psychoanalysis. By the same token, psychoanalysts would do well to reread this Sartrean debate concerning "knowledge," "consciousness," and "being" when they try painstakingly to define the other, confining it within strategies of knowledge and knowing intersubjectivity.

If it is true that Sartre stopped to consider the Freudian discovery and the as-yet-unexplored terrain it opened up, we might also say that what he calls the scandal of the plurality of consciousnesses is precisely what leads him to literature, specifically to the novel, whose fabric is constituted of singularities: fragmentation, separation, and the conflict of consciousnesses. Only literature can restore "my hawthorn blossoms," "my characters" (Mme Verdurin, M. de Charlus, etc.), singularities issued from my own and altered. Being then disperses its generality and, in the pages of Proust, for example, as in *Nausea*, dissolves in the superimposition of characters and sensory words such as "nausea."

Mit-Sein: *Sartre, Reader of Heidegger*

Let us continue with Sartre but alongside Heidegger this time: a Heidegger who profited from the philosophy of Husserl and Hegel, particularly in *Being and Time*. In order to remain within the Hegelian problematic of the other, Sartre stopped at the notion of *Mit-Sein*: "being-with." Heidegger interests him here insofar as he is thinking about the accessibility or inaccessibility of the other. "Being-with" is the test of my being. Note that it is neither my knowledge nor my consciousness but an "essential being" on which "human realities" depend, insofar as the other "throws me outside of myself" toward structures that, as Sartre pointed out, both escape me and define me and originally reveal the other. It is thus by examining myself in my being, in my singularity, that I find myself originally other, that is, different and irreducible. However, Sartre's reading of Heidegger, this solitude of being, cast out, does not stop at this observation. Being still looks for a way toward the other. *Being-in-the-world* is structured on the mode of "being-with." The structure does not come from outside, in a totalitarian manner, as in Hegel. Although Heidegger does not start from the *Cogito*, he discovers *being-with* at the same time that he observes *being-in*: "I discover the transcendental relation to the Other as constituting my own being, just as I discovered that being-in-the-world measures my human-reality." And again: "the Other is the test of my being inasmuch he throws me outside of myself toward structures which at once both escape me and define me; it is this test which *originally reveals the Other* to me" (p. 245; emphasis mine). It is no longer a matter of recognition or conflict between *me* and *the other*, as in Hegel. The other is not an object; it is what makes me *interdepend*. I am not "mired" but "alongside," "in the world." "In" can be seen as "with" in the sense of *colo* and *habito* and not *insum*. In other words, *being*, according to Sartre's reading of Heidegger, would be to "make oneself be" in the form of the "they": the inauthentic mode of "they" or the authentic "they" of relations between unique personalities (p. 246). Think of the "anyone," that in Sartre remains inauthentic but in Giorgio Agamben has the positive values of a modest community, the scrutiny of "theys" essential in their inessentiality, which preserves only the tenuous and random link of being-in-with.[31] In the "they" of the Heideggerian *Mit-Sein*, Sartre appreciates the opposite of the conflict that characterizes the Hegelian dialectical link, namely, the connotation of the crew, which does not work for knowledge but works in rhythm (such as the rhythm of rowing). Although being-unto-death abruptly reveals the "common solitude" and the negative in "concern," it is the coexistence of consciousnesses in the untranslatable *Stimmung* that seduces Sartre, reader of Heidegger, and suggests a humanity linked in its solitude, pluralities that create connections.

"We attempt somehow regarding the Other what Descartes attempted to do for God with that extraordinary 'proof by the idea of perfection.'" This is exactly what we do in psychoanalysis, and exactly what we do in literary theory when we decipher the work of a writer, for it is the otherness of the thought of the patient or writer that calls us. Read: we do not know if God exists, but we need the idea of perfection, and we situate it in the place of God; we do not know if the other is approachable, but we strive to apprehend the interiority of our consciousness or the possibility of *Mit-Sein* through an "intuition of transcendence" concerning others, "the external negation" that reveals the other to the Cogito as "not being me." This is where the notion of revolt and rejection appears. I can only penetrate the specificity of the other by confronting him in myself: my foreignness, the nausea that surrounds me.

Ultimately, Oedipus says the same thing. In the oedipal revolt of the child, when he contrasts himself to the other in order to posit himself as such, the other is only apprehended through external negation: the other appears to the Cogito as not being me. But this process is accompanied by an internal negation, because the subject only *is* (*I am* faced with *I think*) by investigating the being of this self and finding alterity there. A double interiority is then posited through a double movement of negation: mine and that of the other. I oppose myself to the other, and, by this movement of opposition, I oppose myself to me in split, pluralized being. This infiniteness of negativity is the only way to posit the other and the self. Thus the notions of negation and nothingness are justified as perpetual, as processes. From then on, the totality that we posited at the beginning—the same and the other can only be contemplated, mediatized, within the totality of being—becomes a detotalized totality. The access to existence for the other involves the observation of the impossibility of the other as well as the impossibility of any synthesis. All that I can do to attain the other is to look within myself, negativize myself, and negativize the other, so that we never arrive at a peaceful community, whether mental, social, or ideological.

You will note that this line of thought leads first to a refusal of philosophical totality and to being as totalizing; then to a sociological stand against every totalizing society, whether totalitarian or feebly democratic and unitarian, if it crushes the radicality of the same and the other and erases the right to singularity, if only in the guise of human rights; and finally to the recourse to the imaginary and to the role of the gaze thanks to which the process of nontotalizing totality will inscribe itself in the order of the visible.

I will spare you this voyage into the imaginary and instead look at the Sartrean personal imaginary that is ambiguous to say the least and came to light with *What Is Literature?* (1948) and *The Words* (1963).

Is Writing a Neurosis? No Doubt, but . . .

In *The Words*, Sartre examines memories in biographical form and shows how literary meaning is constructed with a double focus, words and childhood, the convergence of which is produced by neurosis. "For the last ten years or so I've been a man who's been waking up, cured of a long, bitter-sweet madness."[32] For ten years, since the nineteen fifties, he has been waking up: everything that happened before that date could be taken as a sort of madness, from which he would purge himself through the literary farewell to literature that is *The Words*.

Henceforth Sartre will relentlessly disparage the imaginary in favor of action, particularly political action, in an approach that seems salutary at the outset, because he denounces with a vigorous and pitiless irony certain psychological errors and political errancies as well as the solipsism of literary brilliance so prized in the French tradition. This flagellation quickly turns into an auto-da-fé, however, because the political activities in which Sartre continued to engage, despite their incisive impact in a France settling into consumerism and the spectacle, seemed to lack the density and polyphony that once accompanied the splendors of the master of Saint-Germain. Deprived of the imaginary, political engagement is fleshless, cut off from its emotional and unconscious substratum, castrated, in a way, of its fateful connotation.

In 1960, in *Critique of Dialectical Reason*, Sartre replaced the other as past, as memory, and perhaps even as language, by praxis and service rendered to others; this led him to leftism, an admirable physical engagement "here and now" in the city.[33] The philosopher-militant sought at that moment to localize—he himself said "objectalize"—history and intersubjectivity, recollection and intersubjectivity, the same-other relationship, and everything that he contemplated in *Nausea*, his theater, and *Being and Nothingness*. He strove to localize them in the search for an *agent of history*: what agent of history could embody the negative? Thus he renounced negation as a force at work in the imaginary (being-as-other deployed in language through the characters and themes in his plays and novels or in the pages of *Being and Nothingness*) and aspired instead to embody it.

Although this temptation to "localize" never left him—he was a fellow traveler of the Communists well before the war, and the dramatic beginning of *On a raison de se revolter* retraces the history of it—it now took place without the imaginary "madness" that opened an infinite abyss in each (necessarily erroneous) position he took, thereby saving it.

"At Any Rate, the Social Order Rests Upon a Mystification"

Take, for example, *What is Literature?* (1948). Art as a matter of flesh and emotion (we are almost on Proustian terrain), literature as a fabric of significations beyond words, all these assertions of Sartre's, of great subtlety and discernment, were received during the formalist years as so many rejections of technique, of signifying materiality. It is true that Sartre often evaded literary formality and did not refrain from scoffing at the linguistic obsessions of future structuralists.

But there were also advances here: a call to seize, beyond the text, what I have personally tried to define as *experience*. I will not elaborate on these points in this book, but if you read Sartre's text, you will find fascinating pages on the destiny of the writer in the Western world; the secularization of the writer in the eighteenth century, when the notion of "taste" replaced that of "faith"; surrealism and the impasses of the surrealist revolt; and the utopia of socialist literature and the absurdity of socialist realism, which like Barthes, he rejected.

I will limit myself to looking at the conclusion of *What is Literature?* to bring up two rather interesting points raised there: first, the observation of a situation that is continually worsening, namely, the decrease in the number of readers; second, the observation that some writers write only for movies and television and the world only wants writers as signatories (though we cannot say that Sartre abstained from the role of signatory!).

It is on the basis of this dual observation that Sartre maintained his utopia. The notion of being, the transcendental whole that corrects the rationalism of those who believe in knowledge—and that, in Sartre, ended up seeming like a utopia because he unveiled its perpetual conflict—emerged once again in the form of the old Kantian myth of the City of Ends. In this case, the City of Ends was a utopic society of communication made up of readers. Through its very demands, the readers were included in the concert of good will that "thousands of readers all over the world who do not know each other are, at every moment, helping to maintain."[34] But Sartre, a realist nonetheless, added that it was necessary to correct this utopia: the Kantian City of Ends, reconstructed by readers who had momentarily replaced the proletariat, the third world, women, and other providential agents of History, was not all that obvious. He did not say whether readers would realize this humanitarian ideal; they had to maintain their singularity and historicize themselves, not forget their concrete presence, their physical experience, or the concrete movement of history in which they found themselves.

More importantly, the reader had to be a demystifier. The notion of the negative once again comes into play: reading was a deciphering, a demystification. It is Barthes, and not Sartre, who would develop this capital point in order to envisage semiology as a semioclasm and taste the true pleasure of the text. But the idea is already found in Sartre: the true man was a reader who nevertheless distrusted and demystified the text. And to give some examples of great mystifications accomplished in the recent past by totalitarian communities, those who adhered to socialist ideals (a personal confession?) ceased to be suspect if they managed to remain suspicious. "At any rate, the social order today rests upon the mystification of consciousness, as does disorder as well.

Nazism was a mystification; Gaullism is another; Catholicism is a third. At present there can be no doubt that French Communism is a fourth" (p. 211).

What is to be done? "And as our writings would have no meaning if we did not set up as our goal the eventual coming of freedom by means of socialism, it is important in each case to stress the fact that there have been violations of formal and personal liberties or material oppression or both" (p. 211). A vibrant call to rise up against all forms of mystification, no matter where they surface, *What Is Literature?* concludes with a defense of literature as the last "chance" for Europe, socialism, democracy, and peace, although this chance is threatened: "Of course, all of this is not very important. The world can very well do without literature. But it can do without man better still" (p. 220). By defining literature as the means by which "the *collectivity* passes to reflection and meditation" and "acquires an *unhappy conscience*" (p. 220), Sartre already seemed to be preparing a renunciation of the individual act (which prevails in writing before its "collective" aim) and imaginary freedom (Orestes did not have an "unhappy conscience").

The Sartre of later years thus returned to the cherished Hegelian idea of negativity as demystification, and one cannot help but love the rebel that he did not cease to be, provided that the imaginary experience, this form of demystification that is writing, was abandoned in favor of what he called "social *praxis*." The active life—with its variants labor, work, and action, which Hannah Arendt subtly analyzed in *The Human Condition*—is contrasted in our metaphysical tradition with the contemplative life. The philosophers most concerned with the moral disaster of World War II believed they could reject this "contemplative life"—philosophy, literature—that lent itself to easy compromises in the great thinkers and writers of the century. But by dismissing the arduous task of demystification through writing, doesn't social praxis, far from avoiding the madness that sustains literature, run the risk of coming up against new dead ends, falling into the old errors of Promethean optimism?

I will conclude with a final remark on *Critique of Dialectical Reason* (1960), which it seems to me can be summed up as devoted to the task of humanizing the world. Sartre, the nonhumanist of long ago, asserted that it was necessary to wrest men from their natural inertia by helping them to totalize their respective praxis and avoid reified totalization and alienation in the inhuman forms of what he called the "practico-inert."[35] To reflect, to demystify and reunite, to totalize at a higher level, to find *Mit-Sein* on the level of social practice equivalent to a permanent calling into question: the project was grandiose, but Sartre pursued it with the strange suspension of the imaginary experience of which *The Words* marked both the apogee and the end. It indicated the contraction of the destiny of sense and the sensory that he deciphered from Aeschylus to Heidegger and insufflated into French existentialism.

Technological development would not take long to marginalize political groups that strived for a political praxis free of all imaginary (or so they thought). Soon the political would be cast into the spectacle, and the question of the sense of the imaginary reactualized. It is precisely at this point that the work of Barthes that awaits us.

8

Roland Barthes and Writing as Demystification

A Theory of Sublimation

Degree Zero

Although self-hatred continues to be a very French speciality—could it be the bitter fallout of Cartesian doubt?—and continues to devalue refractory works, and although in this climate Barthes's writings undergo attack and denigration, I will try to demonstrate to you that he is not a nihilist who might have contributed, along with other so-called structuralists or theorists, to killing the French novel (no less!). Not a nihilist but a sober tragic figure, because, starting in the early fifties, he would devote his reflection to the misadventures of meaning.

The bankruptcy of ideology and the misery of philosophy had already become apparent to most. There is meaning, and it can be analyzed: this was not Barthes's position, for he was too subtle to take a position, but his intuition, which he transformed into savor, music, the meaning of fashion (yes, indeed!) and the pleasure of the text, threading his way through the rigidness of concepts and enchanting them in a mode of writing sensitive to malady, absence, and irony.

To start by advancing that writing had reached its "degree zero" was not an introduction to arouse consensual sympathies. The unified consciousness of the bourgeoisie (which, Barthes suggested, was "undivided," by including in it the classics and romantics) was followed by a "tragic awareness" (around 1850). This was manifested in the disintegration of literature, of which Flaubert was the major embodiment, literature becoming entirely a concern of form, a "problematics of language." This movement, both a "reconciliation with" and "aversion from" the Form-Object, reached a "concretion" that led writing to assume the same status as a piece of "pottery" or a "jewel," depending on tastes. But from the objectifying "gaze" to reifying "creation," the path ended in "murder." And writing "has reached in our time a last metamorphosis, *absence*" (emphasis mine). In "neutral modes of writing" and the "absence of all signs," Barthes located a relationship to meaning that seemed to him a realization of the "Orphean dream," unballasting literary phantasms and philo-sophical messages: a writer "without Literature," blank writing, that of Camus, Blanchot, and Cayrol. This zero degree of writing, a symptom of what would become the current French novel's well-known—and unfortunate—minimal-ism, is nevertheless *thought* of by Barthes as a *sign*, which is also tragic. He de-ciphers "an Ethic of language" here that, in its negative ventures into abstrac-tion, indeed, into the abolition of meaning, can be read in two ways: as a "Passion" for writing and as a "disintegration of bourgeois consciousness." The issue at hand is nothing less than a jouissance of meaning, through meaning, through a revolt against what henceforth appears as a stage or monovalent structure of the mind that we could call "consciousness" and that the "bour-geoisie" wants to guard and defend.[1] All the ingredients of Roland Barthes's subsequent path are already in place: historical concern, the emphasis on form-language as Ethic and, for that very reason, as pleasure.

I will not outline Barthes's biography (b. November 12, 1915, d. March 26, 1980); he has written one himself in the form of *Roland Barthes by Roland Barthes*.[2] Like other rebels, he was fatherless. Barthes resolved this uncertainty by finding his roots in language, but he sought in it neither the paternal au-thority of a norm nor the filial revolt of a son "punching out" the law. Rather, he searched only for the secret rules of what is presented as normal but is sim-ply false. Though not a seeker of truth—such a task would have tired or re-pelled him—he ceaselessly tracked down the *false* in order to discover the mul-tiple networks that the false censures. Barthes was not a revealer of truth; he was a detractor of censure, and if a certain ephemeral, provisional, and thus ironic truth emerged in this unveiling, well, that was a plus, the icing on the cake, not to be glorified but allowed to resonate, to hit you broadside: taste is an infinite, mocking satisfaction.

So, although it may be surprising, I propose reflecting on the sense and non-sense of revolt in Roland Barthes's critical undertakings and will start by exam-ining his first book, *Writing Degree Zero* (1953). I will try to demonstrate that this experience of interpretation can be understood as an experience of revolt.

Barthes's elegant and reserved persona does not exactly evoke the figure of the rebel. His somewhat outmoded or even obsolete discretion resists com-parison with the hysterical tone that the theme of revolt might conjure. Yet this writer's interpretative approach was a demystification that consisted in creat-ing new objects of meaning and ways of deciphering them, foremost of which was *écriture*. Barthes's notion of *écriture*, which the current generation has heard a lot about, was a completely bewildering innovation. Perhaps still ob-scure today, it was much more so when Barthes proposed it in 1953! But what if the creation of new objects of interpretation were the most discreet, most invisible variant of revolt? For that very reason, it might also be the most radical one remaining to us in a specular universe saturated with the visible. As I have said many times throughout this book, it is time to ask ourselves this question: what sense can we give that which imposes itself as obvious and visible and substitutes itself for thought? It is this apparently anodyne question that Barthes raised when he began to distrust the meaning that his contemporaries considered natural and that he chose, on the contrary, to undo and displace.

Beneath "Natural" Meaning: Impossibility or Profusion of Meaning

In this world dominated by popular culture—"popular culture" denoting a certain U.S. complacency rather than a culture of the people—in this world of TV screens and channel surfing, hard sex and silicone, where thrills are found in murder trials theatricalized to the point of dissolution, we have a hard time imagining the delicate intellectual force of a man speaking in—for and against—culture and asserting that culture exists and keeps us alive, but only provided we ceaselessly decipher it, that is, critique it in order to displace it endlessly. Barthes started down this path with an absolute and serene anguish. He maintained the modest role of interpreter not only of great literary texts but also of myths, behaviors, stupidity, and love, without ever identifying himself with "the great writer." His respect and admiration for writing was immense but regulated, starting with a subtle distance that only certain patients are able to preserve vis-à-vis the generality as well as themselves, causing the depth of the obvious to emerge continually, making what is unspoken speak.

Barthes thus placed himself in an apparently secondary role that nevertheless led him to see what most of his contemporaries remained stubbornly unaware of: the fact that human beings in the second half of the twentieth century had arrived at an experience of meaning that overthrew not only beliefs in God or some other value but also *the possibility of meaning itself*. Is there a unity—an "I," a "we"—that can have meaning or seek meaning? This is pretty much the question Barthes raised, revealing, under so-called natural meaning, the abyss of a polyvalence of meaning, as well as a polyphony internal to subjects investigating meaning. Polyvalence for better or worse: for better, over-meaning, oversignification, a multitude of significations; for worse, the fragmentation of certainty, whether that of the existence of a Self or the existence of a signification. Barthes was convinced modernity had come to this point: to this *mise en abîme* of the possibility of signifying. For him, the crisis of God, the crisis of values, was, fundamentally, nothing other than this impossibility of unitary meaning that prefigures the germination of meaning and its revival and renewal. To this observation Barthes added the conviction that a certain

critical thought, inspired by both semiology and literature, was capable of accompanying or, better yet, of revealing this radical transformation of man's relationship to meaning.[3]

"Transformation" was in fact the word Barthes used: "A transformation," he
wrote in *Criticism and Truth* (1966), "perhaps as important as that which
marked . . . the transition from the Middle Ages to the Renaissance."[4] Clearly,
he was in no way questioning the importance of history, an accusation frequently leveled at structuralists, of whom Barthes is thought to be the emblematic figure; on the contrary, he was rooting criticism in historical reflection. Barthes worked out the question with all the meticulousness of the
southwestern Protestant that he was (an affiliation he sometimes made reference to), who had read not only Flaubert (he, too, a meticulous writer resistant to bombast), the hypersensitive Michelet, and Loyola, a man of order and
power and rituals, but also writers who still rattle conventions of all sorts, such
as Sade. Thus armed, Barthes threw himself into interpretative writing the way
others throw themselves into music, with a sense of going against the natural—
against natural language, which seemed false to him or seemed to conceal the
deceitful unsaid. In doing so he made (ultra- or infralinguistic) laws more fully
his own, laws he considered indispensable to the human condition, linguistic
rules conveying not only the laws of meaning but also the body beneath meaning. This mirage of the body always shimmered on the horizon of Barthes's
theory, like a secret that was not apparent but audible, signifiable, that the interpreter had to acknowledge in his voyage through the laws of language and
writing.

Semiology as Deception

Thus *to decipher* at the very moment that meaning was being lost seemed to
Barthes the last revolt remaining when ideologies revealed their lethal stupidity (well before the fall of the Berlin Wall). We have to understand that the interpretive adventure that semiology is had already taken into account the collapse of ideologies. Most of those who engaged in it then were dubious,
critical, or else disappointed by the great ideologies, particularly Marxism.
This assertion may seem paradoxical to those who see easy comparisons between structuralism and disengagement or even between structuralism and
dogmatism. In reality, we tried—Barthes before others—not to adhere to
Marxist dictates but to exist side by side with movements of the left—Hegelo-
Marxism, Brechtianism, leftism, Maoism—as so many critical ways to divert
bureaucracy and seek a national renewal of socialist generosity.

At this point, we would do well to recall the fate of those interested in semiology and interpretation in Eastern totalitarian countries, a fate curiously ignored by mass-media detractors of so-called "structuralist terrorism": they were dissidents of Marxism, thinkers who did not accept the Marxist doxa of meaning as a superstructure subordinate to economy, who dissolved Communist certainties with the help of structural analysis. The Stalinist regime took note of this, seized them, prevented them from studying and teaching, and persecuted them. I do not wish to go into the political and social history of that period here, but I do want to underscore that the semiological adventure did in fact constitute a revolt against the utter dejection of the supposedly rebellious discourse that issued from the Communist revolution, as well as against its symmetrical double, bourgeois moralism, whose hypocrisy the West has endured.

Why This "Exquisite Crisis" in Paris?

Why was this interpretive revolt possible in France? What happened around Roland Barthes, the review *Communications,* and the Ecole des Hautes Etudes? What took place around *Tel Quel,* whose energy radiated beyond France, seduced U.S. universities and continues to mobilize interest today?

The end of the Algerian War was no doubt a factor: France was tending its wounds, and its intellectuals were looking for a rebirth in terms of moral and philosophical revolts—existentialism, Hegelo-Marxism—while at the same time already seeing their obstacles. A cultural tradition, unique in Europe, of the cult of the Word was a factor as well, from the medieval tradition of the Sorbonne and its *disputationes* to the central place of intellectuals in the eighteenth century, the Encyclopedists who analyzed the most elusive meaning and emotion and never yielded on the overdetermining role of the formative Word, Idea, or the presence of philosophy at the heart of the City. This is a heritage that is probably to be found nowhere else. Another factor was no doubt the Gaullist grandeur that made Paris a timeless crossroads where Freud, Marx, Hegel, and Heidegger, not to mention Saint Thomas and Saint Augustine, converged. Given this heritage and the cultural ferment of Gaullean grandeur, there were several favored meetingplaces: the Ecole des Hautes Etudes, in particular, and publishing houses like Seuil that brought together, merged, and assembled ways of thinking that elsewhere remained divided. In this climate of Paris as a centuries-old capital of art and literature, there was room for an individual in the sixties and seventies to devote himself to the "exquisite crisis" of which Mallarmé spoke, which led one to the borders of madness without causing one to topple into it, from which one returned, instead, the bearer of an "imaginary trophy" (Mallarmé again), which was nothing other than the ability to express the dissipation and near loss of the self.

The Samurai

I have called this semiological adventure at its most excessive the samurai adventure.[5] Although it finds its justification in the hyperbole of fiction, I use this image again here, for its violence reflects the iconoclasm inseparable from interpretive work that I am trying to convey. Beneath the apparent technical nature of the discourse, a veritable war was being waged against the opacity of the identical, the social norm, the bourgeois norm, the individual norm, of meaning as one and indivisible that no one had the right to question. This war against the opacity of identity took place both internally and externally: externally, in work, discussion, behavior, and social life; internally, because everyone keenly experienced this crisis state—this was the message of the samurai—in personal existence, in the excesses likely to affect health, sexuality, and life itself, sometimes at the risk of death.

This may strike you as a bit ponderous, but I am trying to give you a faithful description of my experience of this period. It is no doubt difficult to imagine today, even though as I write this France is enmeshed in a serious social crisis that, despite certain striking commonalities that I will mention in passing, certainly has nothing to do with May '68. Beyond the economic and political protests, the necessity for reform and the cleanup of public finances, and the future of the European Community, this strike, in December 1995—for the strikers as well as everyone affected by it—expresses the need to rethink the dignity of the individual. By making us confront the various ways we live and die, work or don't work, play and connect with others, the strike shows how difficult it is to maintain this dignity. The gravity of these questions suddenly springs forth, creating a rare current of solidarity, even if there is a good chance it will soon dissipate. Yesterday, a patient of mine expressed her delight in participating in a demonstration but was sorry it wasn't "silent." If this complaint becomes an issue—namely, that once the economic problems are raised and perhaps resolved, we will still have to find the words for a more profound malaise—then we will in fact be experiencing something similar to the crisis of May '68. It will not only be a matter of an embryonic crisis that dissipates by itself but a stage in the reconquest of psychical life. This strike, whose duration we cannot predict, shows that the French are far from having lost the taste for freedom, which begins with the safeguarding of psychical life, and that they wonder how to continue living psychically in the modern world, how to escape automation, how to express and foster the need for intimacy, self-respect, and the respect of others. This will no doubt be an arduous task.

All this is to say that the ingenious forms of revolt represented by interpretation (such as literary criticism and theory or psychoanalysis) are faced with the demand to excavate meaning in everything that is said and that is being demonstrated today in the street, from social security to retirement pensions. Perhaps because—if you will allow this oversimplification—life is the search for meaning.

To get back to *Writing Degree Zero*, in which Barthes defined his notion of *écriture*, I will start with a warning: this is not an easy text. What is writing? Barthes's reflection made a cut in the literary text that was a reinterpretation of the literary object starting with language, as you might expect. He did not approach this question in terms of linguistic, grammatical, or stylistic categories. The reinterpretation Barthes proposed brought into play a listening process that strove to make language emerge from the substances that idealities or linguistic and stylistic categories represent—subject, verb, object, metaphor, metonymy, etc.—in order to come closer to what I have called the secret that haunted Barthes, namely, the body, which is always the body in history.

Negativity and Freedom: Against Subjectivism

To summarize: between the substance of linguistic categories, on the one hand, and the body and history, on the other, Barthes tried to define *écriture* as a negativity, a movement that questions all "identity" (whether linguistic, corporeal, or historical). Barthes's metaphors—"hit broadside," "knot," "cut," "recasting"—operate on three levels: language, the subject and his body, and history, so that the dimension of *writing as negativity* appears as an intermediary between the subject's drives, on the one hand, and social practice in language, on the other.

Nevertheless, for Barthes, this investigation, no matter how subjective, had very little to do with psychoanalysis, which always seemed to him a science of pathology: neurosis and psychosis. Writing, though placed side by side with these pathologies and hand in hand with drives, was irreducible, according to Barthes, to the psychoanalytical approach. For "drives," "biology," "the body"—again, his terms—are always already objectified through literature and transmuted in a mode of writing, a communication, that is historical. A mode of writing is historical in two ways: first, because the one who writes inserts himself in a rhetorical tradition and confronts the laws of language, genre, stylistics, and so forth; second, because writing is a social practice that targets communication here and now. Writing as Barthes conceived it is in part a force of destiny dependent on passions; it is sustained by the abysses of pathology, dependent on the hazards of the signifier or drives that are its substratum. But, at the same time, it is a locus of freedom, and moreover it is perhaps the turning point where the destined signifier is transformed into freedom.

With Barthes, then, we are not in a psychoanalytical perspective. When it does not fail, the analytical experience is supposed to give the subject access to freedom. But for Barthes, as his text demonstrates, what turns the subject's dependence vis-à-vis the signifier into freedom is not analysis at all: it is writing as proof of freedom. In other words, writing is the intermediary that incorporates the tensions of the ego into history, insofar as it desubjectifies its subject. Writing becomes a sort of objectified "outside ego," at once *infra*language because linked to the body, biology, and passions and *ultra*language because of its aim, praxis, including history, present ideas, and the future. If writing is a translanguage, then the subject of writing, if there is one, cannot be confused with the psychiatric or even psychoanalytical subject. The subject can only be apsychological, indeed, asubjective, which can be compared to my notion of a "subject-in-process," which seems to me to be nothing other than that of sublimation.[6]

To illustrate the notion of writing as a "recasting" or "knot" between the signifying drive, on the one hand, and freedom in history, on the other, I would like to underscore two propositions in *Critical Essays*: First, "the work of art is what man wrests from chance."[7] The subject-history dimension is subjacent to the insistence on the wresting from chance: to wrest from the chance of birth, biology, dependence, what? a gift that writing destines as necessity/form/toss of the dice/laws to other men and that characterizes the specious premeditation that is the work.

Now, to this submission of chance to the rules of a particular logic, add the following proposition: writing "speaks the locus of meaning but does not name it" (p. 219). Barthes dissociates the logic of the work—the place of spoken meaning—from any linguistic harnessing that names: the work does not name meaning, the semiologist asserts. Writing suggests a translinguistic meaning that is never verbalized in the categories of language. In short, do not look for writing in the linguistic substance of language. Writing does not offer itself in the verbal immediate; it is to be interpreted through the immediate, next to the appearance of signs, in addition to the named. It is the inexhaustible aspect of meaning, accessible only through infinite interpretation. As you can see, Barthes was indeed searching for a new object, one that, for the layman, is extracted with difficulty from his early texts.

Neither Style Nor Language

In the first pages of *Writing Degree Zero*, Barthes strives to dissociate writing from two superimposed notions that cloud our comprehension of its specificity: writing is neither language nor style. "Language is therefore on the hither side of Literature. Style is almost beyond it . . . , style has always something crude about it: it is a form with no clear destination, the product of a thrust, not an intention, and, as it were, a vertical and lonely dimension of thought." Impersonal, archaic, and unnamable, "style is properly speaking a germinative phenomenon, the transmutation of a Humour. [In other words, this is not writing as Barthes envisions it.] . . . Style is always a secret."[8] As for language, it has a flatter dimension, that of linguistic categories that organize the linearity of the signifying chain, which we recognize in Saussure's signifier and, differently, Lacan's.

The issue, then, is to find a place for writing that is neither "the horizon of language, nor the verticality of style." Language is the horizon, while style refers to a biological verticality. Between language and style, there is room for another formal reality: a mode of writing. "A language and a style are blind forces; a mode of writing is an act of historical solidarity" (p. 14). We are quite far from those who claimed that structuralist theoreticism and its so-called interpretative excesses were antihistorical. But there is a fundamental difference: we are dealing not with a cursory history that strings together sociopolitical events but the history that Nietzsche called monumental history: the history of mentalities, mutations in man's relationship to meaning.

"A language and a style are objects; a mode of writing is a function" (p. 14). Writing in the sense of "function" allows the subject to find freedom, for function should be understood as action, dynamic, relationship, correlation, faculty, aptitude, consequence. It is nothing other than the realization of the freedom that only becomes such when the trauma is *traversed*, inscribed in a certain law. What Barthes asks us to ponder is complex: it is not a matter of fleeing the secret or obeying the universal legality of an inert praxis and subjecting oneself to the collective imperative; it is a matter of making a crossing, which must indeed be described as dialectical and leads from the secret to freedom. Several parameters are established that could be described as registers of the pathological or of social constraint but that, on the contrary, Barthes rejects in order to find their diagonal, hence the true vertigo that his notion of writing provokes. And I still see no other way of grasping this dynamic of writing-as-freedom according to Barthes except to think of it in light of the Hegelian dialectic, at the crossroads of Force and Law, as I proposed in 1971.[9]

The Morality of Form

Here, now, are several examples Barthes drew from literary texts to show how different styles can be a part of the same mode of writing: "Mérimée and Fénelon, for instance, are separated by linguistic phenomena and contingent features of style; yet they make use of a language charged with the same intentionality." That is to say, the will and the desire of the two writers are identical at the place of language. "Their ideas of form and content share a common framework, they accept the same type of conventions, the same technical reflexes work through both of them. Although separated by a century and a half, they use exactly the same instrument in the same way: an instrument perhaps a little changed in outward appearance, but not at all in the place and manner of its employment. In short, they have the same mode of writing."[10] Mérimée and Fénelon therefore do not necessarily have the same style, or the same biology, or the same subjectivity, or the same social practice, but they do have the same relationship to meaning and, consequently, the same *écriture*. "In contrast, writers who are almost contemporaries, Mérimée and Lautréamont, Mallarmé and Céline, Gide and Queneau, Claudel and Camus, who have shared or who share our language at the same stage of its historical development use utterly different modes of writing." In effect, if you compare Mérimée and Lautréamont (a man of the nineteenth century but whose writing is still unusual and scandalous), you will immediately note the difference between their relationships to meaning: Mérimée conforms to the demands of conventional comprehension, employing immediateness, clear imagery, and syntactic regularity; Lautréamont, on the other hand, plays with paradox, with these oneiric hieroglyphics in which the surrealists recognized themselves. As Barthes points out, "Everything separates them: tone, delivery, purpose, ethos, and naturalness of expression: the conclusion is that to live at the same time and share the same language is a small matter compared with modes of writing so dissimilar and so sharply defined by their very dissimilarity. These modes of writing, though different, are comparable, because they owe their existence to one identical process, namely the writer's consideration of the social use which he has chosen for his form, and his commitment to this choice" (pp. 14–15). There is, then, a use for form that, although personal, has a social destination (by "social" we should understand the manipulation of the rules of language as a fundamental social link as well as the modification of the communal link that results). This is why Barthes does not seek a psychoanalytical scope in this use of form, which is for him the locus of the writer's freedom, but sees a moral value in it, which confers a historic dimension to his notion of writing: "Writing is thus essentially the morality of form" (p. 15).

In sum, writing is a matter of translating a certain secret—stylistic, personal, and, ultimately, pathological—but inscribing it in a law (society, tradition, manners). This "morality" is not to be suffered as obedience to a group or a code of moral imperatives: position in meaning and the link it implies goes beyond the question of choice, for it gives free reign to negativity or revolt. "It is not a question for the writer of choosing the social group for which he is to write." The "morality of form" has nothing to do with Marxist or Sartrean "engaged literature," and I have already underscored that Barthes's interpretative thought, which would lead him to semiology, was a reaction to the impasses of the dominant ideologies, including those of the left. The writer "knows that, save for the possibility of a Revolution, it can only be for the self same society. His choice is a matter of conscience, not of efficacy. His writing is a way of conceiving Literature, not of extending its limits" (p. 15). Which means this: the writer is not there to make the masses literate, to educate them, to influence the redistribution of power in society much less to dominate as a "master of thought"; rather, his function is to modulate the relationship to literature, which is nothing other than the profound link that unites the subject to meaning: literature manifests the multiple logics of the mind, from the sensory to the intelligible, in the complex *organization* of the linguistic flesh (the word "structure" will come later).

This historic and not historical value of writing is better expressed this way: "It is because the writer cannot modify in any way the objective data which govern the consumption of literature . . . that he voluntarily places the need for a free language at the sources of this language and not in its eventual consumption" (pp. 15–16). The writer devotes himself to the "need for language" and not to the modalities that will make it fit for "consumption." This need leads him to the sources of language and to the architectonics of meaning, to its heterogeneity.

Between Blanchot and Sartre

Barthes's search for a mode of writing between the intimate and the social is a process of trial and error: he thinks in front of us, is surprised by the novelty of what he discovers, and seeks to share with us the dynamics of the thinking body in history. He situated himself in a very personal way between two great authors to whom he was greatly indebted and who placed the experience of writing at the center of their preoccupations: Blanchot and Sartre.

In *The Space of Literature*, Maurice Blanchot devoted himself to a veritable contemplation of writing.[11] Writing—the paradoxical act par excellence, devoted to "time's absence" and traversed by the negative *and* the affirmative—is defined as "the loss of being, when being lacks," which in a way evokes the intimate pole of Barthes's reflection when the "relinquishing" of earlier expression offers the promise of freedom. In a more psychological way, the formulation of phenomenological inspiration in Blanchot evokes the states of solitude, depression, and indeed dereliction that are concealed in the act of writing. From this place of lack or loss of being, writing, according to Blanchot, leads to a dazzling light that is faceless and nameless. We can decipher a metaphor for God here, the Jewish God in particular, the most demanding God in truth. At the same time, it is an attempt to lay out the territory of the sublime as entirely Other, extracted and different from the psychosexual path: the space of the Absolute, "They" with a capital T, the impersonal.

This is what "resonates" with Barthes's search for a detour through writing that leads individual disarray toward a *formula* that is impersonal and divisible: "formal truth," "equation," "necessity," indeed, "law": "The man is put on show and delivered up by his language, betrayed by a *formal reality* which is beyond the reach of his lies, whether they are inspired by self-interest or generosity." "If the writing is really *neutral*, and if language, instead of being a cumbersome and recalcitrant act, reaches the state of a pure *equation*, which is no more tangible than an algebra when it confronts the innermost part of man, then Literature is vanquished." "The social or mythical characters of a language are abolished in favour of a *neutral* and inert state of form." "If Flaubert's writing enshrines a Law, if that of Mallarmé postulates a silence, and if others, those of Proust, Céline, Queneau, Prévert, each in its own way, is founded on the existence of a social nature, if all these modes of writing *imply an opacity of form* and presuppose a problematic of language and society, thus establishing speech as an object *which must receive treatment* at the hands of a craftsman, a magician or a scriptor, then neutral writing in fact rediscovers the primary condition of classical art: instrumentality."[12]

However, what is of interest to us in Blanchot's reflection, although he is situated on the phenomenological rather than psychoanalytical plane, is the following argument: the impersonal "They," prefiguring the sublime Law, soon takes on a maternal connotation. First the dazzling light and shattering mirrors where "space is its vertiginous separation," the place of writing is revealed to be dependent on the maternal radiance supporting the subject on his path toward the light on the horizon. Consider this: "Perhaps the force of the maternal figure receives its intensity from the very force of fascination, and one might say then, that if the Mother exerts this fascinating attraction, it is because, appearing when the child lives altogether in fascination's gaze, she concentrates in herself all the powers of enchantment." It is because the mother was fascinated, Blanchot tells us, that the writer can be fascinated in return. He mirrors the maternal fascination. And this exchange of gazes, more archaic and fundamental than the mirror stage, already stabilizing, will support the subject in the course of his trials when he later feels the loss of being on his path toward light. "Fascination is fundamentally linked to neutral, impersonal presence, to the indeterminate They, the immense, faceless Someone." Once again, the prototype of the invisible God, this nonfigure, is very explicitly reflected in the maternal figure. "To write is to enter into the affirmation of the solitude in which fascination threatens."[13] Solitude and fascination mark the intra- and extrareligious experience of the subject in meaning. Subjectively, they are traces of the reciprocal mother-child fascination, which organizes our preobjectal, prefigurable, presignifying relations, the memory of which resurfaces in our subsequent derelictions. The fascination of the indeterminate "They" in Blanchot is a maternal fascination; beyond it lies the continent of the amorous link and writing as "a lover's discourse" (1977).[14] Those who have read Barthes know how explicit this theme would eventually become, particularly in *Camera Lucida* (1980).

Nevertheless, having pointed out Barthes's proximity to Blanchot, I would now like to point out his differences with him. Writing, for Barthes, was less a dazzling light where the subject vanishes in the mother than the logical process accompanying/preceding/exceeding this dazzlement. And it is indeed the process of dazzlement and its path that he would track in the semantic density of language, in the networks of the characters and themes of S/Z (the voice of the castrato condensing "loss" and "fascination," for example), and that he would expose in the rigor of its formalisms.[15] This program of a putting-into-law of fascination was set forth in *Writing Degree Zero*: through the symbolic order of language, writing is a recording of this dialectic of displacement, facilitation, discharge, the investment of drives (up to the carrier wave of the death drive) that activates-constitutes the signifier but also exceeds it. It is added to the linear order of language, using the most fundamental laws of *significance* (displacement, condensation, repetition, inversion), and, using other supplementary constellations, produces an overmeaning. Barthes wrote in 1953:

> Writing, on the contrary, is always rooted in something beyond language, it develops like a seed, not like a line, it manifests an essence and holds the threat of a secret, it is an *anti-communication*, it is intimidating. All writing will therefore contain the ambiguity of an object which is both language and coercion: there exists fundamentally in writing a "circumstance" foreign to language, there is, as it were, the weight of a gaze conveying an intention which is no longer linguistic. This gaze may well express a passion of language, as in literary modes of writing; it may also express the threat of retribution, as in political ones . . . [in] literary modes of writing, [. . .] *the unity of the signs is ceaselessly fascinated by zones of infra- or ultra-language.*[16]

Allow me to emphasize that these lines, written in 1953, would become a method of analysis applied in 1970 in S/Z.

Writing-as-praxis, on the other hand, should be compared with Sartre's vision of it. Though resistant to Sartrean bombast and his philosophical density, Barthes showed great esteem for Sartre's thought and not only in order to distinguish himself from it. Recall the dialectical conception of writing in Sartre, as objective praxis: "The work poses questions to the life. But we must understand in what sense; the work as objectification of the person is, in fact, *more complete, more total* than the life."[17] Think again of the Barthesian "ethics of form" and a surpassing of the biological/biographical secret to reach a formulation that would be a sort of objective law; recall what I said about Barthes's desire not to "pathologize" or "psychologize" writing. Sartre expressed himself in much more sociological and philosophical terms to discuss analogous preoccupations: that the text far exceeds biographical realization, even if it is social and historical. For Sartre, the reason for the work is found in the work itself; similarly, for Barthes, writing displaced the biographical in a universality of another, translinguistic order. Sartre went on: "[The work] has its roots in life, to be sure; it illuminates the life, but it does not find its total explanation in the life alone" (p. 142). We could not reduce Proust's texts to his homosexuality or his relationship to his mother; rather, it is the opposite that the work requires, as I tried to show in *Time and Sense*.[18] "But it is too soon as yet for this total explanation to become apparent to us," Sartre continued. "The life is illuminated by the work as a reality whose total determination is found outside of it."[19] This "outside" (which for Sartre is the idea, the philosophical option, the message) was situated for Barthes in the play of forms and in the placement of the subject vis-à-vis meaning. This would lead him to seek a more refined structuring of literary construction insofar as it manifested the complex and heteronomous logics of meaning.

Yet the similarities between the two authors should be underscored: "The life is illuminated by the work as a reality whose total determination is found outside of it—both in the conditions which produce it and in the artistic creation that fulfills it and *completes it by expressing it.* Thus the work—when one has examined it—becomes a hypothesis and a research tool to clarify the biography. . . . But we must also know that the work *never* reveals the secrets of the biography" (p. 142). In other words: the work has its secrets, which are not those of the life. Finally, Sartre sees language as praxis (Barthes says writing is the ethics of form): "Language as the practical relation of one man to another is *praxis*, and *praxis* is always language (whether truthful or deceptive) because it cannot take place without signifying itself."[20] The attention that Sartre accorded linguistic theories and philosophies has never been sufficiently underscored, it seems to me, although *The Words* is an accessible representation of this in the form of a novel. " 'Human relations' are in fact the inter-individual structures whose common bond is language and which *actu-*

ally exist at every moment of History" (p. 99). That language is the structure
or the form of human praxis and the compost of History is what Sartre placed
in a phenomenolo-dialectical systemization but also what he put into practice
in his experience as a writer, orator, and militant. It is writing-as-praxis that
Barthes auscultated, more intimately and more positively, when he defined it
as an "ethics of form."

A last word on history, in which Barthes wanted to situate what he called a
mode of writing. In his *Michelet* he evoked a "cordial history."[21] Think of "cordial" not in the romantic sentimental sense ["of or relating to the heart," obsolete in English. — Trans.], but in the sense of an appeal to subjectivity at its
most "savory" (another key word of Barthes's), its most unformulatable. Writing that addresses History does not ignore the praxis Sartre spoke of but is
lodged there, in an attempt to formulate this "cordial history," some not very
tender examples of which I will soon provide.

Semiology and the Negative

Polymorphous Writing: A Coercion

What does the accusation of "technicality" mean? Is it a way to impugn a lack
of interest in the so-called fundamental problems, whether ideological, metaphysical, vital, or human? Is it a criticism of a sort of obsessional ritualism, a
keen interest in details to the detriment of "great subjects"? Roland Barthes
would find in language a privileged object of the universal and the intimate,
at the crossroads of constraint (the linguistic norm, rhetorical tradition) and
freedom (imaginary invention). His meticulous pointillism, his concern to
auscultate the infinitesimal signs of the ailing body or bodies in ecstasy, led
him first to invent the notion of *écriture*, then to move toward its clarification
through semiology, and finally to write it in turn, in a generous, fragmentary,
savory way. This was done without ever abandoning what he posited in *Writing Degree Zero*; the notion of a mode of writing involved attention to the materiality of language, from which apparently flat and one-dimensional categories (which so frustrated both metaphysics and literary enthusiasm) gathered
a polymorphous experience. Barthes's conviction was that it was here alone
that a place still existed for the dignity and freedom he himself practiced secretly, modestly, and amiably.

Almost fifty years after the publication of *Writing Degree Zero*, it is still difficult to make people understand that writing is not a communication.
"Whom are you addressing? What do you want to say?" a journalist will ask

some lucky writer, culled from the ranks of the invisible and catapulted into the media. And we are always surprised when answering seems difficult. Yet the rebellious Barthes would continuously stress that, while employing the universal language-tool of communication, writing stamps it with another economy. Which? "Closure," "strangeness," "introversion," these are the words that mark the way, that allow us to seize the issue at hand.

"All modes of writing have in common the fact of being 'closed' and thus different from spoken language," Barthes said at the outset, but this is not a matter of the difference between the written and the oral. What is being described here is a *position* of the subject that is not that of communication. "What makes writing the opposite of speech is that the former always appears symbolical, introverted [The meaning of writing is to be deciphered *in addition*, beyond or within the immediate message of communication.] . . . whereas the second is nothing but a flow of empty signs, the movement of which alone is significant."[22] The signs of spoken language take on a value in the movement of communication, but, in themselves, they are empty; in writing, on the contrary, each sign acts, already full of its past in the history of the language and the memory of the writer ("symbolical, introverted"). Writing operates with full elements, it explores a "closure"; this enigmatic practice is *self-referential*, it refers only to itself. This last feature will be repeated indefinitely, to the point of becoming a sort of catchword of thought termed structuralist or modern, a tiresome cliché: everyone has heard it said that "Godard makes images of images," "Sollers writes of writing," and so on. But if you transcend your lassitude, in rereading Barthes's inaugural text, you will appreciate the freshness of his definition. This introspection, this advance is sustained in particular by Flaubert and Mallarmé and acknowledges the essential fact that writing analyzes itself, presents itself, saturates itself, and exhausts itself with this very fullness. "All writing will therefore contain the ambiguity of an object which is both language and coercion" (p. 20).

Barthes uses another metaphor—"coercion" (Lautréamont said "basalt")—to refer to this extreme condensation that evokes closure, intimacy, and self-referentiality and is, for this reason, a "circumstance foreign to language." This is what is so interesting, not least because it prefigures semiology: Barthesian semiology does not analyze literature by copying language but by finding translinguistic models of it.

Linguists (some of the best) first devoted themselves to doing semiology by exporting linguistic models and grafting them onto texts; this was the initial path of semiology. But in Barthes's conception—where writing is foreign to language—semiology would consist of finding other models, issued from linguistics, certainly, but modified, because writing is an *other* language. It is therefore not a matter of tracing cinema, painting, or literature onto language as linguists study it and dismantle it but of forging other models inspired by this model to make *several* languages, a typology of languages. "[In writing] there is, as it were, the weight of a gaze conveying an intention which is no longer linguistic. This gaze may well express a passion of language, as in literary modes of writing; it may also express the threat of retribution, as in political ones: writing is then meant to unite at a single stroke the reality of the acts and the ideality of the ends" (p. 20). We are in a translinguistic dimension: "the reality of the acts and the ideality of the ends" joined by a hypotenuse that stems from language in that language is the intrinsic index of the speaking being but that, *through* language, concerns the realities of the *infra-* or *ultra*linguistic mind (its psychological as well as moral and historical motivations). Writing is a sort of diagonal line that, through language, inserts the intimate into the historical. This is what I brought up earlier, in discussing Blanchot, for whom writing as exploration of the intimate was dependent on a fascination with archaic states of subjectivity (mother/child fascination where the speaking being breaks free from the other and finds his autonomy) and Sartre, for whom writing was praxis, where the dialectical negativity of the subject occurs in the other and the group. As for Barthes, he would seek to recast these two poles and situate them in a new dimension of meaning that emanated through language, which he would call a mode of writing.

How Do You Write the Revolution?

Let us consider an example of a mode of writing Barthes analyzed that is necessarily inscribed in this inquiry into revolt: political writing. He commented on two examples of it: the writing of the French Revolution and that of Marxism. Everyone is familiar with the classical style of the 1789 revolutionaries: read a few pages of Saint-Just to appreciate the magnificence and clarity of the phrase, the rhetoric, the argumentation. "Classical writing was a ceremonial which manifested the implantation of the writer into a particular political society. . . . To speak like Vaugelas meant in the first place to be connected with the exercise of power." Barthes immediately attached classical writing to the exercise of power that it subtended and surpassed but that, at the same time, consolidated it. On the other hand, Barthes told us, in the midst of this great classical form, truly revolutionary writing was being forged, "defined not by its structure [Barthes used the term "structure" here in the sense of style.] (which was more conventional than ever) [None of the writers of the Revolution avoided academic style.] but by its closed character and by its counterpart, since the use of language was then linked, as never before in history, to the Blood which had been shed" (p. 21).

Some speak of Barthes's formalism; on the contrary, his brilliant stroke was the immediate leap from classical style (from the reasoning applied to the use of revolutionary language) to historical reality: the Terror. Right away, the analyst allowed himself the luxury of evoking the guillotine and the pikes through an image directed at the senses: not as a political appreciation but as an image, it conveys all the aggression, violence, and deadly passion behind the political and moral petitions of the writing in question. Without any social or historical development, strictly speaking, simply by according attention to the play of metaphors, Barthes suggested that beneath the rhetoric, this writing had the particularity of taking into account the blood shed. How? Is it the presence of the signified or signifier "blood"? Not really. A dynamic transversal to words (for which semiology would later try to specify exact figures or models), revolutionary writing signified the blood shed, this historical singularity, through theatrical amplification: while it spoke explicitly of human rights, the oratorical emphasis, such as a pathetic gesture made by a body, referred outside discourse to another passionate and political gesture, that of shedding blood. This revolutionary body, which could have appeared in the classical theater, exceeded the register of the latter and inflated it, a presentiment of romanticism. Barthes deciphered the presence of this emphatic gesture within the revolutionaries' classical style itself—just as the gesture of Chinese calligraphy is inseparable from Chinese writing and inherent in its meaning—for it is this gesture that gave revolutionary writing its true impact, and not academic style. I am using the word "gesture" here not only to anticipate Barthes's interest in China and Japan or to make you appreciate the heroic pose—the "extravagant pose," he said—of the guillotines but, above all, to draw your attention to this dimension of writing that, like gesture or anaclitics (i.e., demonstrative pronouns such as "this" or "that"), establishes the hiatus between *signs* and *reality*, *discourse* and *history*. Although classical in terms of grammar and stylistics, revolutionary writing was bombastic, pathetic, and inflated. Yet this excessiveness was its one and only precision, because it existed in unison with the excessiveness of real history. And this is the referent, apparently banished from writing, that gives it its definitive value. The gesture of writing is its ability to allude, beyond the signs of language, to historical reality. In one paragraph, before our eyes, Barthes constructed a figure with three equal components: classical style, rhetorical bombast, and terror, at once sensorial and historical. It is in the intersection of these three components that the singularity of revolutionary writing is crystallized.

The short revolutionary extract in the following quotation will help us appreciate this synthesis—through language—of a scene, an act, and a moral: the scene where the subject of the utterance, Guadet, refers to his own person, his head, and his executioner; the act of bravura against the tyrants; and the moral of the historical message where a man sacrifices himself in the name of an ideal that is no longer transcendental but democratic. A condensation of these three registers, the writing solicits a plural approach ("pluridisciplinary," it will later be termed). Semiology would eventually seek to detail the various translinguistic logics internal to this coercion, but in 1953 the issue was to show the strangeness and complexity of the process, not to explain it. Listen to Barthes's felicitous definition:

> This writing, which bears all the signs of inflation, was an exact writing: never was language more incredible, yet never was it less spurious. This grandiloquence was not only form modelled on drama; it was also the aware-ness of it. Without this extravagant pose, typical of all the great revolution-aries, which enabled Guadet, the Girondin, when arrested at Saint-Emilion, to declare without looking ridiculous, since he was about to die: "Yes, I am Guadet. Executioner, do your duty. Go take my head to the tyrants of my country. It has always turned them pale; once severed, it will turn them paler still," the Revolution could not have been this mythical event which made History fruitful, along with all future ideas on revolution. Revolutionary writing was so to speak the entelechy of the revolutionary legend: it struck fear into men's hearts and imposed upon them a citizen's sacrament of Bloodshed.   (p. 22)

Until Barthes, revolutionary writing was justified externally by its contents: rev-olutionaries were ideologues in favor of the third state, human rights, and so forth. No one had considered the polysemy of the writing until Barthes ap-proached the enunciation of 1789 with the help of the notion he was in the process of forging.

I am not discussing the notion of writing as later found in Derrida that refers to an intrapsychical functioning, to the architrace subjacent to every trace, in the graphic sense of the term, because it articulates the register of the uncon-scious. I am describing the *practice* called "writing" that allows us to decipher the decentering of the subject and of history by means of a cut in the texts, lan-guage, and style. Because it is a mode of writing, the extravagant pose of the revolutionaries and their classical grammar are neither ridiculous nor out-dated but *exact*.

The Marxist writer, something else entirely, was spared none of the lucid-ity of Barthes the subtle rebel. Even if blood continued to flow, "one" did not see it. Neither blood nor violence served as a reference; it was the functional, the technical, that were important: this is the sphere of the robotization that henceforth constituted the modern. The issue was no longer to give a moral justification to bloody law or to raise it to a scriptural and ethical formulation; it was to enunciate rupture as if it consecrated knowledge, if not science. After

Marx, the revolutionaries in Russia asserted the scientific change of society and, based on this scientific presupposition, their writing fell into reduction, cliché: it was a "litotic" writing, Barthes would say. The litotes is a rhetorical figure of omission: by omitting, or suggesting enigmatically, one can be dazzling, stir the senses, stir up meaning. But this was not the intention of Marxist writing. The Marxist litotes was a censure: it served to hide, to not-say, to abstain from truth. Thus entire pages of the *Soviet Encyclopedia* would be destroyed because, when a certain personage had fallen from grace, the "writing" required that they disappear, purely and simply, from History. The litotes here became a deliberate act of murder, at once symbolic and real. In a similar way, under the pretext of scientific method, silence was imposed on discourse. From then on, so-called Marxist writing appeared as a series of dry algebraic signs liable to lead to the death of language through the extinction of polyvalent meaning. Yet this "scientific" meaning was far from neutral: bloodless to start with (unlike that of the French Revolution), Stalinist writing ultimately charged each word with a value and thus imposed a mandate that was at once knowledge *and* ideology. The result was a strange situation where language did not *construct* values but *carried* prefabricated values within it: it cut itself off from its function of producing values and was content to convey them. Thus "cosmpolitanism" bore within it a negative value that exempted the speaker from elaborating on when, how, why, and under what circumstances "cosmpolitanism" was bad. Always-already, the sign "cosmpolitanism" meant "the plotting of Jews, foreigners, capitalism against the system." The word was self-sufficient, its value relieved it of demonstrating its meaning in syntax, figures of speech, and the like: this was contained within it. "Internationalism," on the other hand, was positive. And so forth. The language of Communist writing was emptied of its *meaning* because it was weighed down by "values." And Barthes concluded that this writing was a perfect tautology: it was defined by itself; there was no alternative to the meaning it indicated because it prohibited any alternative. This was the dogmatic closure of language in which no other gap, no other space, slipped between "naming" and "judging": the named was already judged; there was no use elaborating on it.

Once again, the analysis took its point of departure in linguistic data but was anchored at the outset in social and ideological experience. Yet the latter, illuminated in the tiny details of the *enunciation* (a word that in linguistic and semiological terminology would take on the subjective scope of the polymorphous object that is writing), would alert us to the most intimate injuries that totalitarianisms have inflicted.

Finally, Barthes took pleasure in mocking intellectual writing. Ironic and caustic but not without sympathy, he outlined the portrait of "a new type of scriptor" (a new sort of user of writing) situated "halfway between the party member and the writer" (p. 23). This concerned nothing less than the difference between "writers" and "intellectuals." The intellectual, who is not a writer but a scriptor, has ideas to defend, generally on the left, of the *Esprit* or *Les Temps modernes* variety [A left-wing Catholic monthly and Jean-Paul Sartre's review, respectively. — Trans.]. They reflect a particular ideology that the scriptor upholds; the fact that he writes — novels, pamphlets, mandates, or manifestoes — comes second. However, what unites these diverse activities is that, in all cases, including his fiction, an intellectual "takes a position," he "signs on." Which led Barthes to define this intellectual mode of writing as being, above all, a "sign" of signatories: "the sufficient sign of commitment" (p. 26).

What does this footnote concerning signatory scriptors mean? That the writing in question and consequently the scriptor-intellectual are institutions, constituting a state within the state, a power. This writing is the opposite of writing-as-risk, the novel or essay, lost in remembrance of things past. On the contrary, "form thus becomes more than ever an autonomous object, meant to signify a property which is collective and protected" (p. 27). In effect, if I sign on with fifty people, or if I write a book that is supposed to express the opinion of the group whose power I share, then my form is not my form; it is collective property. Beneath an apparent assertion of singularity, I dilute myself in the collective, I am the property of the institution in whose name I speak. And Barthes, targeting Sartre, asserted that certain writers, in so doing, do not hesitate to "scuttle" the writing itself, to renounce writing, and to propagate archaic models: think of leftist intellectuals and their taste for the nineteenth century, for example. "The intellectual is still only an incompletely transformed writer, and unless he scuttles himself and becomes for ever a militant who no longer writes . . . , he cannot but come back to the fascination of former modes of writing" (p. 28). Intellectual modes of writing are unstable writings, situated between the literary and the political, but the scriptor finds an advantage in them insofar as this "scripting" offers him a reassuring image of the collective.

Once again, the argument here may seem abstract, neither truly rhetorical nor political. But it "broadsides" social standing and, strictly speaking, the use of language. These "intellectual writings" are mocked as so many blind alleys situated between complicity and impotence.

Here Barthes forgets to be prudent and becomes slightly caustic. . . .

The Novel: A Euphoric Sorting

How will this intersection of language, intimacy, and history that Barthes examined shift in the writing of the novel? Again, he starts with formal criteria such as verb tense or the personal pronoun and arranges them as political questions. The preferred tense of the realistic novel is the preterite; Barthes calls this the "unreal time of cosmogonies, myths, History and Novels," "a ritual of Letters" (p. 30). What is the meaning of this ritual? he asks in an argument at once linguistic and already semiological. First of all, the novel uses the preterite because it articulates a distance through which a past may be arranged. A demiurge, extracted from the fray, speaks through the voice of this preterite and constructs a world of order. Barthes takes into account the psychical mechanism that underlies the verb tense of the novel and describes the dramaturgy of the time and space deployed there. This ordered world, he explains, is called euphoria.

The interpreter as he manifested himself here was in fact proposing a psychological analysis, but perhaps I should say a novelistic analysis, for it was as a novelist that Barthes proceeded. I will come back to the idea that he developed later with regard to the relationship between *criticism* and *truth*: criticism cannot unveil truth unless it becomes the critic's subjective expression, unless it becomes a novelistic mode of writing unlimited by the supposedly objective reconstruction of facts and meanings. For now, keep in mind that *Writing Degree Zero* already introduced this intimate part of the writer Roland Barthes, internal to the interpretation that the theoretician elaborated.

So, the preterite is "the expression of an order, and consequently of a euphoria." The link between "order" and "euphoria" is not immediately apparent; it is inscribed through Barthes's insistence, it is a creation of his writerly touch: "Thanks to [the preterite], reality is neither mysterious nor absurd; it is clear, almost familiar, repeatedly gathered up and contained in the hand of the creator; it is subjected to the ingenious pressure of his freedom" (p. 31). The order established by the preterite may evolve toward a sort of calming that is not evident right away but that the particular subject who is the novel writer modulates discreetly. The preterite, constructed and ordered, procures pleasure and euphoria; it becomes *narrative past*: the bourgeois novel needs it in order to provide an image of the world as secure and creative. Barthes supposed that our perception of the bourgeois world resonates with this image and with that of the novelist, all aspiring to a secure, creative world. The preterite of novelistic writing ceased to be a linguistic category, beneath Barthes's pen, and, through psychology and sociology but also beyond their limits, became a veritable category internal to the psychical apparatus. "The teleology common to the Novel [and to the bourgeois mentality it brings to the fore] . . . is the alienation of the facts: the preterite is the very act by which society affirms its possession of its past and its possibility." It took all Barthes's freedom and dilettantism, placing him at the crossroads of several disciplines, for this very polymorphous notion of *writing* to be sketched out and for it to allow us to read the preterite in this surprising way, as this past tense so necessarily French and yet totally prepared to fall into the moneybag of the bourgeoisie: "It is thanks to an expedient of the same kind that the triumphant bourgeoisie of the last century was able to look upon its values as universal" (p. 33).

Let us now look at the pronoun "he."

The Solid "He," the Crumbing "He": Balzac or Flaubert

Unlike the pronoun "I," which Barthes calls "less ambiguous" and "thereby less typical of the novel," the pronoun "he" is "a typical novelistic convention, like the narrative tense," a conglomerate of several "hes," a construction made in order to rid "I" of its "humours and tendencies" that allows the traits that interest the writer to be condensed without at the same time constituting a "complex" person (pp. 35–37). Thus even Balzac's characters appear to the critic as "slight in terms of solid flesh," but this "slightness" conceals an advantage: it allows the narrator's "I" to retain its own moral density and its own tendencies. Later, semiology would in turn reflect on the novelistic "he," starting with the linguistic definition of personal pronouns. Benveniste defined the "he" as the "nonperson," one exterior to the circuit of communication established between "I" and "you," which explained its "objective" charge of abstraction and distance.[23] For the semiotician, the "he" will be a "shifter," thanks to which the writer may, on the one hand, extract himself from the plenitude of the "I" in order to glue together the heterogeneous elements that constitute his characters and, on the other hand, construct the archetypes of bourgeois society. Barthes suggested this in *Writing Degree Zero*: "The appearance of the 'he' is not the starting point of History, it is the end of an effort which has been successful in extracting from a personal world made up of humours and tendencies, a form which is pure, significant, and which therefore vanishes as soon as it is born thanks to the totally conventional and ethereal decor of the third person."[24] And when the bourgeois universe finds itself in crisis, the character in the novel will also lose the compactness and homogeneity the "he" conferred on him.

Barthes nevertheless sketched out a typology of novelistic "hes": "Between the third person as used by Balzac and that used by Flaubert, there is a world of difference," he suggested, "that of 1848," once again pointing out the historical reflection, the political preoccupation (which, though always present, never raises a red flag, as in Sartre). In Balzac, "we have a view of History which is harsh, but coherent and certain of its principles, the triumph of an order; [in Flaubert], an art which in order to escape its pangs of conscience either exaggerates conventions or frantically attempts to destroy them." On the one hand, the consistency, the homogeneity of these "hes"; on the other, the crumbling, the emphasis on their status as "convention." Barthes concluded: "Modernism begins with the search for a Literature which is no longer possible" (p. 38). It was with Flaubert that this impossibility would explode, which Barthes analyzed in Jean Cayrol in the form of a crisis.

"Desubstantifying" Linguistic Idealities

The essential features that characterize writing according to Barthes are thought *with* but especially *beyond* language, which is the object of linguistics. Writing and the other signifying systems Barthes considered (cinema, painting, photography, fashion, etc.) are and are not of a linguistic order: the profound unity that characterizes apparently very different books like *Writing Degree Zero* (1953), *Elements of Semiology* (1964), and *The Fashion System* (1967) brings to the fore this contradictory tension always at work in Barthes's thought.

On the one hand, because language is the first of the signifying systems and the best defined, Barthes suggested the following modification of Saussure's position: "Linguistics is not a part of the general science of signs, even a privileged part, it is semiology which is a part of linguistics."[25] (Here we recognize a necessity clearly dictated by a concern for rigor and positivity.) On the other hand, and at the same time, signifying systems are *translinguistic*: they are articulated in great unities that traverse the phonetic, semantic, syntactic, and stylistic order and organize another combinatory with the help of these same linguistic categories, functioning, however, at a second power, in another system activated by another subject. We have come full circle: the passage through the Russian formalists allowed a return to the translinguistic, or even antilinguistic, positions of *Writing Degree Zero* (there is "in writing a 'circumstance' foreign to language") while it simultaneously established them.[26]

Reduction of the complexity of the signifying practice to a neutral and universal intelligible? This supposed "ideology" of Barthes's approach has been criticized. But one must not neglect his willingness to specify a typology (communication is not writing) and his persistence in comparing semiological systematization to a critical writing that breaks with the "neutral and universal" status of metalanguage.

Barthes's semiological texts—and they are all semiological if one uses the term to refer not to formalization but to a search for dialectical laws of *significance*—impose above all a desubstantification of the signifying ideality. That is to say, the import of these texts is first negative ("[there is] no semiology which cannot, in the last analysis, be acknowledged as *semioclasm*"), a negativity that works against the transparency of language and the symbolic function in general.[27] The phenomenological idealities that linguistics finds in language are, for Barthes, a façade veiling another order that remains to be established. Behind opaque, substantified linguistic categories and structures functions the scene where the subject, defined in the topos of his communication with the other, begins by negating this communication in order to formulate another plan of action. In contrast to the first so-called natural language, this new language is no longer *communicative* but *transformative*, when it is not *deadly* for the "I" as well as the "other." It ends in the border experiences you are familiar with, in an antilanguage (Joyce) that is sacrificial (Bataille) that also bears witness to the social structure in upheaval. Although still understood as signifying, this other scene of writing is only partially linguistic: because it is only partially communicative, it pertains only in part to idealities established by linguistic science. Instead, it accesses the process of formation of its linguistic idealities by unfolding their phenomenal structure; linguistic unities and structures no longer determine writing, because it is not only—or not specifically—a discourse addressed to someone. Displacements and facilitations of energy, discharges and quantitative investments logically anterior to linguistic entities and to their subject mark the constitution and the evolutions of the ego and are manifested by transforming the linguistic symbolic order. An analogous desubstantification affects mythic idealities, recrystallized in the practice of subjects in history: "Myth is not defined by the *object* of its *message*, but by the *way* in which it utters this message: there are formal limits to myth, there are no '*substantial*' ones" (p. 109; emphasis mine).

If this position has a marked affinity with the structuralist approach, where Barthes willingly ranked himself, his project differs radically: to be a structure, myth is only intelligible as *historical production*; its laws will therefore be found in history and not in phonology: "One can conceive of very ancient myths, but there are no eternal ones; for *it is human history which converts reality into speech*, and it alone rules the life and the death of mythical language. Ancient or not, mythology can only have an historical foundation, for myth is a type of speech chosen by history" (p. 110; emphasis mine). Contrary to a structuralism that sought in myth "the permanent structures of the human mind," Barthes targeted, through the discursive phenomenon, the question of social and historical overdetermination.

I hope I have shown how his position differs from structuralism and especially how distant from it his point of departure is: history, for Barthes, is inseparable from a deep unfolding of the signifying subject through which it is readable: "History, then, confronts the writer with a necessary option between several moral attitudes connected with language; it forces him to *signify* Literature in terms of possibilities outside his control."[28] This obligatory but uncontrollable necessity that commands *signifying* is delivered to us by a privileged experience: "esthetics." "Structuralism does not withdraw history from the world: it seeks to link to history not only certain contents (this has been done a thousand times) but also certain *forms*, not only the material but also the *intelligible*, not only the ideological but also the *esthetic*."[29]

Language as Negativity: Death, Irony

Desubstantified, or rather deidealized, in this way, language becomes the frontier of the subjective and the objective, of the symbolic and the real; it becomes the material limit on which the dialectical constitution of the one and the other occurs: "Language functions negatively, as the initial limit of the possible."[30]

Barthes was probably one of the first, within structuralism, to consider language as negativity, not because of a philosophical option (deconstruction, antimetaphysics, etc.) but because of the very object of his inquiry, literature being for him at once experience and proof of the negativity proper to the linguistic operation. "A writer is someone for whom language constitutes a problem, who is aware of the depth of language, not its instrumentality or its beauty."[31] Experiencing the trajectory of this negativity, writing is contestation, breakage, theft, irony. In writing, negativity acts on the unity of language and on the agent of this unity: it literally pulverizes the subject as well as its individual representations, which are contingent and superficial, making them "clouds, a passing vapor,"[32] the savors of meanings, a dust haze of elements, of fragments: "Today, there is no language site outside bourgeois ideology. . . . The only possible rejoinder is neither confrontation nor destruction, but only theft: fragment the old text of culture, science, literature, and change its features according to formulae of disguise. . . . [Writing] exceed[s] the laws that a society, an ideology, a philosophy establish for themselves in order to agree among themselves in a fine surge of historic intelligibility."[33]

Precisely because it operates in the language of the subject, this negativity exists alongside a positivity. The materiality of the language that obeys strict rules, bearers of the concrete body and history, blocks the movement of absolute negativity that could only support itself as such in the excess of ideas and through a negative theology. Keep this in mind: *writing formulates the negative*. At the heart of the national language, negativity organizes itself as a new *signifiance*: language is remodeled in a writing whose novelty, seen at first as scandalous, ultimately emerges as revelatory of a universal, international, and transhistorical logic. Barthes chose authors who are classifiers, inventors of codes and languages, topologists, logothetes, architects of new languages who list, enumerate, synthesize, articulate, formulate. And we read our aberrations there as if they were laws, scriptures. At least this is the axis that Barthes sought in them—from *Writing Degree Zero* to *Sade, Fourier, Loyola*, by way of *S/Z*—making his way through the "flesh" of their writings in order to find new syntheses of new languages.

The critic, for his part, also crosses this explosion of meaning in language that is internal to writing and whose only pole of transference is linguistic or referential. But the formulating operation of *critical* writing is distinguished from that of the *writer*: in the critic, the operational negativity of writing is seized by an *affirmation*. It is ultimately blocked by the concern to find meaning, which, in the end, reveals that the critical writing is entirely triggered, supported, and determined by the discourse of the other in the dialectic of the relationship of transference. "While we do not know how a reader *speaks* to a book, the critic for his part is obliged to adopt a certain 'tone,' and this tone, when all's said and done, can only be affirmative."[34] Literary critical discourse "openly and at its own peril adopts the intention of giving a particular meaning to the work" (p. 73). Unable to dissolve the self in this turbulent cloud that produces writers, creators of modes of writing, whom Barthes calls logothetes, the critic remains riveted to his "I," which absorbs polyvalences and signs without, however, openly asserting itself. The critic is the one who cannot produce the He of the novel, but who is also unable to reject the I of pure private life, that is, to renounce writing: he is an aphasic of the I, while the rest of his language remains intact, yet is marked by the infinite detours imposed on the word (as in the case of the aphasic) by the constant blockage of a certain sign. In a perfectly *homonymic* journey, from his opaque "I" interested in the writing of an other, the critic returns in fact to this same "I," no longer a person because along the way it has objectively become *language*. He "confronts . . . his own language"; "In criticism, it is not the object which must be opposed to the subject, but its predicate" (p. 85). "The symbol must go and seek the symbol" (p. 89).

By implicating himself in the negative operation that is language through the intermediary of the other (the author), the critic retains a weakened but persistent effect from the negativity of writing: the *death drive* of the writer becomes *irony* in the critic, because there is irony each time an ephemeral meaning crystallizes for a certain recipient. Freud demonstrates this economy of laughter in *Jokes and Their Relation to the Unconscious* (1905); it is a discharge in a dual sense between sense and non-sense. For a fleeting moment, a semblance of meaning must be sketched out. This is the task of the critic, one of the more amusing ones, to crystallize an island of meaning in a sea of negativity. Thus, for Barthes, the critic may "develop precisely what is lacking in science; this one could sum up in a word: *irony*. Irony is nothing other than the question which language puts to language" (p. 89). This irony, by which the critic, with the help of his "I" and without putting it at risk, participates in the process of writing, is only a moment (among others) of the process in question: for Rabelais, Swift, Lautréamont, and Joyce are only ironic when one posits them (or when they posit themselves) as subjects recording an always-already ancient meaning always-already exceeded, as peculiar as it is ephemeral. Without this critical position, left to its own evolution once called "inspiration," their writing is not really an irony but an infinity that is seeking its laws. As for the critic, caught in an opaque "I," the aim of "one" meaning, and irony, no one eluded the traps better than Barthes himself, through writing that has joined knowledge and singularity, truth and virtuosity.

Atheism as Pleasure of Texts

The moment has come to appreciate in just measure this semioclasm that dissolves apparent meaning and apprehends writing as negativity: an endless refraction and reformulation of the system of language, the unity of the speaking subject, and the transparency of the social link itself. If the notion of atheism has a sense, it can only be realized in this practice that destabilizes the elementary bases of signification that are the unities and rules of language. Do you question faith and God? Know at the outset that it is your aptitude for meaning itself that is in question: do natural meaning, "one" meaning, and their subject, their guardian and possessor, exist at all, or are they a fiction, inconsistency crumbling away in repressed or shameful versions before ending in silence? Barthes did not hesitate to underscore the atheist impact of his experience as an interpreter and semiotician, dissolving apparent layers of significations one after the other. In his reading of Saint Ignatius of Loyola's *Spiritual Exercises*, emphasizing the void saturated with sensations and the ritualistic beacons of "the development of thought" for the benefit of language, he concluded with the "suspension" of the (divine) sign in Loyola: the silence of God. The sign of the response was inevitably late, divinity spoke but did not mark, the respectful dialogue was sent back to the "void" in which the question without an answer and the meditative hearing that was its own answer was resolved. Thus, "returning the deficiency from sign to sign," the mantic act—Loyola's or Barthes's?—managed to "[include] within its system this empty and yet significant place called the zero degree of the sign."[35]

Yet listen to Barthes's conclusion, which both realizes and reverses its atheism. For even in interpreting the absence or the loss of meaning, the semiotician gives meaning to nonmeaning; in other words, he replaces "divine

threat," as well as its threatening absence, with the pleasure of a writing sustained by "the plenitude of a closed language": "Restored to signification, the
divine vacuum can no longer threaten, alter, or decentralize the plenitude
which is part of every closed language" (p. 75). Having shown the zero degree
of signs—their plural stratification and even their non-sense—Barthes gives
his atheism the savory plenitude of a jouissance in immanence, which is simply language. From then on, this atheism avoids the traps of nihilism and—in
"the plenitude which is part of every closed language"—opens the infinite
pleasure of the text.

NOTES

[All texts have been cited from the editions listed below. In the case of French works that have not appeared in English, I have translated all passages from the original.—Trans.]

1. What Revolt Today?

1. For those interested in the subject, I recommend Alain Rey, *Révolution: Histoire d'un mot* (Paris: Gallimard, 1989), particularly pp. 21–32, which I refer to here.

2. Corneille, *Selections; or, Polyeuctus/The Liar/Nicomedes*, trans. John Cairncross (Harmondsworth: Penguin, 1980), act 5, scene 6, p. 309.

3. Corneille, *Polyeuct*, trans. Noel Clark (Bath, U.K.: Absolute, 1993), act 1, scene 4, p. 157.

4. Voltaire, *The Age of Louis XIV*, chapter 4.

5. Rey, *Révolution*, p. 34.

6. In 1636, in Father Monet's *Dictionnaire français-latin*; see Rey, *Révolution*, p. 36.

7. The word is used in the sense of "conflict" in Bossuet ("Fatales révolutions des monarchies," *Oraisons funèbres*, sermon 71). Montesquieu uses it to mean "social upheaval" ("upheavals which plunge rich men into destitution and swiftly raise the poor, as if on wings, to the height of opulence" [*Persian Letters*, trans. C. J. Betters (Harmondsworth, U.K.: Penguin, 1973), letter 98, p. 182]), and La Rochefoucauld uses it to describe changes in taste ("Une révolution générale qui change le goût des esprits aussi bien que les fortunes du monde," maxim 259, quoted in Rey, *Révolution*, p. 53). [The Fronde was an insurrectionary French political party during the minority of Louis XIV and the ministry of Cardinal Mazarin. Members were called *frondeurs*, from the French for "slingshot."—Trans.]

8. Rey, *Révolution*, p. 54. See also p. 56, where Rey quotes Voltaire: "Il se peut que notre monde ait subi autant de changements que les états ont éprouvé de révolutions" (from *Essai sur les moeurs*).

9. I will not probe these legal matters any further, but those interested in the topic can do so in a very good book by jurist and University of Paris I professor Mireille Delmas-Marty: *Pour un droit commun* (Paris: Seuil, 1994). In it, she details the status of law in the contemporary world, its banality, its theatricality, and the invisibility of power, along with the punitive proceedings that have resulted.

10. Julia Kristeva, *The Old Man and the Wolves*, trans. Barbara Bray (New York: Columbia University Press, 1994).

11. I will examine the timelessness of the unconscious in volume 2, *Intimate Revolt*.

12. Sigmund Freud, *Totem and Taboo: Some Points of Agreement Between the Mental Lives of Savages and Neurotics*, trans. James Strachey (New York: Norton, 1950). The German text dates from 1912–1913.

13. Quoted in Ernest Jones, *The Life and Work of Sigmund Freud* (New York: Basic, 1957), 3:204. At the end of his life, Ludwig Binswanger drew closer to the phenomenologists, particularly Heidegger (from whom he is nevertheless very different) and maintained his ambition to combine psychoanalysis and phenomenology.

14. One can—and I have done so elsewhere—call on other texts to highlight the radical evolution that is related to this new stage of what Nietzsche called "monumental history": not the linear, cursory history of sociopolitical events but fixed psychological attitudes, beliefs, and religions. And I could have—should have—spoken of Albert Camus; *The Rebel* is essential, and *The Stranger*, with its blank writing, incites an unsettling strangeness that goes well beyond humanistic testament. The current return to Camus has revived the moralist and the metaphysical importance of his writing.

15. Francis Jeanson, *Sartre: Les Ecrivains devant Dieu* (Paris: Desclée de Brouwer, 1966).

2. The Sacred and Revolt

1. See Julia Kristeva, *Powers of Horror: An Essay on Abjection*, trans. Leon S. Roudiez (New York: Columbia University Press, 1982).

2. Bernard-Henri Lévy, *La Pureté dangereuse* (Paris: Grasset, 1994).

3. See Julia Kristeva, "The Obsessional Neurotic and His Mother," in *New Maladies of the Soul*, trans. Ross Guberman (New York: Columbia University Press, 1995).

4. Julia Kristeva, *Revolution in Poetic Language*, trans. Margaret Waller (New York: Columbia University Press, 1984). This work first appeared as *La Révolution du langage poétique* (Paris: Seuil, 1974).

5. Georges Dumézil, *Mitra-Varuna: An Essay on Two Indo-European Representations of Sovereignty*, trans. Derek Coltman (New York: Zone, 1988).

6. He takes his name from **Guhedh*, "to have a passionate desire for," hence "jouissance" (ibid. p. 208).

7. Georges Bataille, *Oeuvres complètes*, vol. 3 (Paris: Gallimard, 1971).

3. The Metamorphoses of "Language" in the Freudian Discovery

1. Sigmund Freud, *On Aphasia* (1891); "Project for a Scientific Psychology" (1895), in *The Standard Edition of the Complete Psychological Works of Sigmund Freud*, trans.

and ed. James Strachey (London: Hogarth, 1953–74) (hereafter referred to as *SE*), 1:295–397. This volume also includes the letters to Fliess.

2. Sigmund Freud, *The Interpretation of Dreams* (1900), in *The Basic Writings of Sigmund Freud*, trans. A. A. Brill (New York: Modern Library, 1938).

3. See Sigmund Freud, "Analysis of a Phobia in a Five-Year-Old Boy" (1909), *SE*, 10:5–147. [*Infans* = Latin for infant, but also: not capable of speech, not eloquent.—Trans.]

4. He will take this up again in "Appendix C: Words and Things," *Papers on Metapsychology* (1915), *SE*, 14:209–215.

5. Freud, "Project," *SE*, 1:366.

6. Julia Kristeva, *Time and Sense: Proust and the Experience of Literature*, trans. Ross Guberman (New York: Columbia University Press, 1996).

7. Freud, *The Interpretation of Dreams*.

8. Think, for example, of Artaud or of Apollinaire's *Calligrammes*.

9. W. R. Bion, *Attention and Interpretation: A Scientific Approach to Insight in Psycho-Analysis and Groups* (New York: Basic, 1970); Kristeva, *Revolution in Poetic Language*; Piera Aulagnier, *La Violence et l'interprétation* (Paris: Presses universitaires de France, 1975).

10. Sigmund Freud, *The Ego and the Id*, trans. Joan Riviere, ed. James Strachey (New York: Norton, 1960).

11. Lacan will rely on this formulation, without ever citing Freud, in order to assert that "the subconscious is structured like a language." With this postulation, Lacan hardened and dogmatized the Freudian position, but it is incontestable that he legitimately relied on it.

12. Freud, *The Interpretation of Dreams*, p. 518.

13. Sigmund Freud and Karl Abraham, *Correspondence, 1907–1926* (Paris: Gallimard, 1969). Letter of January 9, 1908.

14. "The Antithetical Meanings of Primal Words," *SE*, 11:155–161. See Emile Benveniste "Remarques sur la fonction du langage dans la découverte freudienne," in *Problèmes de linguistique générale* (Paris: Gallimard, 1966), pp. 75–87.

15. Freud, *The Interpretation of Dreams*, p. 518.

16. See my commentary on *Totem and Taboo* in chapter 1, where I discussed the brothers' revolt against the father, a revolt that constitutes the symbolic pact as the cornerstone of hominization and thus of the culture that is born of this revolt.

17. Sigmund Freud, "On Narcissism: An Introduction" (1914), *SE*, 14:69–102.

18. André Green elaborates on the definition of narcissism by exploring its value as an intermediary structure, or state, an unstable element of identity, in *Narcissisme de vie, narcissisme de mort* (Paris: Minuit, 1983).

19. A certain reading of Lacan could lead us to think that the notion of the subject goes without saying in Freud, but that is not the case. Some Freudians have, in turn, considered it a Lacanian artifact. Why discuss the subject, given that the term is not found in Freud? they argue. Indeed, Freud talks about the ego, the id, and the super-

ego but not the subject, except, precisely, in his work on metapsychology (1915, 1917), translated into French by J. Laplanche and J. B. Pontalis, where the term appears linked exclusively to the drive and not to symbolic construction, much less to language.

20. In Sigmund Freud, *Papers on Metapsychology*.

21. Cf. André Green, *La Déliaison: Psychanalyse, anthropologie, et littérature* (Paris: Belles-Lettres, 1992).

22. Freud, *The Ego and the Id*, pp. 12–13. Emphasis mine.

23. Perceptions that neither the Saussurian linguistic model (signifier-signified) nor Peirce's triangular semiotic model takes into account.

24. Sigmund Freud, *Constructions in Analysis* (1937), SE, vol. 23; idem, *An Outline of Psycho-Analysis*, trans. James Strachey (New York: Norton, 1949).

25. Freud, *An Outline of Psycho-Analysis*, p. 19. For those interested in the question of language, I recommend John Forrester's *Language and the Origins of Psychoanalysis* (New York: Columbia University Press, 1980), a richly detailed work on Freudian thought and language. The author emphasizes Freud's discovery with relation to psychosis and the problem posed by hallucination: desires and anxieties can take internal paths and crystallize in words that have nothing to do with the objective reality perceived elsewhere. See also Freud's *Moses and Monotheism* (1939), SE 23:3–137.

26. The term is not that of Lacan, who speaks instead of the "paternal function."

27. Freud, *The Ego and the Id*, p. 33.

28. I spoke of this with regard to the subject in process in *Polylogue* (Paris: Seuil, 1977), pp. 55–107.

29. ["Singing tomorrows," a slogan of the French Communist Party. — Trans.]

30. Catherine Clément, *Les Fils de Freud sont fatigués* (Paris: Grasset, 1978).

31. Debord committed suicide on Wednesday, November 30, 1994, at the age of sixty-two. [Debord, author of *The Society of the Spectacle*, was a founder of the Situationist International (1957–1972). — Trans.]

32. See Freud, *The Ego and the Id*, p. 26; and Julia Kristeva, *Tales of Love*, trans. Leon S. Roudiez (New York: Columbia University Press, 1987), pp. 24–38.

33. See Claude Lévi-Strauss, "Introduction à l'oeuvre de Marcel Mauss," in M. Mauss, *Sociologie et anthropologie* (Paris: Presses universitaires de France, 1950), pp. xlv–xlvii.

34. Jacques Lacan, *Ecrits: A Selection*, trans. Alan Sheridan (New York: Norton, 1977), pp. 1–7; Didier Anzieu, *Le Moi-peau* (Paris: Dunod, 1983).

35. Freud, *The Ego and the Id*, pp. 24–25.

36. See Hanna Segal, "Note on Symbol Formation," *International Journal of Psycho-Analysis* 37 (1957): part 6.

37. André Green, *Le Travail du négatif* (Paris: Minuit, 1993).

38. "Negation," SE, 19:235–239. See Jacques Lacan, "Introduction and Reply to Jean Hyppolite's Presentation of Freud's *Verneinung*," and Jean Hyppolite, "Appendix: A Spoken Commentary on Freud's *Verneinung*," in *The Seminar of Jacques Lacan, Book I*, ed. Jacques-Alain Miller, trans. John Forrester (New York: Norton, 1991), pp. 52–61, 289–97.

39. Freud, *The Ego and the Id*, p. 35.

40. See. Julia Kristeva, *Black Sun: Depression and Melancholia*, trans. Leon S. Roudiez (New York: Columbia University Press, 1989).

41. In *New Maladies of the Soul*, I pose the question of the translatability of the image in language.

42. See Donald Meltzer and M. H. Williams, *The Apprehension of Beauty* (Strath Tay, Scotland: Clunie, 1988).

43. I will come back to the fact that all narrative is intrinsically sadomasochistic, and not only in transference; Sade, with the accuracy of the visionary, saw something inexorable here.

4. Oedipus Again

1. Jean-Paul Sartre, *Being and Nothingness*, trans. Hazel E. Barnes (London: Methuen, 1958; rpt., London: Routledge, 1996), p. 251.

2. "The idealist branch of Freudian research is as threatening today as the *objectivist* one. We have to wonder whether it is not essential to psychoanalysis—i.e., to its existence as *therapy* and as verifiable *knowledge*—to remain, not a cursed attempt and secret science, but at least a *paradox* and an interrogation" (Merleau-Ponty, preface to A. Hesnard, *L'Oeuvre de Freud et son importance pour le monde moderne* [Paris: Payot, 1960], p. 8; emphasis mine).

3. Sigmund Freud, *Extracts from the Fliess Papers, The Standard Edition of the Complete Psychological Works of Sigmund Freud*, trans. and ed. James Strachey (London: Hogarth, 1953–74) (hereafter referred to as *SE*), 1:265.

4. Sophocles, *Oedipus the King*, in *The Complete Greek Tragedies*, vol. 2, *Sophocles*, trans. David Grene (Chicago: University of Chicago Press, 1991), 2:70–71.

5. Sigmund Freud, *The Interpretation of Dreams* (1900), in *The Basic Writings of Sigmund Freud*, trans. A. A. Brill (New York: Modern Library, 1938), pp. 308–9.

6. Composed of three parts: "A Special Type of Choice of Object Made by Men" (1910), "On the Universal Tendency to Debasement in the Sphere of Love" (1912), and "The Taboo of Virginity" (1918), *SE*, 11:165–175; 179–190; 193–208.

7. Sigmund Freud, "The Dissolution of the Oedipus Complex," *SE*, 19:173. Emphasis mine.

8. Sigmund Freud, "Analysis of a Phobia in a Five-Year-Old Boy" (1909), *SE*, 10:5–147; and "From the History of an Infantile Neurosis (The Wolf Man)" (1918), *SE*, 17:7–123.

9. Sigmund Freud, "The Infantile Genital Organization: An Interpolation Into the Theory of Sexuality" (1923), *SE*, 19:142.

10. Sigmund Freud, "Beyond the Pleasure Principle" (1920), trans. James Strachey (New York: Norton, 1961), p. 14.

11. Freud, "Dissolution of the Oedipus Complex," 19:173.

12. See Hanna Segal, "Note on Symbol Formation," *International Journal of Psycho-Analysis* 37 (1957): part 6.

13. Those interested in the details of Freudian thought on Oedipus should consult Roger Perron and Michèle Perron-Borelli, *Le Complexe d'Oedipe* (Paris: Presses universitaires de France, Que sais-je? 1994).

14. See Julia Kristeva, *Revolution in Poetic Language*, trans. Margaret Waller (New York: Columbia University Press, 1984).

15. Built in the first half of the second century B.C, the floors and walls of this villa are decorated with landscapes of the Nile Valley, miniatures of Egyptian figurines, characters from the Dionysiac cycle, and scenes showing initiation rites of the Dionysian or Orphic mysteries on the Hellenistic model of the third or fourth century B.C

5. On the Extraneousness of the Phallus

1. Sigmund Freud, "Female Sexuality," (1931), *The Standard Edition of the Complete Psychological Works of Sigmund Freud*, trans. and ed. James Strachey (London: Hogarth, 1953–74) (hereafter referred to as *SE*), 21:227–28.

2. Sigmund Freud, "A Child Is Being Beaten: A Contribution to the Study of the Origin of Sexual Perversions" (1919), *SE*, 17:179–204.

3. Jacques Lacan, *Le Séminaire*, book 8, *Le Transfert* (Paris: Seuil, 1991).

4. In Greek, the word *kairos* refers to the point that touches the end, suitability, appropriateness, the dangerous critical point, the advantage, the right moment; that which is à propos, suitable; in modern Greek, it means time, epoch. We can see the etymology in "to encounter" or "to cut." To encounter oneself is also to cut oneself, with the reunification and possible loss that this supposes.

5. Sigmund Freud, "The Infantile Genital Organization: An Interpolation Into the Theory of Sexuality" (1923), in *The Standard Edition of the Complete Psychological Works of Sigmund Freud*, trans. and ed. James Strachey (London: Hogarth, 1953–74) (hereafter referred to as *SE*), vol. 19.

6. Sigmund Freud, "Some Psychical Consequences of the Anatomical Distinction Between the Sexes" (1925), *SE*, 19:257.

7. Lacan, *Le Transfert*, p. 274.

8. Donald Woods Winnicott, *Home Is Where We Start From* (New York: Norton, 1986). One could also evoke the "atoxic" or detoxicating mother, Wilfred Ruprecht Bion's mother-excitation barrier. See his *Learning from Experience* (New York: Basic, 1962); *Elements of Psychoanalysis* (New York: Basic, 1963); and *Second Thoughts: Selected Papers on Psychoanalysis* (New York: J. Aronson, 1967).

9. These observations might be considered in light of recent discoveries concerning the greater participation of the right hemisphere in the female brain than in the male brain in the exercise of language. More lateralized, the male brain would be more likely to treat language as a logical system, whereas, because the right hemisphere is implicated in perception and sensation, the exercise of language in the woman would be

more associated with sensoriality. Nevertheless, the fragile nature of biological discoveries as well as our knowledge about the interhemispheric organization of the brain and the interconnectedness of neurons require the greatest circumspection in interpreting these data.

10. With his reference to "the Minoan-Mycenean civilization behind the civilization of Greece," Freud is designating the archaic mother-daughter relationship. See "Female Sexuality" (1931), *SE*, 21:226.

11. From *illudere*, "to make light of."

12. Freud, "Female Sexuality," *SE*, 21:229.

13. Freud, "Some Psychical Consequences of the Anatomical Distinction Between the Sexes."

14. Freud, "Female Sexuality," *SE*, 21:239.

15. To the point of atheism. I will come back to this.

16. Freud, "Female Sexuality," *SE*, 21:230: "We should probably not be wrong in saying that it is this difference . . . which gives its special stamp to the character of females as *social beings*." Emphasis mine.

17. Picasso said that the artist must become a "dyke." See Geneviève Laporte's *Un Amour secret de Picasso* (Paris: Rocher, 1989).

6. Aragon, Defiance, and Deception

1. The review *Tel Quel* was published from spring 1960 to winter 1982 by Editions du Seuil. A good book on the subject is Philippe Forest, *Histoire de Tel Quel* (Paris: Seuil, 1995).

2. Arthur Rimbaud, *Complete Works*, trans. Wallace Fowlie (Chicago: University of Chicago Press, 1966), p. 199.

3. [Paul Claudel, the French dramatist and poet, rediscovered his Catholic faith in Rimbaud's *Les Illuminations* and *Une Saison en enfer*. Claudel wrote the preface to the 1912 edition of *Illuminations*, in which he "Catholicized" Rimbaud. — Trans.]

4. Lautréamont, *Les Chants de Maldoror* (1868), second canto, and *Poésies* (1870), part 2, in *Maldoror and the Complete Works of the Comte de Lautréamont*, trans. Alexis Lykiard (Cambridge, Mass.: Exact Change, 1994), pp. 105, 234.

5. This is a reprise of Pascal, who wanted to write "[his] thoughts without arranging them, but not perhaps in deliberate disorder; that is the proper order, and it will convey my intention by its very want of order. I should be doing too high honour to my subject if I treated it with order, since I wish to show that it is incapable of that" (*Pascal's Pensées*, trans. H. F. Stewart [London: Routledge, 1950], p. 13).

6. [*The Origins of the World*, Courbet's painting of a woman's vulva. — Trans.]

7. Louis Aragon, *Paris Peasant*, trans. Simon Watson Taylor (Boston: Exact Change, 1994), p. 202.

8. Charles Baudelaire, "Saint Peter's Denial," trans. Richard Howard, in *Baudelaire*

in English, ed. Carol Clark and Robert Sykes (Harmondsworth, U.K.: Penguin, 1997), p. 182.

9. "The literary types . . . have in general limited themselves to exalting the resources of the dream at the expense of those of action, all to the advantage of the socially conservative forces that discern in it, and quite rightly, a precious distraction from rebellious ideas," Breton writes in *Communicating Vessels*, trans. Mary Ann Caws and Geoffrey T. Harris (Lincoln: University of Nebraska Press, 1990), p. 7.

10. André Breton, "Characteristics of the Modern Evolution and What It Consists of," in *The Lost Steps*, trans. Mark Polizotti (Lincoln: University of Nebraska Press, 1996), p. 108.

11. Tristan Tzara, *Seven Dada Manifestos*, trans. Barbara Wright (London: John Calder, 1977), p. 15.

12. André Breton, *Notes sur la poésie*, in *Oeuvres complètes* (Paris: Gallimard, Bibliothèque de la Pléiade, 1988), 1:1018.

13. André Breton, "Situation of Surrealism Between the Two Wars," in *Free Rein (La Clé des champs)*, trans. Michel Parmentier and Jacqueline d'Amboise (Lincoln: University of Nebraska Press, 1995), p. 58.

14. Breton, *Notes sur la poésie*, 1:1018.

15. Louis Aragon, *Treatise on Style*, trans. Alyson Waters (Lincoln: University of Nebraska Press), p. 104.

16. See Julia Kristeva, *Time and Sense: Proust and the Experience of Literature*, trans. Ross Guberman (New York: Columbia University Press, 1996).

17. Louis Aragon, *La Défense de l'infini* (1923–1927), followed by *Les Aventures de Jean-Foutre la Bite*, with an introduction and notes by Edouard Ruiz (Paris: Gallimard, NRF, 1986).

18. Louis Aragon, second preface to *Le Libertinage*, 2· ED. (PARIS: GALLIMARD, 1964), p. 13.

19. Aragon, *Treatise on Style*, p. 9

20. Aragon, *Paris Peasant*, p. 66.

21. Aragon, *Treatise on Style*, p. 105.

22. Louis Aragon, *Blanche ou l'oubli* (Paris: Gallimard, NRF, 1967).

23. Aragon, second preface to *Le Libertinage*, p. 14.

24. In Louis Aragon, *The Libertine*, trans. Jo Levy (London: John Calder; New York: Riverrun, 1987), p. 18.

25. "To create is to conceive an object in its fleeting moment, in its absence" (from "Music and Literature," in *Mallarmé: Selected Prose Poems, Essays, and Letters*, trans. Bradford Cook (Baltimore: Johns Hopkins Press, 1956), p. 48).

26. Think here of Duchamp and his interest in the relationship between the real and the possible. See also André Breton: "The question of reality in its relations with possibility, a question that remains a great source of anxiety, is resolved here in the most daring manner: possible reality is obtained by a lax approach to the laws of physics and chemistry." *Oeuvres complètes*, 2:112.

27. Aragon, *Paris Peasant*, pp. 114, 116, and 118.

28. Stéphane Mallarmé, "Crisis in Poetry," in *Mallarmé*, p. 42 [The quotation appears in the following: "When I say: 'a flower!' then from that forgetfulness to which my voice consigns all floral form, something different from the usual calyces arises, something all music, essence, and softness: the flower which is absent from all bouquets."—Trans.]; idem, letter to H. Cazalis, October 1864, in *Mallarmé*, p. 83.

29. Louis Aragon, *La Défense de l'infini*, pp. 41–95.

30. See André Breton, *Nadja*, trans. Richard Howard (New York: Grove Press, 1960). See also the book by Jean Decottignies on surrealist poetry, *L'Invention de la poèsie: Breton, Aragon, Duchamp* (Lille: Presses universitaires de Lille, 1994). I also recommend the work of Xavière Gauthier on the surrealists and women: *Surréalisme et sexualité* (Paris: Gallimard, 1971).

31. André Breton, "Soluble Fish" (1924), in *Manifestoes of Surrealism*, trans. Richard Seaver and Helen R. Lane (Ann Arbor: University of Michigan Press, 1969), p. 63.

32. "*Individual sexual love*, born of this *superior form of sexual relations that monogamy is, [is] the greatest moral progress* accomplished by humans in modern times," wrote Breton in *Mad Love*, trans. Mary Ann Caws (Lincoln: University of Nebraska Press, 1987), p. 77.

33. Villiers de L'Isle-Adam, "L'étonnant couple Moutonnet" (1890), in *Chez les passants*, in *Oeuvres complètes* (Paris: Gallimard, Bibliothèque de la Pléiade, 1986), 2:405–9.

34. Breton, *Soluble Fish*, p. 106.

35. Aragon, *Paris Peasant*, p. 170.

36. Louis Aragon, *Anicet ou le Panorama* (Paris: Gallimard, NRF, 1921).

37. Aragon, *Paris Peasant*, p. 196.

38. Aragon, *The Libertine*, p. 171.

39. Aragon, *Paris Peasant*, p. 110.

40. *Littérature*, no. 13, p. 22, reproduced in *Littérature: March 1919–August 1921* (Paris: Place, 1978). The review was published from 1919 to 1924.

41. "Le Mentir-vrai" is the title of a 1964 short story in a collection of the same name (Paris: Gallimard, NRF, 1980).

42. Daniel Bougnoux has emphasized "the perpetual motion" of the century in Aragon's work and persona. See *Encyclopaedia Universalis*, s.v. Aragon, and *Annuel*, the supplement of 1983. [*Le Mouvement perpetuel* is a collection of poems.—Trans.]

43. Louis Aragon, second preface, *Le Libertinage*, p. 14.

44. See Pierre Daix's insightful biography, *Aragon: Une Vie à changer* (Paris: Seuil, 1975; 2· ED., PARIS: SEUIL, 1995), which examines the life as well as the literary work.

45. Louis Aragon, "Et comme de toute mort . . . ," in Elsa Triolet and Louis Aragon, *Oeuvres romanesques croisées*, 42 volumes (Paris: Robert Laffont and Amis du livre progressiste, 1964–1974), 1:13.

46. Louis Aragon, "Vie de Jean-Baptiste A.," *Feu de joie*, followed by *Le Mouvement perpétuel* (first published in 1920 by Au Sans Pareil) (Paris: Gallimard, 1980), p. 43.

47. Louis Aragon, *Henri Matisse* (Paris: Gallimard, NRF, 1971).

48. Aragon, "Et comme de toute mort . . . ," in *Oeuvres romanesques croisées*, 1:14.

49. Louis Aragon, *Les Voyageurs de l'impériale* (1937–1939; first publication censored, 1942) (Paris: Gallimard, NRF, 1947). This book is part of the Monde réel cycle. [It appeared in English as *The Century was Young*, trans. Hannah Josephson (New York: Duell, Sloan, and Pearce, 1941).—Trans.]

50. Louis Aragon, "Le mot," from *En étrange pays dans mon pays lui-même* (1942), preceded by *La Diane française* (Paris: Seghers, 1979), p. 135. The French reads in part:

Le mot n'a pas franchi mes lèvres
Le mot n'a pas touché son coeur
Est-ce un lait dont la mort nous sèvre
Est-ce une drogue une liqueur

Jamais je ne l'ai dit qu'en songe
Ce lourd secret pèse entre nous
Et tu me vouais au mensonge
        A tes genoux
. . . .
Te nommer ma soeur me désarme
. . . .
Que si j'ai feint c'est pour toi seule
Jusqu'à la fin fait l'innocent
Pour toi seule jusqu'au linceul
        Caché mon sang

J'irai jusqu'au bout de mes torts
J'avais naissant le tort de vivre. . . .

51. These words appeared on the first page of the first issue of *La Révolution surréaliste*, founded on December 1, 1924. The complete collection of the review was published in Paris by Editions Jean-Michel Place in 1975.

52. Louis Aragon, *Lautréamont et nous* (Paris: Sables, 1972), pp. 77–78. Emphasis mine. For more on the signing of this pact, see especially page 164 on. The piece first appeared in *Les Lettres françaises*, no. 1185–86 (June 1967).

53. Philippe Forest, "Anicet, Panorama du roman," *L'Infini*, no. 45 (1994): 79–102.

54. Aragon, *Anicet*, p. 112.

55. Aragon, *The Libertine*, pp. 22–23.

56. Louis Aragon, "Programme," in *Le Mouvement perpétuel*, p. 43.

57. Louis Aragon, *The Adventures of Telemachus*, trans. Renée Riese Hubert and Judd D. Hubert (Boston: Exact Change, 1997); Fénelon, *Les Aventures de Télémaque, suite du quatrième livre de l'Odyssée d'Homère*, in *Oeuvres complètes* (Geneva: Slatkine, 1971), 6:398–566.

58. Aragon, *The Adventures of Telemachus*, p. 32.

59. Founded by Henri Barbusse, *Clarté* was published from 1919 to 1927.

60. Antonin Artaud's *Le Pèse-Nerfs* was published in the collection "Pour vos beaux yeux" in 1927. See also Antonin Artaud, *Oeuvre complètes* (Paris: Gallimard, 1970), 1:99–132. [Parts of *The Nerve Meter* appear in Antonin Artaud, *Selected Writings*, ed. Susan Sontag, trans. Helen Weaver (New York: Farrar, 1976).—Trans.]

61. See Pierre Daix, *Aragon*, pp. 189–190.

62. *Aragon parle*, with Dominique Arban (Paris: Seghers, 1968), p. 62.

63. Louis Aragon, *Le Roman inachevé* (1956; rpt., Paris: Gallimard, Poèsie, 1978), pp. 102–147.

64. Aragon, "Très tard que jamais," in *La Grande Gaîté* (Paris: Gallimard, 1929), p. 19. The French reads:

Les choses du sexe
Drôle de façon de parler
Des choses du sexe
Je m'attendais à tout
Mais aucunement à cela

65. Aragon, "Maladroit," in *La Grande Gaîté*, pp. 43–44. The French reads:

Premièrement je t'aime
Deuxièmement je t'aime
Troisièmement je t'aime
Je t'aime énormement
Je fais ce que je peux pour le dire
Avec l'élégance désirable
Je n'ai jamais su le moins du monde
Inspirer le désir
Quand j'aurais voulu l'inspirer
Un exhibitionisme naïf en matière de sentiment
Un caractère au moral comme au physique
Nom de Dieu tout ça n'est guère amusant
Comme attraction c'est zero

66. See Aragon, *Le Mentir-vrai*, pp. 7–48; see also his *Défense de l'infini*, pp. 185–232.

67. *Les Lettres françaises*, no. 1015 (February 6, 1963).

68. Published by René Bonnel, with five engravings by André Masson.

69. Louis Aragon, *Irene's Cunt*, trans. Alexis Lykiard (London: Creation Books, 1996), p. 84.

70. Louis Aragon, *Je n'ai jamais appris à écrire, ou les Incipit* (Paris: Skira, 1969), pp. 46–48.

71. Philippe Sollers, "Limites d'Aragon," in *La Guerre du goût* (Paris: Gallimard, 1994), p. 393.

72. Louis Aragon, *Irene's Cunt*, p. 33.

73. Daniel Bougnoux points out the anagram "Aragon"/"ouragan" [hurricane]; see his excellent analysis of the kaleidoscopic structure of this text in "La langue ardente de l'orage," *Pleine Marge: Cahiers de littérature, d'arts plastique et de critique,* no. 12 (December 1990): 79–87.

74. Aragon, *Irene's Cunt,* pp. 84 and 85.

75. Mallarmé, "Crisis in Poetry," p. 42.

76. See Julia Kristeva, *Revolution in Poetic Language,* trans. Margaret Waller (New York: Columbia University Press, 1984).

77. Louis Aragon, *Les Communistes,* 6 vols. (1st ed., Paris: Editeurs français réunis, 1949–1951; 2· ED., 1967).

78. Louis Aragon, *Aurélien* (Paris: Gallimard, NRF, 1944) (in English, Louis Aragon, *Aurelien,* trans. Eithne Wilkins [New York: Duell, Sloan, and Pearce, 1947]); idem, *La Semaine sainte* (Paris: Gallimard, NRF, 1958) (in English, Louis Aragon, *Holy Week,* trans. Haakon Chevalier [London: Hamish Hamilton, 1961]).

79. See Plato's *Philebus.*

80. See Jacques Lacan, *Ecrits: A Selection,* trans. Alan Sheridan (New York: Norton, 1977), pp. 388–389, 439; and *RSI* (1974–1975), ed. Jacques-Alain Miller, *Ornicar?* nos. 2–5 (1975).

81. Gilles Deleuze and Félix Guattari, *Anti-Oedipus: Capitalism and Schizophrenia,* trans. Robert Hurley, Mark Seem, and Helen R. Lane (New York: Viking, 1977).

7. Sartre

1. Aeschylus, *Oresteia,* in *The Complete Greek Tragedies,* ed. David Grene and Richmond Lattimore, vol. 1 (Chicago: University of Chicago Press, 1991).

2. Jean-Paul Sartre, *The Flies,* trans. Stuart Gilbert (New York: Knopf, 1947), pp. 79–80, 159.

3. Jean-Paul Sartre, *The Words,* trans. Bernard Frechtman (New York: Braziller, 1964).

4. Jean-Paul Sartre, *The War Diaries, November 1939–March 1940,* trans. Quintin Hoare (New York: Pantheon, 1984).

5. See Jean-Jacques Brochier, *Pour Sartre: Le Jour où Sartre refusa le Nobel* (Paris: Lattès, 1995).

6. Recalling that Sartre, in *The Words,* said he merited a single prize, one "for good citizenship," Michel Contat humorously noted in light of recent documents on the writer's private life that the only prize he would no doubt be refused would be that of transparency, "for he had begun to lie about his feelings to far too many women in an effort not to complicate his life, with the result that it had become enormously complicated" ("Rien dans les mains, rien dans les poches," *Quai Voltaire,* no. 6 [fall 1992]: 82).

7. Ibid., pp. 87–88.

8. Statement translated from the Swedish, Agence France-Presse, October 22, 1964, quoted in Brochier, *Pour Sartre,* pp. 41–45.

9. Jean-Paul Sartre, *On a raison de se révolter* (Paris: Gallimard, 1974), p. 30.

10. Quoted in Brochier, *Pour Sartre*, p. 71.

11. François Mauriac, *Le Nouveau Bloc-notes (1958–1960)* (Paris: Flammarion, 1961), p. 361, quoting from the column in the October 29–November 4, 1964, issue. Emphasis mine.

12. Quoted in Brochier, *Pour Sartre*, pp. 76–77, 78. Emphasis mine.

13. Gilles Deleuze, "Il a été mon maître," *Arts*, no. 978 (October 28–November 3, 1964): 8–9.

14. André Green, "Des *Mouches* aux *Mots*," in *La Déliaison* (Paris: Les Belles-Lettres, 1992) p. 357.

15. Sartre, *The Flies*, pp. 121 and 123.

16. Green, *La Déliaison*, p. 358.

17. Sartre, *The Flies*, p. 159.

18. Sartre, *The War Diaries*, p. 70.

19. Sartre, *The Flies*, p. 140.

20. Sartre, *The War Diaries*, p. 42. *The Flies* was written four years later.

21. Jean-Paul Sartre, *The Devil and the Good Lord and Two Other Plays*, trans. Kitty Black (New York: Knopf, 1960), p. 34.

22. Alexandre Dumas, *Kean*, adaptation by Jean-Paul Sartre, in Sartre, *The Devil and the Good Lord*, pp. 189, 191, and 251.

23. Jean-Paul Sartre, *Saint Genet, comédien et martyr* (Paris: Gallimard, NRF, 1952) (in English, Jean-Paul Sartre, *Saint Genet: Actor and Martyr*, trans. Bernard Frechtman [New York: Pantheon, 1963]).

24. Jean-Paul Sartre, *The Roads to Freedom: The Age of Reason, The Reprieve, Troubled Sleep*, trans. Eric Sutton [*The Age of Reason* and *The Reprieve*] and Gerald Hopkins [*Troubled Sleep*] (New York: Vintage International, 1992). Both *The Age of Reason* and *The Reprieve* appeared in French in 1945 and in English translation in 1947; *Troubled Sleep* appeared in French in 1949 and in English translation in 1951.

25. Jean-Paul Sartre, *Nausea* (New York: New Directions, 1964), p. 122.

26. Jean-Paul Sartre, *What Is Literature?* (1948), trans. Bernard Frechtman (London: Routledge, 1998), p. 217.

27. Julia Kristeva, *Powers of Horror: An Essay on Abjection*, trans. Leon S. Roudiez (New York: Columbia University Press, 1982).

28. Sartre, *Nausea*, p. 12.

29. I refer you here to my *Black Sun: Depression and Melancholia* (trans. Leon S. Roudiez [New York: Columbia University Press, 1989]), which analyzes the melancholic-depressive structure as a border state subjacent to creativity.

30. Jean-Paul Sartre, *Being and Nothingness: An Essay on Phenomenological Ontology*, trans. Hazel E. Barnes (London: Routledge, 1996), p. 239.

31. Giorgio Agamben, *La Communauté qui vient: Théorie de la singularité quelconque* (Paris: Seuil, 1990).

32. Sartre, *The Words*, p. 253.

33. Jean-Paul Sartre, *Critique de la raison dialectique* (Paris: Gallimard, 1960).

34. Sartre, *What Is Literature?*, p. 201.

35. Jean-Paul Sartre, *Critique of Dialectical Reason*, trans. Alan Sheridan-Smith (London: NLB, 1976), p. 67.

8. Roland Barthes and Writing as Demystification

1. Roland Barthes, *Writing Degree Zero*, trans. Annette Lavers and Colin Smith (New York: Hill and Wang, 1968), pp. 3–6.

2. *Roland Barthes by Roland Barthes*, trans. Richard Howard (New York: Hill and Wang, 1977).

3. For a more in-depth discussion of this, see my essay "How Does One Speak to Literature?" in *Desire in Language*, trans. Thomas Gora, Alice Jardine, and Leon S. Roudiez (New York: Columbia University Press, 1980).

4. Roland Barthes, *Criticism and Truth*, trans. Katrine Pilcher Keuneman (Minneapolis: University of Minnesota Press, 1987), p. 66.

5. Julia Kristeva, *The Samurai*, trans. Barbara Bray (New York: Columbia University Press, 1992).

6. See "Le Sujet en procès," in Julia Kristeva, *Polylogue* (Paris: Seuil, 1977), pp. 55–106.

7. Roland Barthes, *Critical Essays*, trans. Richard Howard (Evanston, Ill: Northwestern University Press, 1972), p. 217.

8. Barthes, *Writing Degree Zero*, pp. 10–12.

9. See Kristeva, "How Does One Speak to Literature?"

10. Barthes, *Writing Degree Zero*, p. 14.

11. Maurice Blanchot, *The Space of Literature*, trans. Ann Smock (Lincoln: University of Nebraska Press, 1982). Published in France in 1955, it was still an influence on the author of *Writing Degree Zero*, as parts of it were published earlier.

12. Barthes, *Writing Degree Zero*, pp. 81, 78, 77, 77–78. Emphasis mine.

13. Blanchot, *The Space of Literature*, p. 33.

14. Roland Barthes, *A Lover's Discourse*, trans. Richard Howard (New York: Hill and Wang, 1978).

15. Roland Barthes, *S/Z*, trans. Richard Miller (New York: Hill and Wang, 1974).

16. Barthes, *Writing Degree Zero*, p. 20. Emphasis mine.

17. Jean-Paul Sartre, *Search for a Method*, trans. Hazel E. Barnes (New York: Knopf, 1963), p. 142.

18. Julia Kristeva, *Time and Sense: Proust and the Experience of Literature*, trans. Ross Guberman (New York: Columbia University Press, 1996).

19. Sartre, *Search for a Method*, p. 142.

20. Jean-Paul Sartre, *Critique of Dialectical Reason*, trans. Alan Sheridan-Smith, ed. Jonathan Rée (London: Verso, 1976), 1:99.

21. Roland Barthes, *Michelet*, trans. Richard Howard (New York: Hill and Wang, 1987).

22. Barthes, *Writing Degree Zero*, p. 19.

23. See Emile Benveniste, "La Nature des pronoms" (1956) and "De la subjectivité dans le langage" (1958), in *Problèmes de linguistique générale* (Paris: Gallimard, 1966), pp. 251–57 and pp. 258–66. On novelistic character and personal pronouns, see also Julia Kristeva, *Le Texte du roman: Approche sémiologique d'une structure discursive transformationnelle* (La Haye: Mouton, 1970) pp. 98 et seq.

24. Barthes, *Writing Degree Zero*, p. 37.

25. Roland Barthes, *Elements of Semiology*, trans. Annette Lavers and Colin Smith (New York: Hill and Wang, 1968), p. 11.

26. Barthes, *Writing Degree Zero*, p. 20.

27. Roland Barthes, *Mythologies*, trans. Annette Lavers (New York: Hill and Wang, 1972), p. 9.

28. Barthes, *Writing Degree Zero*, p. 2. Emphasis mine.

29. Barthes, *Critical Essays*, p. 219. Emphasis mine.

30. Barthes, *Writing Degree Zero*, p. 13.

31. Barthes, *Criticism and Truth*, p. 64.

32. G. W. F. Hegel, *The Phenomenology of the Spirit*, trans. J. B. Baillie, in *The Philosophy of Hegel*, ed. Carl J. Friedrich (New York: Modern Library, 1953), p. 502.

33. Roland Barthes, preface to *Sade, Fourier, Loyola*, trans. Richard Miller (Baltimore: Johns Hopkins University Press, 1997), p. 10.

34. Barthes, *Criticism and Truth*, p. 92.

35. Barthes, *Sade, Fourier, Loyola*, p. 75.

INDEX

European Perspectives
A Series in Social Thought and Cultural Criticism
Lawrence D. Kritzman, Editor